Awakening Memory
Copyright © 2021 by Tom Morris
Cover: Painting by permission © Hélène Farrar,
What We Carry: Rain Lady (2019)

All rights reserved. No part of this publication may be reproduced, distributed, or transmitted in any form or by any means, including photocopying, recording, or other electronic or mechanical methods, without the prior written permission of the author, except in the case of brief quotations embodied in critical reviews and certain other non-commercial uses permitted by copyright law.

tellwell

Tellwell Talent
www.tellwell.ca

ISBN
978-0-2288-6382-3 (Paperback)
978-0-2288-6383-0 (eBook)

To the live creature
and its memories and hopes
in each of us

If we could see ourselves, not as we do—
in mirrors, self-deceptions, self-regardings—
but as we ought to be and as we have been:
poets, lute-stringers, makyres and abettors

of our necessary art, soothsayers of the ailment
and disease of our times, sweet singers,
truth tellers, intercessors for self-knowledge—

—From 'The Glass King' by Eavan Boland[1]

---

[1] From Boland, *Outside History: Selected Poems 1980–1990*.

CONTENTS

Introduction 1
Acknowledgements 11

Part I
Getting Started

Chapter 1   What is Memoir Writing?... 17

Memoir writing described. Memoir and remembering. Introducing 'the live creature.' Writing as exploration. Writing as a process. What to include. Why write your memoir? Memoirs as nonfiction, mostly. 'Schooled' versus personal writing. The memoir writing workshop.

Chapter 2   Practical Matters: Memoir Writing Tools,
            Helpful Habits, and Timelines 36

What you need to get started. Some helpful writing habits. Timelines: personal and historical.

Chapter 3   The Wellsprings of Effective Memoir Writing............. 43

An overview of the key elements of memoir writing as exploration.

Chapter 4   Courage 56

The importance of courage for memoir writing. How the writing workshop can bolster courage.

Chapter 5   Finding Our Life Stories: Memoir Source
            Materials and Suggested Writing Topics 60

Materials and techniques for awakening memory. An extensive list of suggested writing ideas.

Chapter 6   Let's Get Writing.. 80

Entering our inner writing room. Turn to what interests you. The small and the solid. Our imagined reader. Four approaches to start writing. William Zinsser on making a beginning.

Chapter 7 Mapping Our Experience 90

What memoir story mapping is and how it works.

Chapter 8 The Memoir Writer's Demons 101

Obstacles to effective memoir writing—self-doubt, egoism, familiarity, normalization, seeing the final result before you begin, the quick fix—and how to fend off their powers.

Chapter 9 Storytelling in a Memoir 115

What is a story? Inner storytelling. The storyteller's invitation. Fiction and non-fiction in memoir. Storytelling as a craft.

Chapter 10 The Personal Essay: Investigations of My Self in
the World 135

What is the personal essay? Formal and impersonal versus informal and personal essays. The personal essayist's method, subjects, and voice. Conversations with self and world. Qualities of effective essays. Types of personal essays. The essay's structure. Beginnings and endings.

Part II
Strengthening Your Writing

Chapter 11 Wonder 159

How attention to wonder helps awaken the activity and results of remembering—and enlivens our writing.

Chapter 12 Bringing Your Experience Alive 174

To show and to tell. Dramatic scenes versus narrative bridges and summaries. Realia. Time. Structure. Attending to our unfolding inner life. Humour.

Chapter 13 'Voice' in Memoir Writing: Finding the
Sound of Who I Am 192

Our speaking voice versus personal writing voice. Developing our own voice. Memoir writing's many voices. Voices to avoid. Voices of our youth. Using voice to redeem the past. Examples of voice in memoir.

Chapter 14 Bats in the Belfry: Figurative Language and Its Uses . 210

What is figurative language? What are figures of speech? A mere piece of cloth made figurative. Dramatic solidity. Finding your own figures of speech. Figurative language versus imagery. Figures of speech have consequences.

Chapter 15 The Writing Process:
              From Rough Draft to 'Good Enough' Final Text...... 219

The trial-and-error zigzag of writing. The first rough draft. Reviewing and rewriting. Revising towards a 'good enough' final text. A reader's checklist for reviewing your work.

Chapter 16 The Memoir Writer's Blues, and How to
              Become Inspired Again 233

Getting beyond procrastination, carping critics, writing challenges, feeling blocked, and self-doubt.

Part III
Finalizing and Sharing Your Memoir

Chapter 17 Bringing It All Together: Organizing,
              Preparing, and Sharing Your Memoir........................ 243

Giving an overall shape to your writing. Considering titles. Reviewing details. Creating a consistent 'look.' The dedication, introduction, and acknowledgements. Today's options for printing and publishing.

Part IV
Further Reflections On Memoir Writing

Chapter 18 The Dust-Covered Shoebox in the Attic:
              Reflections on Memory, Remembering,
              and Creating the Past.. 259

The challenges of memory and remembering. Bodily experience and remembering childhood. Opening ourselves to creaturely memory. Getting at the truth of the past by 'making it up.' Memory and imagination.

A copy of this painting—from a series called *What We Carry* by Hélène Farrar—has been sitting over my desk, like a questioning presence, as I have been writing this book. Farrar calls the woman in the painting the Rain Lady. I often think of her as Mem, the keeper of memories. During the past year or so I have frequently looked up at this figure and found myself wondering: *What is she carrying? What do I carry? What do you, the reader, carry?*

What is inside those many colourful packets? What life experiences? What memories and hopes? What belongings and longings? What voices and silences? What pleasures? What regrets? What concerns? What hunger? The memory of the grip or slap or caress of a hand? An aroma or taste? A satisfying achievement? A time of joy? Of sadness? Of loneliness? Of eager anticipation? A dream of something still to be done? The sensation of feeling at home—or not at home—with the social surround, with yourself, with life?

Where has the Rain Lady journeyed from, and where is she going? Where have you been? Where are you going? How did you become who you are? What journey are you on? Who, importantly, has been with you along your way? What might you tell us about what it means to be you here in this world?

As I look at the woman in the painting, and as she stares out towards me, these are some of the questions that I imagine we ask of each other. They are the same questions that I invite you to ask yourself as you read this book.

The woman pulling the wagon appears to be homeless, a 'street person.' She could also be a war-created refugee, or a person who feels exiled by, or has removed herself from, the conventional world of fixed addresses. She reminds me as well of Mother Courage, after whom Bertolt Brecht named his famous play. In that play, Mother Courage is last seen pulling her goods wagon alone, the Thirty Years' War and her efforts to survive it having devoured her children.[2]

---

[2] In Brecht's anti-war play *Mother Courage and Her Children*, written as he was fleeing Germany in 1939, the main characters are forced into a vulnerable

In discussing her painting, Farrar recalls a woman in her hometown whom she often sees pulling a rolling cart piled with things she appears to value. Farrar has tried to make eye contact with the woman, but without success. That is, until one memorable cold night when the two stare at each other through Farrar's headlights. The painting invites me to experience something of this moment of connection with the Rain Lady, with Mem, with the keeper of memories. It's a connection that feels direct but equivocal, and propitious as well.

Commenting on her complete *What We Carry* series of paintings, Farrar talks about the idea of inner 'containers' of experience. She wonders about how what we carry—'what we cherish, collect, remember and carry'—defines our way of being; 'how our bodies keep score of our life experiences'; how we 'might . . . be carrying with us an entire room of a life,' and how the relation between 'our "load" and [the] "everyday" . . . can tell our stories—what we seem and what we need—like a window into the distant lands that inhabit our physical gestures, human connections, emotions and imagination.'[3]

As the Rain Lady looks out from the painting, she seems to throw back our gaze and invite us to wonder, just as Farrar does. What is it that we cherish, collect, remember, and carry? How has our body 'kept score' of our life? What is inside our own many-shaped, many-coloured packets of memories and dreams, all that 'baggage' of life experience that tumbles around us? Finally, and not least among what it suggests, Farrar's painting is a reminder that a successful memoir leads us, as readers, in two directions: not only into the writer's exploration of their life world, but into an exploration our own life as well.

---

    shelterless existence (German: *obdachlos*: those without a roof over their head), forever shuffling to and fro under the starless sky of the endlessness of the Thirty Years' War.

[3] I have combined comments by Farrar from two sources: her website at helenefarrar.com, and 'From the Curator: Balancing Acts with Hélène Farrar,' an interview with Debra Claffey, July 2016, at debraclaffey.com. More needs saying about the bird in the painting: possibly a representative sign for the world's birdlife that, under war-like attack by humans, has been given refuge in the form of this dreambird amidst all that the Rain Lady carries.

If we sat together for awhile—in the amber warmth of a late afternoon, say, when time slows and curiosity goes for a stroll through our memories and dreams—what stories might we tell, what stories would we find ourselves needing to tell, to better understand and share our lives?

༺❀༻

The subject of this book is memoir writing: how to do it and how to think about it. I could just as readily say it is about autobiographical or personal or life-story writing. The categories don't matter. What matters is the activity of using writing to *explore* what it means to be this 'I' that you call yourself, and to express this as honestly and as eloquently as possible in your own voice. Memoir writing is a journey, and this book has been written to serve as one of your guides. We will walk and explore and learn together.

Along our way I will keep returning to four key ideas:

- First, memoir writing is a *process*, like crossing a river step by step, stone by stone. Personal writing is an ongoing search for what needs saying, and the development of what needs saying into what I call 'good enough' final texts.

- Second, memoir writing worth doing involves a fresh *awakening* of memory and an *exploring* of what is significant among our life experiences. Memoir writing calls for curiosity, wonder, questioning, listening, self-reflection, investigation, digging, unpacking. We will move along the edges of the well-known, the felt but unknown, and the to-be-known.

- Third, memoir writing calls on us to write not only about our cultural self, such as our working life. It also asks us to listen for the tremorings, the felt voices, of what I call our inner *creaturely life*: our unfolding, single-bodied, sensate life with its pleasure and pain, love and hate, fragility, vulnerability, and yearnings, and its refusals to become fully accommodated to cultural norms and prescripts.

- Finally, my view is that the most interesting memoir writers are personal *truth-seekers* and *truth-tellers*. They work towards expressing the truths of their actually lived creaturely life. This is work that can and often must include a questioning of pleasing illusions. Seeking, then voicing the truth takes courage.

⁂

Memoir writing begins with the awakening of memory, followed by the *exploration* of our life experiences. We will have many occasions to reflect on the idea of memoir writing as exploration, in particular how good memoir writers follow the feeling-qualities or energies of their experiences. For the moment let's get a taste of what I mean—'exploration' as following the energies of our memories—by reading 'The Carousel in the Park,' a poem by Eavan Boland. I read the poem as an act of experiential *exploring*, what Boland describes as the activity of *finding*: of locating, piecing together, sympathetically imagining, and thereby bringing alive a memory. She begins by summoning the rememberer inside the self.

> Find it.
> Down the park walks, on the path leading
> past the sycamores.
> There through the trees—
>
> nasturtium rumps, breasts plunging
> lime and violet manes
> painted on
> what was once the same as now littered
> russet on their petrified advance.
>
> Find the sun
> in the morning rising later,
> the chilled afternoons getting shorter and—
> after dusk, in the lake, in the park—
> the downtown city windows scattering
> a galaxy of money
> in the water.

> And winter coming:
> The manhandled indigo necks flexing and
> the flared noses
> and the heads with their quiffed carving.
> And the walks leafless and
> the squirrels gone,
> the sycamores bare and the lake frozen.
>
> Find the child,
> going high and descending there—up and down,
> up, down again—
>
> her mittens bright as finger-paints and holding fast
> to a crust of weather now: twelve years of age in
> a thigh-length coat,
> unable to explain a sense of ease in
>
> those safe curves, that seasonless canter.[4]

The subject of Boland's 'finding' (or exploring) in this instance is finding 'the child' and the experiential places of our childhood. The subject could be any one of the countless memories and dreams that we carry. I have chosen this particular poem in order to show how 'exploration,' as I use the word here, involves a unique way of finding—seeking and bringing alive—the *experiential qualities* of our memories. When I say 'a unique way of finding,' I have in mind the poem's tone of eager anticipation. Remembering as the mobilizing of the senses, as something kindled by curiosity and wonder. Remembering as a re-membering: reconstituting the body of experience with an attentive, empathetic care. The poet's attention to creaturely life's 'rumps' and 'breasts,' its flexing and flaring, ascent and descent. The passing of the seasons and of dawn into dusk. Loving care for the used, handled qualities of things. 'Exploring' here is sensate, it has body and weight and movement. It reminds us that memories, remembering, and

---

[4] From Boland, *Outside History: Selected Poems 1980–1990*. Boland died in April 2020 as I began revising the manuscript of this book. Her poetry has been an informing, inspiring presence throughout its writing.

dreamwork are close companions. It is filled with the energies of both regret and yearning, especially yearning for that 'seasonless' 'sense of ease' and pleasure and safety that remains, for the poet today, in the form of an unforgettable promise.

So, as I use the phrase 'exploring our life experiences,' I mean attending to their felt qualities and energies. I also use 'exploring' in a second, related sense: the activity of searching for the truth—the meaning and consequences—of our actually lived experiences. A memoir may include but is not equivalent to family history and lore. Nor is it merely the description of our experience. Rather it is a *working through* of what our life has been and is about. The best memoirists seek self-knowledge distilled from doubt and questions.

This can be challenging work. Only consider how easily, and often unawares, we can 'adjust' ('forget,' invent, remake, conventionalize) the past to serve some *idea* of our self and 'life'; how readily we can 'edit' memories for enlistment in acts of wishful dissembling; the difficulty of disentangling who our 'I' is from who it has been made to be; how we normalize what shouldn't be adapted to; and the aches, the resentments, the willing of 'wellness' and 'competence,' the emotional blankness, the masking, and the platitudes ('If you want to get ahead with life, you have to get on with life'), each of which is a sign of frustrated life. 'Exploring' as truth-seeking requires ongoing acts of critical self-reflection, a wary questioning of the taken-for-granted, and sometimes a difficult confronting of oneself and others. It is also a process that ends in approximations, producing what Boland calls a 'flawed translucence.'[5] We write *towards* truth.

---

[5] In Boland's poem 'Amber,' an excerpt of which reads: 'The clear air we need to find each other in is / gone forever, yet / this resin once / collected seeds, leaves and even small feathers as it fell / and fell / which now in a sunny atmosphere seem as alive as / they ever were / as though the past could be present and memory itself / a Baltic honey— / a chafing at the edges of the seen, a showing off of just how much / can be kept safe / inside a flawed translucence.' From Eavan Boland, *New Selected Poems*.

'To explore,' as I use the term in the context of memoir writing, has one more meaning: to find our own *voice*. By 'voice' I mean our characteristic way of taking in and pressing out—expressing—life as actually lived in our single-bodied self. The memoirist's *own* voice is not that of a spouse or friend, and not some inner 'should.' Nor is it the voice of 'good' manners and cultural ideals. Yes, the effects of the world of 'should' and cultural precept—the hammer and anvil of social existence—need to be heard in our memoir. But the voice of memoir, at least an authentic feeling voice, emerges from inside the writer's own skin and their actually felt life. Our memoir writing voice is our nervature and fingerprints in words.

This book, then, is an invitation to explore, to *find*, your life stories—and find a voice of your own to tell these stories in the truest form possible.

I hope that the following pages act as a helpful guide for claiming the space you need to explore and voice your life—those lands, as Farrar writes, 'that inhabit our physical gestures, human connections, emotions and imagination.' I hope as well that you will feel encouraged to look anew at, and evaluate, your lived relation to the cultural surround: its choices and demands, its system of rewards, its appeals and conventions, and its possibilities and obstacles for living a fulfilling life. Finally, I hope that you will come to see that memoir writing is not exclusively about looking backwards, an activity that easily leads to the quietism of nostalgia and reverie, and the repeating of the 'tried and true.' More completely done, memoir writing is an active, critical, fresh engagement with the past with the aim of understanding our life anew.

Using this book

Awakening Memory is intended for people who are writing their memoir or engaged in related forms of personal writing. It is also written for people who are facilitating memoir writing workshops. The book is divided into five parts.

Part I introduces our subject. It includes a number of practical considerations and tools to help you begin writing, including the importance of a regular writing space and time. It also lists an array of possible memoir writing topics, considers the important role of 'courage' in memoir writing, discusses how to deal with self-doubt and other obstacles, and looks in detail at the two major forms of memoir writing: life stories and personal essays.

Part II begins with a discussion of the role of 'wonder' in personal writing, then looks more closely at writing as a craft. This includes discussions on how to shape a piece of writing and bring it alive, the development and use of 'voice,' using figurative language, the writing process from rough draft to what I call a 'good enough' final text, and various mid-writing blocks and how they can be overcome.

Part III offers advice on how to bring your memoir materials together into a shareable form, as well as options for printing and publishing.

Part IV widens and deepens how we might think about memoir writing. It includes chapters on the workings of memory, the idea of 'the live creature,' memoir writing as exploration, and the challenging work of 'being true' to our experience.

Part V includes a chapter on how to set up and facilitate a memoir writing workshop. The workshop is a key source of mutual learning and motivation. Part V ends with a Selected Readings list of materials on memoir writing, and a short list of recommended memoirs.

In writing this book I have imagined a reader who is self-reflective and open to the new. Be surprised, be provoked. Ask questions, question yourself. Be inspired. Try things out. This book is my personal take on exploring and writing about our life experience, written from the limits of my own experience. Use what you find here to do your own exploring and find your own voice.

The images in this book

Between each chapter are a variety of images—photographs, drawings, and paintings—along with questions and comments. I invite you to use these images to help awaken your own memories and reflective processes.

ACKNOWLEDGEMENTS

Awakening Memory has had a lengthy gestation that runs through decades of teaching literature and personal writing in university, college, and community settings. Early versions of a number of its chapters were first written for a series of community-based memoir writing workshops for seniors that I have been facilitating in Ottawa. My thanks to participants in the first of these workshops: Herb Brennen, Jean Broadfoot, Rheo Brunet, Lynn Haggarty, Margaret Holubowich, Mary Humphrey, Guy Lajoie, Carol MacLellan, and Dagmar Van Beselaere. You warmed me to my task with your enthusiasm, your questions, your courage, and your stories.

Thank you to Mona-Lynn Courteau for her conscientious editing, encouragement, and always helpful suggestions. Any errors are entirely my responsibility.

This book would not have been possible without the counsel and inspiration of others who have written with such intelligence and wit about the memoir form and its relation to life. I name these writers in the Selected Readings, and hope that I have fully credited their work wherever needed.

Our subject is about exploring our life experiences, about remembering and imagining, about critically understanding our self and culture and the tensions between the two—and about expressing what we find in something of our own voice. For their thoughtful, heartfelt conversations on these matters, and for their friendship, my thanks to Tariq Ahsan, Andrew Bales, Prem Bakshi, Roger Clark, Jim Chalmers, Bob Fraser, Bob Goodfellow, Bill Gilsdorf, Andrew and Kathrine Greiner, Patrick Kavanagh, Ruth Kirstein, Bonnie Harnden,

Deb Patterson, Joyce Patterson, and Brian and Lucy Voss. For their encouragement to develop my own response to the world in my own voice, I am especially grateful for two teachers, writers, thinkers, and dear friends: Art Efron and Jerry Zaslove.

A special thank you to Hélène Farrar for permission to use her painting *What We Carry: Rain Lady*.

In addition to thinkers and writers referred to elsewhere in this book, I am particularly indebted to the writings of T.W. Adorno, Mohammed Arkoun, Mikhail Bakhtin (*The Dialogic Imagination*), Walter Benjamin, Christopher Bollas, Murray Bookchin, Hugh Brody, Wayne Burns, Judith Butler (*Precarious Life: The Powers of Mourning and Violence*), Alex Comfort (*Art and Social Responsibility*), Guy Debord, George Dennison, Stanley Diamond, Norbert Elias, Jacques Ellul, Sigmund Freud, Paul Goodman, Susan Griffin, Václav Havel, Jules Henry, John Holt, Lewis Hyde (*Trickster Makes the World*), Ivan Illich, R.D. Laing, Dorothy Lee, Herbert Marcuse, Carolyn Merchant, Maurice Merleau-Ponty, William Morris, Lewis Mumford, Ashis Nandy, A.S. Neill, Paul Radin, Wilhelm Reich, James C. Scott, Vandana Shiva, Georg Simmel, Peter Sloterdijk (*Critique of Cynical Reason*), Paul Virilio, E.V. Walter, and Colin Ward.

In writing this book I have found myself hearing once again the voices and life stories of human rights defenders met earlier in my life. These stories, of unbending courage often told with such humility, have reminded me of the importance of finding and using our voice to speak the truth of our experience, including truth to power. To these women and men I am deeply grateful.

Thank you to Michael Murphy for many years of stimulating discussions, for his advice and encouragement during this project, and for his friendship.

Above all, for the unencumbered time and experiential space to complete this book—generously given and deeply appreciated—thank you Betty.

A note about the author

Tom Morris has taught literature, cultural studies, and personal writing in a number of university, college, and community settings. He also worked as a publicist and campaigner for Amnesty International Canada for twenty years. More recently he has facilitated community-based memoir writing workshops for seniors in Ottawa, Ontario.

PART I

GETTING STARTED

CHAPTER 1

WHAT IS MEMOIR WRITING?

> I don't write about what I know, but in order to find out what I know.
>
> —Patricia Hampl, *I Could Tell You Stories*

> In memoir the heart is the brain.
>
> —Mary Karr, *The Art of Memoir*

> What writers can do in this symbolic ice age is to preserve and present individual identities, individual existences that you can pick out from the flow and present as something that moves people, or shocks them.
>
> —Imre Kertész[1]

What is a memoir?

A memoir is the writer's personal exploration of a selection of her or his significant life experiences.

Let's begin here, with this definition, and see where it takes us.

The memoirist might introduce her work by saying: Here you will learn about a number of memorable events and experiences in my life,

---

[1] The memoirist-novelist in conversation with Julian Evans in 'A Man Apart,' *The Guardian*, April 2006.

told through stories, essays and other forms, and explored for their personal meaning. She goes in search of answers to questions like this: *What is it like to have been here—and to be here now—on this earth?* And this: *What is my time on this earth adding up to?*

Memoir writers revisit the sites of their continuing life journey. They then return to tell the rest of us stories about where they have been, what they have done and had done to them, who they have met, what they have learned, how they have changed, and what they now wish for. The memoirist says: *This is my way of being in the world. This is life as I understand it.*

Memoirs show the writer in their interactions with others and the larger world, but they do so from a fundamentally personal perspective. Indeed, the best memoirists seem to understand the 'personal' in a very specific sense: as experience lived inside their own skin. By this I mean that they take seriously their *embodied*, or what I call their *creaturely* life. In searching for the truth of their experiences, they are guided not by what their respectable self or culture or an acquaintance says *should* be true. Instead, they listen to the evidence of their single-bodied, carnal, feeling self—their actually lived life. Indeed, as I hope to show, some of the best memoir writing issues from the writer's attentiveness to the tensions between the voices of 'should' and the creaturely self.[2]

---

[2] See Chapter 19 for a more detailed discussion of the concept of 'the live creature,' adapted here from American philosopher John Dewey's *Art As Experience*. I use variations of the phrase 'live creature' to help characterize who we are, naturally, as human beings, and thus as people who write about their personal experiences. For Dewey, the human is an embodied organism with 'natural needs,' 'basic vital functions,' and the 'biological commonplaces' humans share with 'birds and beasts.' Dewey asks us to consider being human as something not above or apart from our natural, animal being (a commonplace idea in the Western tradition), but rooted in and inseparable from it. Dewey's 'human' is, or can be, a thoughtful, reasoning, and practical creature. But it is also, fundamentally, a creature understood by the 'interplay of [its] natural energies,' sense experience, appetites, and 'charged' perceptions. (All passages are from *Art As Experience*.)

Memoir writing, remembering, and exploration

The word 'memoir' is from the Old French *mémoire*, a term borrowed from the Latin *memoria*, meaning memory or reminiscence. Remembering, then, is essential to memoir writing. But what does remembering really involve? The ancient Greeks knew memory as the goddess Mnemosyne, the mother of the Muse of history and eight other Muses, all women, associated with creativity, thinking, and learning. Each of Mnemosyne's daughters is said to have begun life with her heart set to song. For their part, the Greeks recognized that remembering is not simply a descriptive, unbiased telling of the past. Just consider Mnemosyne raising all those daughters. Wasn't she bound to get tired and confused, remembering some things while misremembering and forgetting others? More to the point, the ancient waters of Memory and Forgetfulness (the Lethe) were believed to flow side by side. It was easy to drink from one when you thought you were drinking from the other. More challenging still, the ancient storytellers recognized that there are risks in drinking from either river. Drink from Forgetfulness, they said, and be immediately happy—although also doomed, upon reincarnation, to repeat your past follies. On the other hand, drink from Memory and risk being overwhelmed by painful recollections—although these might make you wiser and perhaps, with the passage of time, able to laugh once again. Remembering, the ancients knew, was no simple thing.[3]

Remembering involves, or can involve, a fascinating cluster of what I think of as 're-' words: refeel, rediscover, reawaken, reminisce, revisit, reconstitute, rethink, retell, rewrite, realize, release, reclaim, restore, reconcile, redeem. It is these 're-' words that suggest how memoir writing can be used to *explore* our life: to search for what is significant among our life experiences, and to ask why 'significant,' what an experience means, and how it contributes with other experiences towards a renewed understanding of our life. Vivian Gornick makes a similar point. 'Truth in a memoir is achieved,' she writes, 'not through a recital of actual events; it is achieved when the reader comes to believe

---

[3] See Chapter 18 for a more detailed examination of memory and remembering.

that the writer is working hard to engage with the experience at hand. What happened to the writer is not what matters; what matters is the large sense that the writer is able to make of what happened' (*The Situation and the Story*).

To describe and to explore

I want to pause for a moment and emphasize the distinction between memoir writing as exploration and as description. Most first-time memoir writers assume that what they are doing—in fact, all they are doing—is describing, reporting on, or giving an account of experiences taken from their life. They are showing what happened, often in a storytelling form and sometimes in very entertaining ways. However, description alone is only part of what memoir writing invites us to do. The other part, to return to Gornick's admonition, is to engage with and make sense of our experience—that is, to critically explore and learn from it. The best memoirs are written in the spirit of these lines from Eavan Boland's poem 'In the Garden': 'I want to show you / what / I don't exactly know. / We'll find out.'[4]

Memoir writing as description typically repeats the writer's well-known and oft-told experiences, ideas, and sentiments. The result is familiar stories and points of view told in habitual ways, a life turned into something like a collection of packages whose surfaces and shapes are copied in words. Such writing often has a tone that suggests complacency, self-absorption, and self-satisfaction. There is little, if any, genuine self-questioning and wonder.

---

[4] From Boland's collection *Outside History: Selected Poems 1980–1990*.

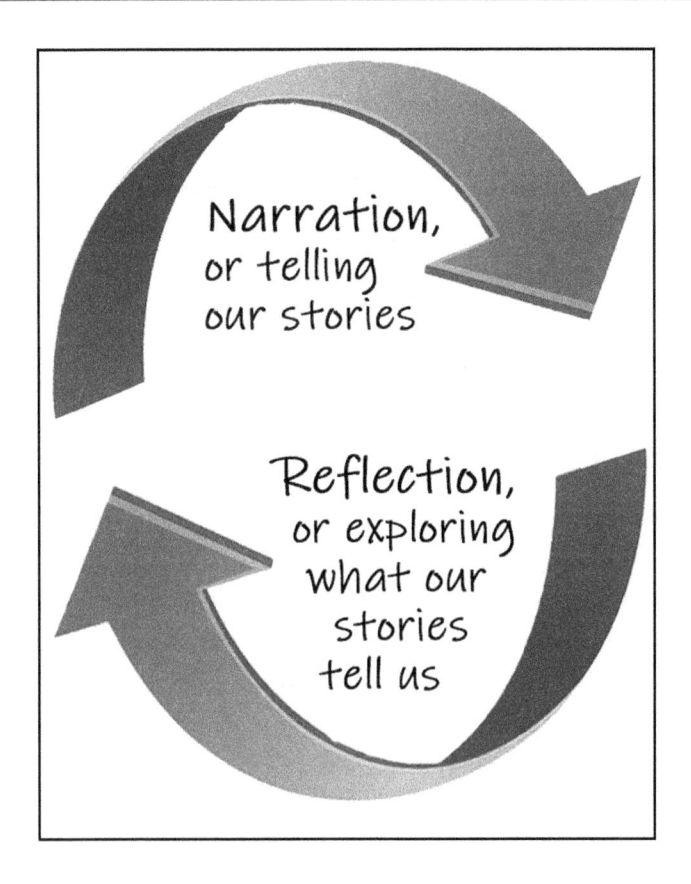

> Narration, or telling our stories
>
> Reflection, or exploring what our stories tell us

More complete memoir writing stems from an exploratory process. The personal essayist Phillip Lopate describes this as 'thinking on the page . . . to question all that might have been transpiring inside and outside [the writer] at the time, and to catch the hunches, doubts, and digressive associations that dart through their brains . . . . The story line or plot in nonfiction [such as memoir] consists of the twists and turns of a thought process working itself out . . . [a 'working out' that combines] 'curiosity-driven research plus personal voice' (*To Show and To Tell*). To explore one's experiences, ideas, opinions, and values is to critically reflect on and search out their meaning. Exploration involves self-questioning, explaining, interpreting, summarizing, research, setting the context, seeing the particular as part of a larger pattern, accounting for alternative views, self-implication, attention to creaturely experience, making judgements, thoughtful guesswork, and imagination.

Many memoir writers are perfectly happy to only describe their life experiences, to stay within the cozy circle of what is familiar, accessible, and reassuring. Indeed, they may find this circle so comfortable that when they are asked to venture into 'self-reflection,' they often reproduce the packaged buzzwords and moral platitudes of contemporary culture or their well-acculturated self.

Memoir writing as exploration is more demanding. It asks us to 'make sense' of something *for ourselves on our own terms* from inside the skin of our own creaturely life. It asks us to interrogate our life, ask it questions—especially questions we do not already have the answers to. Exploration also strengthens personal writing. As Lopate says, few things will engage your reader more than following you in your adventure of figuring things out. 'You must surprise yourself, and, when you do, it will make you elated and your prose elevated. What I want [from the memoirist] . . . is honesty—honesty that will cut through the pious orthodoxies of the moment and ring true. There is nothing more exciting than to follow a live, candid mind thinking on the page, exploring uncharted waters' (*To Show and To Tell*).

To sum up, the best memoirists use description to bring alive their life experiences. But they also take the next step. They reflect critically on these experiences, and in so doing they *use their writing* to learn about themselves and engage their reader in this process of learning. They know as well that memoir writing as self-understanding is always a work in progress.[5]

Memoir writing is a process, like finding our way across a river, stone by stone

Imagine that your memoir is a river you want to cross. There is no preordained way across, nor can we clearly see the far shore. Rather, we must use reflection and writing to find our way, our personal 'way,'

---

[5] For further discussions of memoir writing as exploration see Chapter 20. On writing and wonder see Chapter 11.

forward. It is this exploratory process, taken step by step, that will become our memoir.

Understood like this, the memoir writer is a *wayfinder* and memoir writing is a personal *wayfinding*. Through her stories and personal essays, the memoirist touches on fundamental questions regarding her life. Where have I come from? Where am I now? Where am I going? Who am I? Why am I here?[6] Her 'answers'—revealed obliquely through her stories and reflections—help show us her 'way,' understood as not only who she is, but also the course and meaning and purpose of her life.

We can only cross memoir's river—that is to say, find our way and write our memoir—by feeling for one stone at a time. Some of these stones are too unsteady to stand on. Some will seem solid and safe but

---

[6] These are the questions Michel de Montaigne (1533–1592) asks in his personal essays. Later, Jean-Jacques Rousseau (1712–1778) writes in his *Confessions*: 'I have nothing but myself to write about, and this self that I have, I hardly know of what it consists. I will go in search of it in your presence . . . . To know a character well it is necessary to distinguish that which has been established by nature, to see how he has formed himself, what occasions have developed him, what sequence of secret affections has rendered him thus and how he has modified himself to produce on occasions the most contradictory and most unexpected results.' One hundred years before Montaigne, we discover Margery Kempe reflecting on her life in a similar manner—the memoirist's way—in *The Book of Margery Kempe*, a manuscript that the illiterate Kempe appears to have dictated to a scribe in the early fifteenth century. Mother of fourteen children, business woman, pilgrim, Christian mystic, and accused heretic, Kempe describes with remarkable candour 'hyr felyngys and revelacyons and the forme of her levyng' [her feelings and revelations and the form of her living]. Long before Kempe, the Catholic bishop Augustine announced in his fourth-century *Confessions* that 'I have become an enigma to myself . . . . I do not know where I came from'—remarks that deeply disturbed his contemporaries. Augustine does not say he will merely describe his life. He begins by admitting that he does 'not know.' He begins, that is, by questioning the given orthodoxies (the best memoirists have often been seen as heretics), and with an admission of his need for greater understanding. Indeed, writers and oral storytellers across the ages and in cultures around the world have wondered who and where and why they are—see, for example, Paul Radin's *Primitive Man As Philosopher*.

turn out to be slippery. Others will only become visible mid-steam. One day when you feel stranded, a passing log will suddenly appear, allowing you to leap onto a stone that just seemed to rise from nowhere. Being open to the unexpected is the lifeblood of good memoir writing.

Whatever your way forward turns out to be, make a beginning here and now. Feel around for that first nearby stone—a significant-feeling life experience. Scribble rough notes on this experience, or tell its story in a quick rough form. Take a rest, then search for the next stone, and rough out the gist of the next story. Then find the next stone, then another, and another. We begin by acting on our intention to cross the river. We find what needs saying step by step. Our memoir will be the path we have found, told stone by stone.[7]

What can I include in my memoir?

The memoir is a spacious writing form. In *I Could Tell You Stories*, Patricia Hampl praises its 'mongrel nature.'

Memoirists turn life experiences into narrated life stories. As well, they use the personal essay form to explore their opinions, life questions, values, pet peeves, places visited, moods, and passions. Memoirs combine storytelling and musings. They describe, interpret, and speculate through many jostling voices. Although deeply personal in outlook, memoirs set the personal in its social-cultural context, and they focus at least as much on the people, places, and influences in one's life as on oneself. They also combine documentary and reportorial elements with lyrical re-creations of experience.

In this book I focus on two primary forms of memoir writing: stories and personal essays, examined in more detail in Chapters 9 and 10.

---

[7] Memoir writing is a process in another sense as well. Effective personal writing—writing that is true to our experience and brings it fully alive for our reader—involves a process of revising and even reimagining what we say, starting with a first rough draft and working through to what I call a 'good enough' final version. See Chapter 15.

- *Personal life stories.* These can be about significant experiences, relationships, people, and places in the writer's life. What happened? Who was involved? How were you affected? How do you understand it? Why is it important?

- *Personal essays.* These deal with subjects of significance to the writer: your interests, obsessions, beliefs, values, aggravations, complaints, observations, questions, and wishes.

In practice, writers tell stories in essays and introduce elements of personal essay writing to their stories; hybrids of both forms abound.

Besides life stories and personal essays, you can include any materials that help bring alive and clarify the picture of your life. You might include photographs, copies of documents (first passport), copies of special letters or telegrams (remember those?), pages from a journal, or favourite passages from a poem, novel, essay, speech, or song lyric. Remember to also include, if you wish, examples of your writing (or possibly sketches or paintings) from earlier stages of your life.

Memoir stories and essays can touch on a variety of subjects and themes, a few of which I list here (for a more complete list of possibilities, see Chapter 5):

- Relationships: friends, lovers, partners, children.

- Childhood, youth, 'growing up.'

- Interesting people I have known.

- Life crossroads, turning points, life crises, and opportunities.

- Lives lived: working lives, social activism, volunteerism, my creative or craft life, avocations, interests, passions.

- Travel experiences, memorable places and human encounters, nature writing.

CHAPTER 2

PRACTICAL MATTERS: MEMOIR WRITING TOOLS, HELPFUL HABITS, AND TIMELINES

Memoir writing tools

Portable notebook. Memories and inspiration arrive unbeckoned—during walks, dinner party conversations, as we go to sleep and wake up. Be prepared. Always carry a small portable notebook or add a note-taking app to your phone. Use it to make brief notes or sketches or, if your notebook is a phone, take photographs of documents and special places and people.

Private creative journal. This is your place to write whatever you want, however you want. The essayist Phillip Lopate calls the contents of his writer's journal 'intimate scribbles.' According to Lopate, 'The writer's notebook has been variously compared to a laboratory, a mirror, a brainstorming tool, an icebreaker, a wailing wall, a junk drawer, a confessional, a postcard to oneself, a singing in the shower, a jump-start cable, an aide-mémoire, an archive, an anthology, a warehouse, a tourist's camera, a snooping device, a sharpener of observation, a survival kit, a way of documenting mental illness, a meditation practice, a masturbation, a therapist, a spiritual advisor, a compost bin, a punching bag, a sounding board, a friend' (*To Show and To Tell*).

If you restrict your personal writing to texts that you plan to share with others, you will almost certainly censor your memory and your expressive voice from the outset. A private writer's journal allows you to acknowledge and voice your actual experiences in their true, raw forms. It is a reflective, expressive space that is beyond the reach of the finger-wagging of loved ones and the inner barking dogs of propriety and shame. Write the truth in your journal, then decide whether or not you want to share this, or versions of this, with others.

Let's say that you begin remembering the death of your mother. Go to your creative journal and write in quick, brief form the sensuous, felt elements of your immediate experience of this death. Note whatever comes to mind: the whistle of a kettle, the hush in a room, a voice, the feeling of your dead mother's cheek, the tear stains on your uncle's shirt, your wish to not be there, the last time your mother kissed you goodnight, those other reassuring goodnight kisses, the time you came upon her half-dressed, how unforgivably vile she was to share your secret with others, the pleasure of story-reading together, the erotic jolt that day she rested her hand on your knee, her best-ever macaroni and cheese . . . . Here begins a gradual circling around and through a fateful moment—a circling that gradually widens to include a rich mix of inconsistent and ambivalent memories—bidden, unbidden, forbidden—of having *this* woman as a mother.

If you doubt the generative power of a private journal, try the following experiment: list in your journal five experiences or thoughts that you should not or must not think, or publicly cannot or should not write about. Now go ahead and write a paragraph on each. When you are finished, reflect on where this writing has taken you in your life experiences. What are you discovering about yourself that might belong to the story about your life?

By the way, your journal is also a useful place to 'map' a story and essay (see Chapter 7).

Index cards or digital equivalents. Some people find these a helpful way to organize notes for each story or essay. Each card includes one story or essay idea, its key words, and possibly quotations and samples of people's voices.

Reference tools. These include a good dictionary, thesaurus, etymological dictionary, and historical and other reference material. Most of these resources are available online. Among the many helpful books on writing well, I recommend Strunk and White's *The Elements of Style* and William Zinsser's *On Writing Well*.

Recording device. Some people find it easier to tell their life stories through speech rather than writing. Consider creating an audio memoir library. Or use your spoken stories as a starting point for redrafting them in written form.

Helpful habits

Set a routine place and time to write. Think of the value of a routine for going to sleep and then develop a routine for writing. Build your writing time into existing routines. Make this time necessary and natural feeling. Think small: 20 or 30 minutes each day, including 5 to 10 minutes for reflection—get yourself into the zone of memory and personal experience—then 20 minutes for 'writing,' whether this means mapping, note-making, drafting a paragraph, or rewriting.

Experiment with various writing places, times, and prompts—and use whatever helps you write. Create a place that says *This is where I write*: a particular table or desk, being near certain pictures, the right lighting, listening to a type of music, or having complete silence. No interruptions, no distractions. Choose a regular time of day: perhaps on waking or the quiet hours of late evening. Set writing in a sequence of activities, for example after a walk, cycle, yoga session, or period of meditation.

Take a step forward each week. Map a story and write a rough draft each week, or revise an existing draft. Work in small units, say 200 to 500 words. Yes, there will be days when the tank is dry, or the rest of your life calls you elsewhere, or some enticing inner voice reads off the many reasons why you needn't 'get on with it.' Yet even in times like these you can move your memoir forward. Make brief notes on a memory of a voice, a place, a person, a taste, or a touch. Thumb through photo albums. Talk to family and friends about their life and your own. Above all, claim regular personal time for your writing.

Remember that creativity is fickle. Be prepared. Carry around your portable notebook everywhere. Memories, key words and phrases, images, sensations, voices—the generative stuff of life stories—come tap-tap-tapping on consciousness at any time, like unexpected visitors. Have the welcome mat ready.

> **Back up your writing files**
>
> You have precious personal stories in your computer files. Prevent their loss by backing them up daily or weekly. This means more than simply saving your files. Copy your work to an external drive and/or store your files in one of the many online 'cloud' services. Store external drives in a secure place. Ensure that if something happens to you, your family or friends know about your memoir writing files and where to find them.

Timelines

A timeline is a list of significant personal or historical details associated with our life. They set these details in simple chronological order. Done early in the memoir writing process, timelines help clarify, confirm, and organize key life events and dates, at least in their initial, provisional form. A combined personal and historical timeline placed at the end of your memoir is also a useful reference tool for your reader.

Timelines:

- Create a sense of our life organized into phases and important moments, and suggest possible connections between various experiences.

- Begin to identify possible memoir writing subjects: significant experiences and life moments, milestones, crossroads.

- Set our personal experiences in social-historical context and help recall connections between the personal and the cultural.

- Fill in details about our birth and childhood worlds and the world in which our parents parented.

- Help create an emerging rough sketch of the possible key elements and overall shape of our memoir.

Best of all, a timeline frees us from any need to take a chronological approach in our week-to-week writing. Instead, we can go to what really interests us among our life experiences, and it is this interest—this care, curiosity, excitement—that energizes good writing. Finally, because a timeline serves as an orienting reference for our reader, it gives us greater freedom to organize our overall memoir as we wish—whether by themes, influential relationships, working lives, travels, key turning points, or other means.

There are two types of timeline: personal and historical.

Personal timeline

Begin with your birth date or perhaps earlier. List significant events, dates, places, names of people involved, and other relevant details. Begin by keeping the entries brief. As needed, you can add further details and associations along the way. Be careful about highlighting life events that others around you say are significant. You are setting out the key markers of your life as *you* understand them and as suggested by *your own* experience.

Historical timeline

Consider adding a historical timeline to your personal timeline. Use a different typeface to add 'historical' items at the end of or alongside the appropriate year or decade in your personal timeline. Include social-cultural forces, events, people, and influences (such as books or films) that have shaped how you think about and understand the world, your fears and hopes, your life choices, and your values and beliefs. Historical timelines can also identify moments where you have influenced, or worked to influence, events around you.

Each personal and historical timeline will be unique. Because of your birth year, you will experience a historical event at a particular stage in your life—or experience it indirectly, say, through your parents or historical records. Remember that we also experience the world through different bodies and social-cultural contexts, such as female or male, skin colour and other body characteristics, income and class, city or country, this country or that or many. As well, each of us uniquely responds to and is affected by specific external influences.

Select social-cultural details that have significance for how your own life has unfolded, who you have been and are, what you have done, and how you have made your mark. Include influences from your hometown, the world, your country, cultural movements and fashions, books, films, music . . . whatever has helped shape your life.

Further reading

For recommended books and essays on writing memoir stories, personal essays, and memoirs, see the Selected Readings at the end of this book.

Rheo Brunet: 'Made by an inmate at the Kingston Penitentiary in 1952, this old wallet has been with me all along. You'll find more memories than money in it.' Courtesy © Curtis Brunet, from his video *This Old Wallet*. Some objects—a wallet, a bookshelf, a screwdriver, a sewing pin cushion, a chair, an ice cream scoop—become containers filled with our life stories, like a memento-filled trunk. What special objects contain stories from your life?

CHAPTER 3

THE WELLSPRINGS OF EFFECTIVE MEMOIR WRITING

Effective memoir writing requires that we attend to matters of craft: the intentional reworking and shaping of each life story or personal essay.[1] But craft cannot identify or explore our significant life experiences. Craft can't find that crack in things where, as Rumi said, the light of new revelation or insight comes in. Nor can craft alone bring alive our stories, tell them in our voice, and make them feel like the real thing—like *our* story. For this we need to attend to other matters—what I call the *wellsprings* of effective memoir writing. I briefly introduce a number of these here and examine the issues they raise in more detail in later chapters.

Write, then write some more. Effective writing takes practice—like dancing the tango or quilting or using a hammer or hitting a baseball. We learn to write, and write better, by writing.

Listen to your writing. Read your writing to another person or to yourself. Feel its rhythms, its points of emphasis, its energies. Ask how and whether specific words and phrases work, and whether the writing conveys the moods and meanings you want. Be open to your listeners' responses.

---

[1] For discussions of craft, see especially Chapters 8 and 12–15.

Read well-written, thoughtful memoirs. Ask yourself how and why they work. Learn from the writing of others. See the reading list at the end of this book.

Write with integrity. Make a serious effort to find, explore, understand, and communicate your significant life experiences. 'Serious' does not mean that you ban humour from your writing. Serious effort says *I mean this. This is the real thing as I understand it. This is my best effort to say what's true.* The most interesting memoirists have flaws and doubts, they live amidst uncertainty and paradox, they are confident enough to be self-deprecating, they implicate the self in life's quandaries and missteps, and they learn from (or show themselves refusing to learn from) their experiences. That is, they write with integrity. See Chapter 21.

Write with courage. Writing a memoir, especially with integrity, can feel like entering a lion's cage. We need courage—courage of heart, courage to be true to one's heart (the Old French *corage* means heart or innermost feelings). In memoir writing, courage calls on us to expose our uncertainties and vulnerabilities, to be true to our actually lived experience and, as Brené Brown says, speak one's mind by telling one's heart (*The Gifts of Imperfection*). Write with courage. And be encouraging toward other memoir writers.

Write from within your own skin—or what I call your embodied or creaturely self.[2] The memoirist Mary Karr writes, 'One can't mount a stripper pole wearing a metal diving suit' (*The Art of Memoir*). The arbiter of what is 'real,' 'significant,' and 'true' in your life is not what others or convention or some voice inside you says *should* be significant. 'Should' is one form of the metal diving suit, as are the concepts 'nice,' 'upright,' and 'proper.' Don't write as if you are someone else's echo. Truth and significance sit uniquely somewhere inside your single-bodied self, as something *grasped* or lived by the sensate self. When we write from within our own skin, we write in our own voice. Our writing comes alive. It feels like the real thing. See Chapters 19 and 21.

---

[2] See the more detailed discussion of the 'creaturely self' in Chapter 19.

Listen to the evidence of all your senses—or what I referred to in the previous point as your creaturely self. We modern adults are socialized to favour our sense of sight and to belittle the other senses, along with our animal selves. And yet despite what consciousness might claim, our entire perceptual system—how we interpret or make sense of the world through the senses—depends on how the medley of our senses *touch* and thereby *grasp* our environment, in the same way that a dog, released into a field, will learn about that field through its nose, ears, tongue, paws, bones, and muscles. As live creatures, we embrace some things, spurn others, and become anaesthetized to still others. Our sensing body is always telling us how we actually are in the world. Good personal writers take into account the full spectrum of their sensuous life—sight, hearing, touch, smell, taste—when reflecting on their experience and understanding. Theirs is a 'grounded intelligence' that uses a 'sensuous reasoning.'[3] When writing about your earliest experiences in particular, remember that, quite unlike adults, children live in a world where touch, taste, smell, and hearing are the primary sources of experience. On memory and the senses, see Chapters 18.

Draw your own circle. One of Picasso's favorite assignments for new artists was to have them try to draw a perfect circle. It can't be done. Each of us draws a circle with some particular distortion. That circle is your circle, a window onto your shaping experiences, your expressive writing style, your voice. As Picasso said, 'From errors one gets to know the personality.'[4]

Explore your life experiences. I have already touched on this point in Chapter 1 and will return to it in Chapter 20. For the moment, let me put the issue this way. Among the greatest challenges facing all memoir writers, and especially those over 60 or so, is the appeal of

---

[3] This language is from E.V. Walter's *Pathways: A Theory of the Human Environment*. Walter continues: 'For the mind includes more than intellect. It contains a history of what we learn through our feet. It grasps the world that meets the eye . . . the places we know in our hearts, in our guts, in our memories, in our imaginations. It includes the world we know in our bones.'

[4] I have taken this example from Lewis Hyde, *Trickster Makes This World*.

playing back the familiar, set-piece life stories we've always told. Sure, some of these stories are brilliant. Go ahead and tell them. Often, though, simply repeating the same old is to write like a sleepwalker. Be awake to your experiences. Be like the archaeologist excited by and keen to make sense of what she's unearthing—the evidence of life—down through the layers of time. Ask What? But also ask How? and Why?

'Memoir,' William Zinsser writes, 'is the best search mechanism that writers are given. Memoir is how we try to make sense of who we are, who we once were, and what values and heritage shaped us' (*Inventing the Truth*). 'Write about what you know' is oft-repeated and good advice for memoir writers. The best writers do this, but they go further. They not only question the familiar. They explore the unthought but felt, what they already know but don't know they know, and those other knowns that need more understanding. That is, they explore what they know and what they don't know. Many memoirists begin by thinking that they are more intelligent than their writing. Others—the ones I find myself wanting to spend more time with—listen for the new forms of intelligence, of awareness, that can be generated through the activity of writing itself.

Pause to reflect and learn. Many novice memoir writers keep moving their narrative forward, pell-mell fashion, adding new scenes and other elements one after another. They don't slow down to wonder about, ask questions of, the experiences they are chronicling. *Why is this important to write about? Why did I do or say or think this? What does this scene suggest—about a character, about me, about a relationship—beyond its mere description?* The best memoir writers move back and forth between narrative forward movement and lingering, meditative reflection. They pause, step back, and ask How? and Why? They are seeing what they might learn from their experiences. And as readers, we see them thinking and learning on the page.

Be wary of common sense. Or 'level-headedness,' 'realism,' 'prudence,' and similar ideas. These are the voices of culture and its ideals of 'practicality' and 'maturity.' 'Life' might have persuaded you of the worth (or at least the necessity) of such concepts, but our actually lived lives follow the push and pull of more varied, contradictory forces. Consider for example how asbestos mining was seen for decades from the perspective of mine owners, stockholders, 'jobs,' and 'the economy.' Then consider the same thing by listening to the breath of the miners. Good memoirists don't ignore the forces of cultural common sense and realism. But the best ones take the next step. They examine and judge the claims of these forces in terms of the needs of the live creature. When someone says *Be realistic*, the best memoirists listen for the breath of life.

Acknowledge the potholes. If life is a journey then little of it takes place on a superhighway. If you write as if the going is always smooth and straight ahead and ends in some happy place, no one will believe you. Effective memoir writing includes the washed out, washboarded, and potholed stretches—and the many byways, dead-ends and empty gas tanks as well. The best memoirists don't take detours around life's significant times of grief or hurt or anxieties or sheer lostness. Nor do they wallow or whine. Instead, they tell it as it is—and work at figuring out, in the writing process, what it might mean. In fact, the true voicing of pain is often the best antidote to wallowing, as well as to pain's hoary grip.

Go to what is personally significant. Take schooling for instance. Culture sees significance in our schooled successes, failures, and certifications—that is, its attention is on the institution. By contrast, when I think of my 'schooling,' I remember the ungraceful, chalkdust-enshrouded figure of Mr. Kapinsky, our Grade 11 math teacher, and how he mesmerized we 17-year-olds with the coolest number-based card tricks. Another example: cultural histories record and analyse the 1950s–1960s Cold War and arms race. I know about that, but my creaturely memory pulls up televised images of enormous fiery explosions and a ravaged place called 'Hiroshima'—their fearsomeness, their inexplicability, my sense of dread (*existential dread* I would have called it, if I had had the words)—and during those same years, the pulsing, teenage, fully intelligible truth of songs like 'Great Balls of Fire,' and the enticing angora-wrapped form of my maybe girlfriend Maggie who, as we parted each day at the laneway end, would make a half-turn, smile, and say with words that also burned, *If I don't see you in the fall, I'll see you in the bedsprings*. The 'significant' in memoir writing is how life's experiences—those fires inside and outside—are lived close and immediate, in the writer's creaturely self. This is the gold of memoir writing.

Stay within yourself. The good memoirist follows the advice of the goalkeeper going for World Cup gold: *Stay within yourself*. Turn off the hectoring, cautioning voices of the crowd. Write as if no one is watching. Or write as if dead. Writing posthumously is advice Christopher Hitchens said he was given by the South African Nobel Laureate Nadine Gordimer. He understood her to mean that 'one should compose as if the usual constraints—of fashion, commerce, self-censorship, public and, perhaps especially, intellectual opinion—did not operate.'[5]

Be attentive. Take your cue from the Zen master Ikkyu. It was he who advised that the highest wisdom can be summed up in one word: 'Attention.' When his listeners were not satisfied, he said: 'Fine, two words. Attention. Attention.' Notice the energy centres of your memories: where they move you, make you shake, bring tears, make you want to repeat an experience. Ask questions of others and yourself—then listen, really listen. Hold your fixed ideas, ideals, and habits lightly; be open to the surprising, to what you are not prepared for. Being attentive means far more than observation, with its inference of seeing from a cool distance. Being attentive is, importantly so, an act of observant care, of consideration, even of concern, as when we attend to the well-being of an infant. Attend with observant care to how your lifelong friend moves her hands. Attend to the voices of the children playing. Attend with compassion to your own bungling. Attend to how that perfume makes you weep. Be attentive with creaturely, empathetic care.

---

[5] Referred to in Jeffrey Eugenides's essay 'Posthumous,' *The New Yorker*, December 21, 2012.

Openness, readiness, patience. Memories come unbeckoned—while tasting smoked cheese at a dinner party, or during a phone call, drifting off to sleep, on a stroll, that uncanny look on your daughter's face. Be ready: keep some note-taking device nearby. Always. At the same time, don't force memory. It will turn mischievous on you and play dumb. Make like you are not remembering. Go for a walk, enjoy the spring blossoms, say hello to that stray cat. Return now and then to the life story ideas in Chapter 5. Carry one or two tucked away in your thoughts. Follow Picasso's advice, 'I do not seek, I find.' Or his comment that his object in painting was to show what he found and not what he was looking for.[6]

Find what really needs saying. Each piece of personal writing, no matter how complex and many-faceted, has a true, deeply personal subject, purpose, and point. I call this its 'aboutness' or true subject. Just as stone sculptors talk of 'letting the stone speak,' so good personal writers talk of 'discovering' their true subject during the process of writing. As they write, some voice in them asks *Why is this really worth writing about? What really needs saying here? What does it mean? What words most precisely name this meaning?* (Words, says Edmund Carpenter, 'are like the knife of the [stone or bone] carver: they free the idea, the thing, from the general formlessness of the outside.'[7]) To begin finding the 'aboutness' of a story or essay, use the 'mapping' technique described in Chapter 7, and see Chapter 15.[8]

Be choosy. Novice writers tend to flit along the surfaces of an experience. Details and anecdotes are included simply because they 'come to mind.' Worse still, each is given equal value. As suggested in the previous point, more practiced writers use the writing process to find what really needs saying—a story or essay's 'aboutness'—then build and rebuild their writing out of this. They slow down and go deeper into what matters, and they scoot forward through the necessary but

---

[6] From Lewis Hyde, *Trickster Makes This World*.
[7] Carpenter, *Eskimo Realities*.
[8] The seed of my use of the concept 'aboutness' comes from Marion Roach Smith's *The Memoir Project*.

incidental. They use writing to find their necessary story, and they set the focus and rhythm of their writing accordingly.

Go to the concrete and 'small.' Many subjects, like schooling, are too unwieldy and impersonal for a memoir. To make them alive and meaningful you need to bring life back to a human scale. In the case of school, you need a chalk-dusted Mr. Kapinsky and his number tricks. Or take that baseball game you find so memorable. Sure, tell me the final score and that the fans were noisier than usual. But first sit me down in the bleachers right beside you and your friend. Let me see that hotdog mustard drip onto your fancy white pants. Involve me in your speculations about why baseball players spit. Tell me a joke about the mystery of signs. Let me actually hear how the fans were noisy. Remember the sense of solidity and weight, and the many defining colours and shapes of those bundles carried by the Rain Lady.

Give your experiences context. None of us is an island. We live in a changing, half-understood web of interactions and influences. I include here family members, friends, co-workers, neighbours, and other acquaintances as well as a variety of cultural, economic, and historical forces and events. Memoir is naturally mediated through the life of the 'I'—like a singular tree in the forest. But the best memoirists are attentive to how the other flora and fauna of the forest can shade, shape, dwarf, and nurture each tree. Attend to the specific texture of place, time, and circumstance. The living, interacting, changing surround or context is critical to each story we have to tell.

Tell a good story. Model the telling of your experiences and viewpoints on the techniques of good storytellers. Shape your material into a dramatic, engaging form. Use suspense, direct voices, anecdotes, and the tensed arc of dramatic development. Make your reader an intimate, as if they are there with you, overhearing a conversation, feeling the joyful beauty of that sunrise, listening in on both your expressed and your private thoughts. See Chapter 9 on storytelling in memoir writing.

Allow for the shadowlands of experience. Life—its experiences and our remembering of these—rarely takes place in a brightly lit room where everything can be seen. Some things 'work out,' others don't, still others do but in utterly surprising ways. Actual life, lived in the rushing midstream, is always 'something to be continued' amidst the uncertain, the contradictory and contingent, the overwhelming and the unknown, good and bad fortune. In actual life we are always stepping into the half-known or unknown. Something similar can be said of the house of memory, with its meandering hallways, its hidden corners, and its shadowlands of candlelit rooms. Fully lit, neatly packaged versions of life are false and boring. Use your writing to acknowledge, explore, and be surprised by what is in the shadows. And begin every writing project by recalling the personal writer's most reliably generative phrases: *I don't know, I'm not sure.*

Find the extra in the ordinary. Not all of us grow up with a drunken mother or creepy uncle, those mainstays of so many recent, and especially American, memoirs. Nor have many of us had missiles destroy our home or been kidnapped or done jail time. What do we who live 'ordinary' lives write about? I suggest beginning by taking a second look at the ordinary. Sure, your father was a good 'provider,' but he was never, ever 'present.' Why? What did it mean, and where did it lead? Or yes, you grew up in an ordinary, 'well-off,' 'everything in its place' house, but one of your greatest pleasures was to flee into the nearby wild woods or to the fusty, helter-skelter, goat-at-the-door home of your best friend Bobby Flanagan. It is also true that everyone around you was well schooled and reasonable, always chattering, as family legend has it, about 'everything under the sun'—except for some things, like the mysterious, danger-laden silence around everything sexual. As these examples are meant to suggest, the 'ordinary' is never completely ordinary. Somewhere there is an 'except that,' a 'but,' some secret or diversion, the *extra* in the ordinary, the thing that made your life the complex unique thing it actually is. It's here that good memoirists go for their material.

Visit your life's thresholds and crossroads. The *threshold* of a house is a place of entry and exit, a crossing place between what lies behind and what lies ahead. A *crossroad* is a place of alternatives, of choice. Both are places of in-betweenness, transition, movement, change, fate, accident, possibility, uncertainty. Life includes many thresholds and crossroads: between childhood and adulthood, especially adolescence; from life to death; struggles between generations; living between two cultures; arriving in a strange land or living as an exile; between the fixed address of domesticity, cultural convention, and routine and a life of wanderlust or of inner discontent.

On the threshold, life is in flux: unfolding, indeterminate. We are between the half-understood past and the unknown future. Certitudes are in doubt. The 'normal' and the made can be unmade and made anew. We are shaping our life, but life is also shaping us. Because of all this, personal thresholds and crossroads offer memoirists some of their most thought-provoking and illuminating materials, as books by Joan Didion, Jan Morris, Maxine Hong Kingston, Vivian Gornick, Doris Lessing, and W.G. Sebald attest (see the Selected Readings). Visit your life's thresholds and crossroads and listen for their stories.[9]

Imagine a curious, thoughtful, empathetic reader. The memoir writer is guided by two competing voices or sets of interests: the voice of truth (*Write true to your experience*) and the voice of discretion (*Be cautious, protect your privacy, don't look stupid or depraved, consider the feelings of others*). Whether these voices originate in other people or within ourselves, and whether or not we are aware of their work as we write, their feuding shapes our writing. It determines what is directly sayable, what can only be implied, what is unsayable and what is even unthinkable. For a variety of reasons, the voice of discretion can easily overrule the voice of truth. Because of this, experiential honesty needs allies.

Here are two ways to offer the voice of truth some extra support. First, imagine reading your mother's or father's memoir. Now ask what you really wanted them to write about that they did not—or they did,

---

[9] I return to the subject of life's crossroads and thresholds in Chapter 11 on wonder.

but in enigmatic or unconvincing ways. Second, imagine a reader of your own work who is really curious, thoughtful, open-minded, and empathetic—a keenly interested 14-year-old great-granddaughter, or even an imaginary, curious, questioning reader inside your own thoughts. What does this reader want to know about your life? Do they want your polite guardedness or your honesty? The upright, mature you or your creaturely you? As you write, remember—as a reader—your appreciation of experiential honesty, then apply this to your own writing. See Chapters 20 and 21.

The ongoing understanding of who we are. There is no key to who we are, no perfect map to this thing we call our self or its making. In comparing memoir writing to feeling or exploring our way across a river stone by stone, I was saying that the memoir we write is the story of 'the way' that we discover. Memoir writing is a form of wayfinding; the memoir writer a wayfinder. Stone by stone, the memoirist deciphers what is important in his life experience, and she asks why and what it means. More than that, the sense we make of an experience when we are 40 years old is a different sense than what we made at 14 or will make at 80 or on our deathbed. It depends on when in our life we cross that river. Indeed, even our choice of an 'important' experience will change.

To change the image, the good memoirist is like the traveller who keeps returning to his hometown after years visiting strange places. Each time he returns—that is, turns to his memoir—he walks streets that are familiar but changed. A street corner seems flooded with a memory he can't immediately unravel, a familiar shortcut has become a dead end, a passing stranger smiles and is surprised she isn't recognized, a house front turns into something—a mask—once seen in the market of another port. A passerby asks: *Where have you come from?* Another asks: *Who are you?* Because for him the names of commonplace things—'house,' 'person,' 'love'—now have many names and meanings, he must constantly interpret and figure out what things mean here.

Even though this is home (or was), the traveller feels that he has landed in a dream place. He is surrounded by those who have never left home—neighbours who over time have come to find their surroundings unremarkable, as naturally changeable as the seasons, hardly worth wondering about. Of course for them the years have also passed, but they have become habitués to the changes wrought by time. The memoirist is a stranger who finds himself repeatedly returning home from afar, carrying with him memories of other worlds, of this port town he calls 'home', and five-spice combinations of both. His is an ongoing journey through the remarkable—that which calls for attention, exploration, and the effort of understanding.[10]

---

[10] The ancient world had words for the traveller and the activity I am imagining here. One of the meanings of the Greek word *theoria* is to see the sights for yourself, learn from them, and thereby develop a broader worldview and wisdom. In the ancient Mediterranean world, the first 'theorists' were understood as thoughtful travellers, like Herodotus, whose collected reports carry the titles *Histories* or *Inquiries*. *Theoria* suggested active observation, asking questions, listening to locals and their stories, and feeling these with all the senses. 'It encouraged an open reception to every kind of emotional, cognitive, symbolic, imaginative, and sensory experience—a holistic practice of thoughtful awareness that engaged all the senses and feelings' (From E.V. Walter's *Placeways*). Memoirists at their most interesting—I think of the work of W.G. Sebald, for example—can be understood as 'theorists' of their life and times.

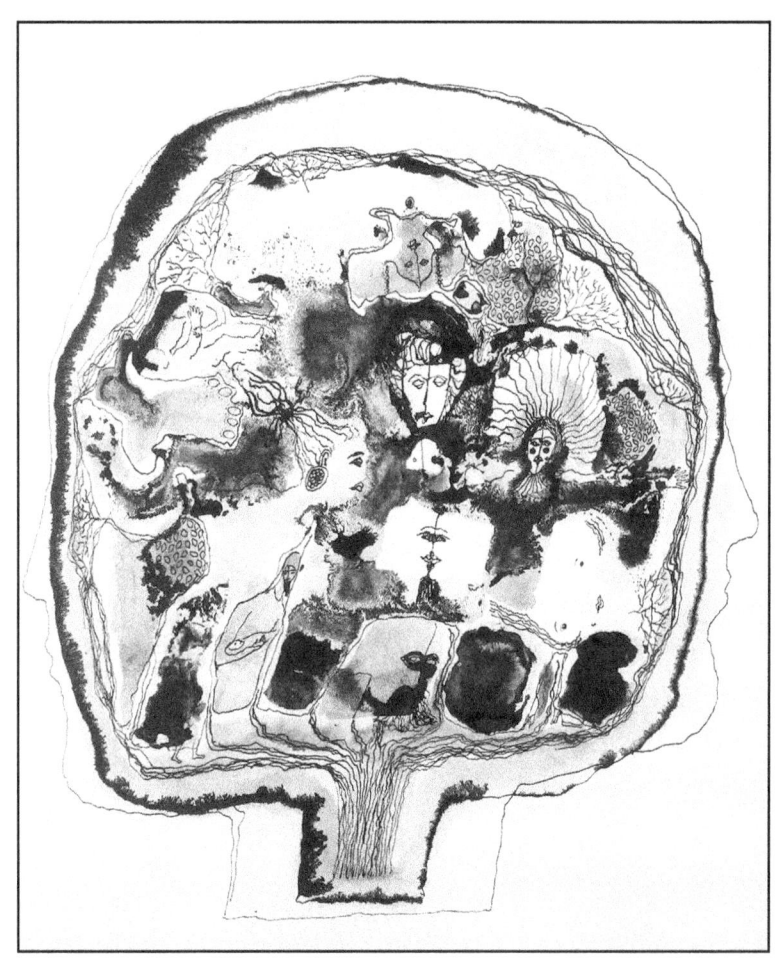

What are your memories of those times when you or someone close to you have shed tears—of sorrow, of joy, or of laughter? The artist Joyce Patterson called this work *Lachrimae Antiquae* (Old Tears). 'Lachrimae Antiquae' is the name of one of seven musical pieces composed by John Dowland in the early 17th Century. Dowland's 'Lachrimae' has the epigram 'Aut Furit, aut Lachrimat, quem non Fortuna beavit' (He whom Fortune has not blessed either rages or weeps.) Dowland points out in his dedication that there are several types of tears. 'The teares which Musicke weeps' can be pleasant, 'neither are teares shed always in sorrow but sometimes in joy and gladnesse.' Although we often associate the word 'tear' (crying) with the identical-seeming word 'tear' (uprooted from a place, ripped apart from a loved one, torn between loyalties or desires), the two words appear not to share a common root. In any case, back to the initial question: What are your memories of those times when you or someone close to you have shed tears? ©Joyce Patterson, author's collection.

CHAPTER 4

COURAGE

> In Bimini, on the old Spanish Main, a girl once said to me: 'Those as hunts treasure must go alone, at night, and when they find it they have to leave a little of their blood behind them.'
> —Loren Eiseley, 'The Mind As Nature' in *The Night Country*

It takes courage to explore our life experiences through writing, and then to share this writing with others.

The word 'courage' is borrowed from the Old French *corage* or heart, the seat of the emotions. Brené Brown, who has written extensively about courage, vulnerability, shame, and empathy, calls courage a 'heart word.' In one of its earliest forms, she writes, it meant 'to speak one's mind by telling all one's heart' (*The Gifts of Imperfection*).

Over time 'courage' has come to have varied meanings: valour (facing danger and trouble without fear); zeal and strength, especially inner strength; confidence; not being afraid or easily intimidated; the ability to do things one finds frightening; encouragement ('Take courage'). Courage, as a word of admiration, would hardly seem necessary if not for those things that make us anxious, fearful, and vulnerable: the threats, dangers, and precariousness of life. 'The saddest thing in life,' writes the poet Robert Frost, 'is that the best thing in it should be courage.'

In the context of memoir writing, courage supports the inner strength and commitment required for us to think, write, and speak honestly about who we are. Even before any thoughts of writing, it can take courage to be alone with and genuinely explore our feelings and thoughts. Later, it takes courage to sit alone in front of the blank page of our journal or notepad or computer screen, a story inside us, but a mind full of inhibiting voices. How to begin? Should I begin? What will people think? Can I even do this? Every really new beginning means knocking at the door of the unknown. We knock with hopeful anticipation. We knock with disquiet. We knock with courage.

Once through the door of personal writing it takes courage to explore our life anew, especially the deep grooves of habits and certainty. It takes courage to differ with loved ones. It takes courage to dissent from the commonly accepted perspectives of family, friends, and society. It takes courage to return to the sites of the bruises in one's life, and to acknowledge one's experiences of vulnerability, the hurt we have caused others, and the times we have betrayed our dreams. It takes courage to call forth the 'monsters.' It takes courage to reveal ourselves as other than the upright, in-control, decent person we present to the world.

It takes courage as well—sometimes extraordinary courage—to read our stories to others, even members of our memoir writing group. It takes courage to listen—really listen—to the responses of others, which are responses to our storytelling, but also felt as judgments on our very selves. We are advised, of course, to develop 'thick skin,' but writers with thick skin don't write much that is worth remembering.

The process of writing, especially memoir writing, involves arriving repeatedly at a personal line which marks the limits of one's remembering and storytelling courage. As is the case with 'being true,' the memoir writer will one moment push this line further out, another moment pull it back, or attempt in imagination to peer beyond it or, in their private journal, leap right across with needful abandon. To adapt an image from Bruce Cockburn, memoir writing by its very nature has us wondering and sometimes fearing where the lions are. And yet one of the miracles wrought by courage is how it helps us come to understand, through writing, that the lions may not be as frightening as they once seemed.

The courage to be true to our actually lived experience calls for understanding and trustworthy companions. This is the value of the well-facilitated memoir writing workshop. Participants are here because we share the preoccupations, aims, and challenges of our fellow memoir writers. We are in the same boat—life raft, perhaps—facing the same uncertainty and risks. Sitting together, each participant hears their own personal storytelling voice being heard by trusted others. In turn, each listens personally, empathetically, and thoughtfully, and each offers feedback in the knowledge of what it takes to 'tell your heart.' Gradually, confidentiality and trust nurture safety, and safety bolsters courage—the courage to think for ourselves and speak the truth in our own voice. It helps to know, at least for a couple hours a week, that we are sitting with the lions in safety.

So . . . cheer each other along. Be encouraging. Have courage to tell your heart—and draw courage from doing so.

The thoughtful memoirist questions the assumed relation between photographs, experience, memory, and truth. 'Before the invention of photography,' writes photographer Sally Mann in *Hold Still*, 'significant moments in the flow of our lives would be like rocks placed in a stream: impediments that demonstrated but didn't diminish the volume of the flow and around which accrued the debris of memory, rich in sight, smell, taste, and sound. No snapshot can do what the attractive mnemonic impediment can.' 'Once photographed, whatever you had "really seen" would never be seen by the eye of memory again. It would forever be cut from the continuum of being, a mere sliver, a slight, translucent paring from the fat life of time; elegiac, one-dimensional, immediately assuming the amber quality of nostalgia: an instantaneous memento mori. Photography would seem to preserve our past and make it invulnerable to the distortions of repeated memorial superimpositions, but I think that is a fallacy: photographs supplant and corrupt the past, all the while creating their own memories. As I held my childhood pictures in my hands, in the tenderness of my "remembering," I also knew that with each photograph I was forgetting.' Photograph courtesy Kelly Lacy (pexels.com).

CHAPTER 5

FINDING OUR LIFE STORIES: MEMOIR SOURCE MATERIALS AND SUGGESTED WRITING TOPICS

This chapter describes a variety of ways to awaken life memories, then lists suggested topics that have been chosen to help you discover your own memoir stories and essays. When using the suggested topics, I recommend narrowing your choices on any given day: choose one category of topics, then one idea from this category. Along the way, whenever you find yourself at a loss for writing ideas, return to the suggestions in this chapter. You might also consider basing your memoir on one category, or using the categories to organize your memoir materials.

Let the stories come

Possible memoir stories and personal essays sit waiting in a multitude of places. In our memory, of course—but also in the many doorways to memories: objects, a word, rooms, aromas in a market or garden, a gripe or wish, the words or rhythm of a song, a photograph, a map, a sudden sensation while picking strawberries, a picture in a book from childhood.

The best memoir writing begins by going to life experiences and thoughts that deeply interest us. Is there a voice inside you that says *I really must write about that*? If so, go there and begin writing. Go to a significant-feeling relationship or person or voice. Hold in your hands or in your thoughts something specific and solid that has personal importance: a brooch, a mustard-smeared hotdog, a lilac blossom, a quilt, a much-used wrench, a stuffed teddy, or a passport cluttered with stamps. Objects like these have an inner, dramatic eloquence. What comes to mind as you touch, listen to, smell, or taste such an object?

Begin with a consequential fact about yourself ('Because I was born at the beginning of the Nuclear Age, I . . .'), then continue writing. Go to your personal and historical timelines (see Chapter 2), circle an important personal crossroad or turning point, a cultural influence, a life stage such as changing from a girl to a woman—and ask your earlier self to tell you the story of this moment.

Visit places from earlier stages in your life, or use online maps and photographs. Interview family members and friends. Find a family photograph that has importance in your life. Try looking at it as if for the first time. What does it say, what doesn't it say? Write its story from the perspective of each person in the image. If you are in the photograph, write about yourself when the picture was taken and then from today's perspective.

The *quality of the energies* in specific memories can be life's truth-tellers—whether the memory is of a particular place, person, relationship, or situation. What was the quality of experiential energy in your childhood home, a secret place of childhood, a job, a marriage? Pleasurable: safe, secure, exciting? Destructive: anxious, lonely, fearsome? Without energy: flat, boring, indifferent? Secretive: suppressed, masked, silent?

I've said that memories and life-story ideas often come unbeckoned—a single word heard from across the room at a dinner party, the smell of mac and cheese fresh from the oven, the touch of a sweater. Make a note at the time. But also take rest days when you just forget about remembering. Read an interesting book, people-watch in the town square, give your garden some love. Often when we stop searching for memories, they find us, right out of the blue.

Memoir source materials

Family is one of the big veins of life stories. George Bernard Shaw offered his own advice on remembering family life: 'If you cannot get rid of the family skeleton, you may as well make it dance' (*Immaturity*). Get out family and personal photo albums and ask these photos questions.[1] *What was happening when I looked so distracted? Why is my brother so terribly sad?* Study video materials, scrapbooks, family member memoirs, genealogies. Talk with family members and friends from various times of your life. Ask questions, compare memories, listen to others' memories of you.

Use family materials such as diaries and journals, family letters, Bibles and other family history materials, recipe boxes, the contents of trunks and suitcases. Yearbooks, heirlooms, postcards, and letters. Childhood books and their images (these are often online if you do not have originals). Newspapers and magazines, music and lyrics. Open a favorite novel, memoir, travel book, poem, or collection of personal essays. Begin reading and see where the writer and your inner responses take you.

Visit haunts and hangouts from childhood and youth. Return to scenes of first dates and important neighbourhoods in your life. Visit the remains of the past: ruins, cemeteries and memorials, old signposts, those shadowy faded photographs of now vanished places. Listen for the *ca-ching* of an ancient cash register from a childhood shop. Read

---

[1] Photographs can both mislead and come to replace actually-lived experience. Like all historical material, they need questioning. On questioning the memories that can be shaped by family albums, see Marianne Hirsch, *Family Frames: Photography, Narrative and Postmemory;* Annette Kuhn and Kirsten McAllister (eds.), *Locating Memory;* and Martha Langford, *Suspended Conversations: The Afterlife of Memory in Photograph Albums*.

local history. Check local newspaper archives. Talk with locals and library archivists.

Draw a floor plan of your childhood home or other significant homes. Imagine approaching this building, walking room to room, sitting down for dinner, gatherings in the evening, stretching out in the dark in your bed. Keep notes on what you feel, and on associated memories, events, voices. Take your cue from Akshay Vasu: 'How ruined the home is, but how vibrant the feelings are in there' (*The Abandoned Paradise*). Draw your childhood neighbourhood, highlighting the experientially significant places. Use your neighbourhood 'map' as a story source—and include it in your final memoir.

Day dreams and rabbit holes

Tell your sensible, logical mind to leave the room. Let yourself return to being 12 years old, or to a time when you felt deeply alone or profoundly complete and happy. Let your bodily, creaturely feelings drop you down the rabbit hole of memory, as Annie Dillard does here in *An American Childhood*: 'Whenever I stepped into the porcelain bathtub, the bath's hot water sent a shock traveling up my bones. The skin on my arms pricked up, and the hair rose on the back of my skull. I saw my own firm foot press the tub, and the pale shadows waver over it, as if I were looking down from the sky and remembering this scene before. The skin on my face tightened, as it had always done whenever I stepped into the tub, and remembering it all drew a swinging line, loops connecting the dots, all the way back. You again.'

Let your personal creaturely remembering lead you down through Bob Dylan's 'foggy ruins of time . . . to dance beneath the diamond sky with one hand waving free' until . . . until, to quote my own remembering, a *werewolf emerges from the dark holding a Kodak home movie camera . . . or a blue bottle, perfume, mystery, strange places, mother, half dressed, that blue bottle my gift, lapis lazuli, small sailing craft under moonlit sky, the words 'southern skies' . . . and now a squat muscular woman appears, child in hand, washing basket in the other, walking across the light beam from a bookshelf lamp, giving birth to sensations of anticipation, tiredness, safety, sadness, tears* . . . . What might you find down your own memory's rabbit holes?

Personal story and essay subjects

■ Childhood, youth, family, friends, and other relationships

- Key moments in childhood and youth that I often think about.

- Our parents are enigmas. Who were they, singly, as a 'couple'? What did I learn from them? Best and worst of my experiences with them.

- One important thing about my mother—or father, grandmother, brother, or sister.

- The challenging, sometimes painful dimensions of relationships: parent to child, child to parent, between partners.

- Use this passage to write your own story: 'I believe that one can never leave home. I believe that one carries the shadows, the dreams, the fears and the dragons of home under one's skin, at the extreme corners of one's eyes and possibly in the gristle of the earlobe' (Maya Angelou, *Letter to My Daughter*).

- A story about something on my father or mother's bedroom dresser, or inside their dresser drawers or closet.

- My first realization that an adult, including a parent, wasn't who they claimed to be, or who I believed they were.

- Childhood games: their settings, voices, interactions, your role among other children.

- Family struggles (battles?) over music, clothes, food, hair.

- First experiences of self-consciousness, being on display, performing: a conversation, a concert, sports, a recital.

- First theft/thieving. First lie.

- Siblings: favourites, differences and conflicts, favourite memories of a sibling.

- Falling crazily in love. First time. Falling (or being thrown) out of love. Finding a 'life' partner. How? And how did I know?

- Experiences of family traditions. Least and best loved traditions. Tell the story of a family tradition through a special event or heirloom (*If it had ears/eyes . . .*).

- My children. First one. Pregnancy, birth, first years. Being a mother, being a father: greatest pleasures and challenges, strongest memories. Loss of a child.

- Grandchildren: first one, special moments with.

- A close friend or family member. Specific experiences that evoke their importance in my life.

- What in my experience is true friendship, and have I had or do I have a true friend? Who? How are they a true friend? What is a true friend?

- First best friend, just the two of us, who she/he was, what we did, secrets we had.

- Encounters with a particularly memorable neighbour.

- A person of great personal influence, living or not, known firsthand or not. Who? How? Why?

■ Personal identity

- The influence of cultural and parental ideas and expectations, and of social practices, on my sense of self as a boy/man, girl/women, gay, bi or transsexual, or a person whose identity has been influenced by race or ethnicity. My responses to these influences. What and how did I learn about who I am in terms of my ascribed identity? How do I understand myself, my own self, in relation to these ascriptions? And how did I come to this understanding? Challenges and pleasures of being me.

- My sense of cultural heritage. Where have I come from? What and how did I learn about heritage? The value, pleasures, and negative dimensions of heritage. Generational conflicts around heritage and traditions.

- Being identified and responded to as a 'minority' or 'different,' either negatively (discriminated against) or positively.

- Having a close friend who is or was identified and responded to as a 'minority' or 'different.' What was/is this like—for my friend, for our relationship, for me?

- Sense of physical self-image at different times of my life. Has this been important? Why and how? Struggles, conflicts, becoming comfortable with who I am physically.

- The life history of a part of my body. A knee: rugby tackles, climbing Machu Picchu, surgery. My nose, toes, buttocks, genitalia, or lips. The life history of a scar (on my body, in my heart), or the lines on my brow. My hands: who they have held, who has held them, their changing appearance, what they have done with great pleasure—or with guilt or regret.

- Living in a sexual body. First or early sexual awareness. How was sexuality dealt with in my family during my childhood and youth? How has living in a sexual body (combined with a culturally defined gender) influenced who I am? Based on my experience, what advice on sexual/gender well-being would I pass along to my readers?

- What do I remember about being 12 years old, or 16 or 21?

- Hugs and/or kisses: memorable experiences of these.

■ Significant objects

- A photo, a favourite pet or other animal, influential books or writers, a favourite childhood toy or game, piece of stitch work, painting, tool, songs and other pieces of music.

- An object that tells a lot about me, or about an important moment or relationship in my life.

- A prized possession: how obtained, its history, uses, beauty, stories associated with it, impact on my life.

- Go to the place where you store things you can't give up. Open up this place. What's there? Finger the objects, smell them, listen to them. Tell their stories.

- A well-travelled trunk, suitcase, backpack—the stories of their contents, labels, worn bits.

- Something I created or invented. The story of the what, how, when, why of this.

- Favourite hobbies, crafts, sports, creative activity, season. Why?

- Book(s) or other creative work(s) that have changed my life or my understanding of life. How?

■ Passions and interests

Passions can fuel our most valued activities, combine the best of all our faculties, offer intense pleasure, create change, and express our 'true' self. Life soars when we live our passions.

- What were my passions as a child and youth? Have they continued in any form? Have they influenced my later life? Were they part of my work life?

- What is a current passion, and what does it feel like to pursue this passion?

- What really irritates me? Why?

- What frightens me? Why?

- My passion for . . . convertibles, baseball, quilting, fishing, playing music, singing, photography, travel . . . .

- Do I have a passion I would still like to realize? What? Why? How?

■ Places

- Stories from a room in a house, especially childhood homes. Places in these rooms: a kitchen table, fireplace, bed, basement, coal cellar, woodshed.

- Secret childhood places: a wood, fort, attic, closet, under bed covers.

- Take us on a walk through your childhood neighbourhood, town, village, farm. If it no longer exists, walk us through what it was like in childhood and contrast this with what it is like now.

- A significant or favourite place today, the place where I most like to spend time.

- Feeling out of place. Feeling that this place is not home. Feeling lost.

- Postcards to a friend from any of these places.

■ **Crises, turning points, 'a-ha!' moments**[2]

- Happiest, saddest, or loneliest time in my life.

- The history of a personal feeling over time, such as grief or anger or love.

- The progression of a set of thoughts over time: beliefs, a radical questioning of one's past, values.

- An 'a-ha' moment or new realization. The time I began to see the world in a new way, or chose a new path, or had a new path suddenly open in front of me. When I came to understand [name your subject here] for the first time.

- The precarious high-wire times of adolescence: testing, experimenting, flinging, flaunting, flirting, fantasizing.

- War or natural catastrophe. Immigrating. Being a refugee. A storm, a flood. Torn from friends and loved places.

- Loss: of a dear friend (by death, by falling out of touch), of an important object, of a place or time.

- A sudden and significant life challenge—and my response.

- A time when I failed. What happened? How? What did I learn?

- Committing a crime. What happened? Why? The consequences.

---

[2] See as well Chapter 11 on wonder.

- Significant goodbyes. Forever, for months, for a day. On the phone, at a doorstep, at a train station, on a street corner. An experience of leave-taking, letting go, separation. What happened, and what happened next? Ache or relief?

- A life turning point. A situation where my life, or sense of myself and life's possibilities, changed direction or took me to a new place.

- The experience of 'first times.' First kiss or erotic touch. First bicycle or car. First moment of shame or embarrassment. First speech or other public presentation. First pay cheque. First death. First funeral.

- An especially influential teacher or mentor, a body of reading, a journey.

- Retirement. How do I understand 'retirement'? Do I consider myself 'retired'? My experience of approaching 'retirement,' its first days and weeks. Has retirement changed my life? If so, how? If not, why?

■ **Working life**

- My first job.

- The time I realized 'This is the job for me!'

- Being 'the boss.'

- Best summer job ever.

- Worst and best jobs ever, and what I learned about the relation of work and life.

- Figuring out the work–life balance.

- The place or significance of work in my life.

- Making ethical or value choices at work: my thinking, my responses.

■ Experience of my historical times

How we experience the forces of our historical times depends on the place and time of our birth; where we grew up; our colour, class, culture, gender; and how our parents related to the larger world. Our surroundings influence who we are even if we are initially unaware of such influences.

- How did historical events during my childhood or youth affect who I became? Did historical events lived by my parents influence how I was raised? If so, why and how? Did historical factors influence my family's or my own social-cultural-economic situation: war, the Great Depression, the 1950s 'boom years,' 9/11?

- If your family was interested in political life, what is the first political event you remember, and what impact did it have on you? Your experiences of your parents' political involvement.

- The first historical event or phenomenon (e.g., the Cold War) I remember. Its influence on me at the time, its influence since.

- The twentieth century and recent decades have seen a number of cultural changes: the roles of women, challenges to racism and discrimination, cultural diversification, urbanization, the increasing industrialization and bureaucratization of work, the climate crisis. Have any of these changes had a significant impact on my life? How? With what consequences?

- Stories of my involvement in civic life, my social activism, including opposition to mainstream social practices (e.g., environmentalism, refugee protection, arms trade, anti-war).

- What was happening immediately around me (a kind of emotional weather report) when I was conceived, or during my first year?

- Where did my love of travel, forests, stitching, reading . . . come from?

- What was/is it like to have a child with autism or other challenge?

■ Travel

Travel, especially when it takes us out of our familiar element, can shake up our understanding of the 'ordinary' and 'normal,' provoke curiosity and questions, expose or reinforce prejudices, and invite us to understand our home culture and life from new perspectives. For children, travel can be a time of intense excitement, anticipation and discovery.

- Walks: a memorable walk, a life-changing walk, a walk I'd like to take . . . .

- What are my first travel memories, especially my first emotionally charged travel memories?

- Experiences of living/working abroad. Highlights. Lasting memories. What I learned. Did this change me and my views about other people and life? How?

- A powerful (emotionally, spiritually) place I have visited.

- Travel experiences that challenged my conceptions of or prejudices about other people.

- The sources of my interest in travelling. What got me travelling? Why do I travel?

- Travel stories that reveal something special about how I became me, or about who I am, my interests and values. How has travel influenced who I am? Has travel or living abroad significantly shaped my worldview? How?

- Travel stories about memorable people met on the road. Who were they? Why memorable?

- What is the best travel-related keepsake I have brought home? Why?

- Postcards to a friend from places I want to share with them.

■ Beliefs and values

Here we focus on what guides our understanding of 'life'—our beliefs and values—and their experiential sources. How do we 'make sense' of life? How do we make ethical choices? How and where do we look for meaning and purpose? Why are we here? How should we be here? Where are we going?

- Times when certain personal beliefs and values emerged, became more conscious, or were challenged, changed, or discarded.

- There but for fortune go I. How have I experienced and come to understand the relation between my wishes, plans, actions, forces out of my control, fate, good luck?

- First 'spiritual' experiences in institutional or non-institutional contexts.

- Experiences of 'pilgrimage' places or pilgrim journeys, or of going on a retreat.

- A place where I experience the 'spiritual,' whatever this means to me. Where? How? Why?

- My values and/or faith in actual practice: comforting the dying, helping to empower the less fortunate, making tough choices . . . . What does 'my faith or values in practice' look like? What does it mean for others, for myself?

- A story about having my beliefs and values tested. Standing up for my values.

- What makes me or has made me lie or withhold the truth? Why?

- What is my idea of happiness as something actually lived?

- What I can't live without. What I can't live with.

- What I can't forgive.

- Choose a word—the word *long*, for example—and use it to write a series of personal reflections. Things I enjoy that are long. Something I have longed for. A voice remembered from long ago. Something that went on far too long.

- Who do I most admire, living or dead, and why?

- Living with and possibly moving through and beyond conflicted ethical choices and values. Money versus vocation or service. Playing a role versus being oneself. Being part of the group versus being true to myself.

- The most difficult ethical challenge I have ever faced and how I responded.

- Ethically speaking, what would make me leave an employer? Or contravene or refuse to obey a law?

- Among everything that circumstance and experience have taught me, what have I learned that feels most important to pass on to others?

- The best advice I have ever received.

- What advice would I give a 12-year-old? A 20-year-old? A 50-year-old?

- Is there a secret to a good life? If so, what is it? And what is a good life?

- This is what I have done to help make the world a better place.

- I might be 60- or 70- or 80-something, but there are still things I'd like to do, things I plan to do. Here's their story: the what, the why, the how.

- The story of an occasion when I felt the inner tremoring of mortality.

- This is my personal credo.

- This is what my epitaph should say—and why.

- If I wrote my obituary today, this is what I would say.

- If there is a celebration of my life when I die, this is what I hope will happen.

■ What if . . .

- A story or essay that begins 'I wish . . .' or 'I once wanted . . .' or 'I like to imagine . . . .'

- If there was a path not taken at an important crossroad in your life, what was it, and how do you remember it now? Why not taken?

- If I could spend a day in someone else's shoes, whose would they be? Why? What might it be like?

- If I could invite any five people to a dinner party—alive or not, known personally or not, from anywhere in the world—who would they be, why these people, what might happen, what would I like to talk about, what conversation would I like to overhear?

- If a genie promised to grant me one wish, what would it be? Why this wish?

- If I had a second chance at life and could use what I experienced and learned from my first life, what would some key elements of this second life look like?

Courtesy López Báez, P, *El salto o la caída* (2015), mixed media on panel, private collection, Israel. López Báez, P writes that in her paintings 'I accumulate layers of images as life accumulates layers of meaning in our memory. My process and technique refer directly to our ability to remember. Our memory is fragile, forgetful and misleading. In my paintings, sometimes the human figures seem that they just appear, other times they seem to disappear, the same happens with our memories.'

Courtesy López Báez, P, *La alegría de vivir* (2017), mixed media on panel, private collection, Spain. View the work of López Báez, P at pilarlopezbaez.com/

CHAPTER 6

LET'S GET WRITING

All my life, I've been frightened at the moment I sit down to write.

—Gabriel García Marquez[1]

No one else can really know what it is like for you to be here on this planet . . . how you experience *being* here. For me, this is the starting point for writing true [memoir] stories: a desire to express how one experiences life—its shape, its texture, its atmosphere . . . you are trying to make words say what it is like to be here in the mystery of existing at all.

—Patti Miller, *Writing True Stories*

This chapter offers practical advice on how to begin writing memoir stories and personal essays. Of course you might be well underway with your writing. Great! But if you want help getting started, this and the following chapter on story/essay 'mapping' have been written for you.

Enter your inner writing room

Think of an activity you enjoy doing—and do pretty well. Preparing a special dish. Practicing yoga. Tinkering with your car engine. Growing

---

[1] From 'Love And Age: A Talk With Garcia Marquez,' an interview with Marlise Simons, *New York Times*, April, 1985.

irises. We first learned to cook or garden by talking to and watching others, trying things out, taking chances. Now each time we are about to begin, we enter something like a little inner world of 'making this recipe' or 'growing irises.' Our mind is imagining the step-by-step process, the ingredients, matters of timing, tools, and the desired outcome. The activity of personal writing is no different. We move to the right workspace, enter into our personal inner writing room, begin imagining what we want to say, and write our first words.

What follows are four tips to help focus your memoir writing imagination.

Turn to what moves and interests you now. Go to an experience that especially interests you, that irritates or delights, that feels important in your life, that kindles your curiosity. Perhaps it's the memory of a sorrowful goodbye, that tarnished ring you found, a shy smile in a photograph. Now use writing to describe—bring alive—and better understand your subject. Give words to its lived qualities: its feelings, energies, setting, atmosphere, voices. Begin telling your subject's story.

Anchor your writing in the solid, small, and specific. Each subject has an inherent smallness and an inherent largeness. A complex lifelong relationship began with a specific kiss. Life and death take the shape of a seven-foot casket along which you are running your fingers. No matter the scale of your subject, or whether or not you choose to use it to also reflect on 'life' or 'fate,' begin and anchor its telling in the solid, small, and specific. The memoirist Anne Lamott keeps a one-inch picture frame on her desk to remind her to build each of her life stories out of 'small,' solid-feeling objects, situations, and anecdotes. However 'large' or abstract your subject, bring it alive through solid things: the slamming of a screen door, a whistling tea kettle, a ghost's aura, unfolding a letter the narrator is about to read, the delicate splish of a fishing lure touching the water.

Your subject might be schooling, but schooling as such is far too unwieldy for personal writing. Instead, surround your reader in one specific scene of what 'schooling' means to you as lived experience. Here's an example of one meaning of schooling from my life: 'In front of me the sneer on Mr White's lips, his raised arm, then a sound, SNAP or THWACK or CRACK or SMACK. Again the raised arm. Again THWACK . . . or SMACK or CRACK. My mind was far away, playing with the possibilities of that sound as my flesh burned and my face froze. I would *not* be here, I would never admit to being here. Later, on the playground, I will be a hero. Now, though, I am learning to send parts of myself, that burning crushed animal self, into distant, playful cerebral wonderlands, and into hiding as well, deep beneath an inner frozen sea.' Begin with moments of sensate life inside Lamott's one-inch frame, keep passing your writing through the specific and sensate, and see where the story takes you.

Write to an imaginary reader. Although good writers do not pander to their readers, they do often find it helpful to write directly to a real-feeling, interested, but imagined reader. When Henry Louise Gates Jr. had difficulty writing his memoir, he suddenly began writing 'twenty or thirty pages in the form of a letter to my daughters, and it just flowed. It was a miracle. I knew I was on to something good.' Because you can have any imagined reader you want, choose one who is inquisitive without being a shaming nag, who respects your courage, and who cares about your success. An imagined reader enters your room as a trusted intimate. 'Let's talk,' you say inwardly. Or 'Let me tell you about . . . .' Then let your writing flow forward on the warm currents of something like a conversation. Tell your imaginary reader about an experience that has long puzzled you—maybe the two of you can finally figure it out. Take them on a walk through childhood haunts. Introduce them to a fascinating person you met on one of your travels.

Just write. As with any skill, we become better writers by writing. We are, as William Zinsser says, 'creating new muscles: memory muscles, writing muscles, storytelling muscles' (*Writing About Your Life*). At the outset, remember that you are creating a first, messy draft that only you will see. At this first stage you are finding out how to best tell your story or write about an idea—or maybe you are still searching for what your true story is. You don't need to 'see'—and probably can't see—everything you want to say. This is a work in progress, the messy work of the self *figuring out* what needs saying. Just begin writing and see where you go.

Four approaches for making a beginning

What follows are four approaches to start writing a memoir story or personal essay. Try them out and see what works—and develop your own approaches along the way. I recommend a 300–600 word limit for each story or essay, at least at the outset. This length will help keep your writing focused and manageable.

1. Simply begin writing

Choose among the following beginnings, or combine a couple:

- Begin with your story or essay's **initiating event or precipitating idea** or a sense-based memory, then develop and follow its inbuilt turns and tensions through to the end.

- Begin with a simple **fact** ('I was born on June 4, 1944 . . .'), then include other related facts that you can use as touchstones for the story or essay's key themes. In my own case, the string of facts includes the following: 'A long-awaited blessed son' (it was said) born to parents in their mid-forties. The parents are finally about to 'get on their feet' during what will turn out to be the 1950s and 1960s Boom Years. Christmas morning opulence. Father Knows Best. Big cars, fast food, 'drive-in' everything, freeways. Red Menace. Whites Only. The permanent state of imminent global catastrophe about to be born in New Mexico, and given the named Trinity. The Cold War phantasmagoria playing to the rhythms of 'Great Balls of Fire' and 'wop bop a loo bop a lop bam boom!'

- Begin with a memory-laden evocative **place:** a house or room, a childhood fort, garden, workshop, office, car, church. Now create one scene in that place that reveals its life and the people in it.

- Begin with a specific **activity or situation** and use it to suggest how it represents a characteristic element of or moment in your life experience. 'Situations' could be: first swimming lesson, a family celebration, unpacking or thinning out your library or Chinaware or tools.

- Begin with a **thought** or **observation**. Here is how Christa Wolf begins *A Model Childhood*: 'What is past is not dead; it is not even past. We cut ourselves off from it; we pretend to be strangers.' Or choose a **thought that is grounded in something more concrete, sensual, and emotional**. Sara Suleri begins her personal essay 'Meatless Days' this way: 'I had strongly hoped that they would say sweetbreads instead of testicles, but I was wrong.'

2. Write in the form of a personal letter

As suggested earlier, imagine an interested reader and write *as if* directly to them in the form of a personal letter. This technique reduces the anxiety you might feel about getting started. It can also make your writing more personable and lively.

3. The 'first sentence' approach

Choose or adapt one of the following unfinished opening sentences—or make up your own. Apply this sentence to a personal experience or idea, then use it to begin a story or personal essay.

Crucial incident or moment:
- I was just a child, but . . .
- I saw my mother (or father) in a new light the day that . . .

Understand why:
- This is a story about my attempts to understand why . . .

I have always liked:
- I have always liked . . . . Continue with some specific object, event, human characteristic, place, art, or sport.

Experiences of discovery:
- I knew I shouldn't, but having drawn open the top drawer of my father's dresser, I . . .
- Suddenly here we were, halfway around the world on the dark outskirts of tropical Medan, stepping . . .

Crossroads:
- That was one of those times when the course of my life . . .
- The spinning coin that would decide whether we would move west or east finally began to . . .

Influences:
- Only now can I see how [person, event, writer, book, piece of music, painting] became such an influence on my life.

Death:
- My first experience of death was when . . .
- As I get older I find myself wondering about the relation between death, writing, and . . .

Places:
- One of the most memorable places in my childhood was . . .

Self-image and identity:
- My father had wanted me to be a 'real man,' so . . .
- Being 13 years old was like . . .

Imagination:
- Even though my family never moved, I lived in several worlds that . . .
- From the earliest days, my storybooks would take me to . . .

Beliefs and values:
- It is easy to have principles until they are tested, as I once learned when . . .

4. Write a story in a series of steps

Choose a subject with significance in your life. Base it, say, on an object, such as a family photo, or a relationship, such as your father or mother and you, or a visit to your grandmother's.

Make the subject 'small,' manageable, concrete, and possibly (although not necessarily) revealing of larger significance. An experience: a typical morning outing to the town market with grandma. A turning point: the days after I nearly killed two friends and myself.

'Map' the experience (see Chapter 7). Imagine key elements of the experience told as a story. Attend to evocative physical details, emotional qualities, specific human interactions and voices. Step back and ask: Given these various elements, what does this experience sound like when told as a written story, from beginning through middle to end?

Write an opening sentence that you will develop through your story. Example: 'I have often wished to speak to this frowning woman in the photo, my 17-year-old sister, her face turned from the camera's eye, turned as well from her parents, one of whom, my father, is proudly holding my newborn self . . . .'

Write the story—quickly, in a rough first draft. Follow the sensuous, felt, sometimes shadow-cast path of the story's situation. Just see where it takes you. Bring its meaning alive through telling details: objects, feelings, tensions, voices, actions. Ignore correct grammar and getting everything 'right.' Your subject is like a meandering streambed. Follow it.

William Zinsser on making a beginning

William Zinsser's advice on starting to write your life stories is among the best I have read. In what follows I quote and paraphrase from his *Writing About Your Life*.

'How should you begin? As always, that's the horrible problem. You've found that old trunk with all the letters and postcards and photographs and diaries, the school and college yearbook . . . wedding announcements and baby shower invitations. Your life is there waiting for you in scraps of paper and scraps of memory. Now all you have to do is put it together.'

Zinsser says that when he teaches life writing, he is invariably asked: How should I begin? The person asking assumes they should start at the beginning ('I was born') and summarize the high points of their life in chronological order. But, Zinsser writes, 'I don't think writing works that way, especially memoir. It doesn't follow the road maps we set in advance.'

Here's the approach he recommends:

'Go to your desk on Monday morning and think of some event that's unusually vivid in your memory: your first day at summer camp . . . an encounter with a teacher . . . the birth of a child, a moment of triumph, a moment of humiliation, a moment of love. Any event will do as long as you remember it vividly.

'Call that memory back and write it up. Describe what happened and how you felt about it. What you write doesn't have to be long: one page, two pages . . . but the episode should be complete in itself: one story with a beginning and an end. When you finish it, put what you've written in a manila folder and get on with your life . . . .

'On Tuesday morning, do it again. Tuesday's memory doesn't need to be related to Monday's memory . . . . Take whatever memory comes knocking. Put entirely out of your mind the idea that you're embarking on a longer project. Write up Tuesday's memory and put it in the folder.

'Do that every day . . . . After a while the entries will begin to add up. They may not fall into any relationship to each other, but they're doing useful work. First, you're exercising new muscles: memory muscles, writing muscles, organizing muscles. Second, you're discovering that the subconscious mind plays a big role in this kind of writing. While you slept, your subconscious mind didn't. It was busy poking around in all those memories you stirred up, dredging up other moments in your past.'

Keep this up, Zinsser continues. Don't be impatient to start writing your 'memoir'—the one you had in mind before you began. Then, after a few weeks or months, take all your entries out of the folder and spread them out on the floor. Here are some things you will likely discover.

'You'll discover that your first entries are quite stiff and self-conscious. That's natural. All of us who write need a certain amount of time, often quite a lot of time, to relax and find our natural voice. Therefore you'll notice that the entries you wrote in the second month are warmer that the ones you wrote in the first month, which are a little wooden, a little impersonal, a little pretentious, a little looking-over-the-shoulder to see who's watching . . . . So you'll gradually begin to find your own style—the person you want to sound like, the person you really are. If you don't find that person, you won't write a memoir that anyone will want to read. All writing is talking to someone else on paper. Talk like yourself.

'You'll make similar discoveries in the area of content. Certain themes and patterns will emerge in what you've written. Your material will begin to tell you: "This is a good direction and a good voice. It's true, it's funny, it's interesting" . . . . It will also tell you: "This is not interesting . . . in fact, it's pretty boring" . . . . [T]rust the process. If the process is sound, the product will take care of itself.'

Our parents. They are so close to us, even inside us, and yet so much about them remains enigmatic. Who are they? Who were they? Who was this man, my father? Or this woman, my mother. How on earth did they become who they were—and contribute to making me who I am? Who were they as a couple: as lovers, as confidants, as helpmates, as working people, as members of a network of friends? Photo: author's collection.

CHAPTER 7

MAPPING OUR EXPERIENCE

> Part of what fascinates us when looking at a map is inhabiting the mind of its maker, considering that particular terrain of imagination overlaid with those unique contour lines of experience. If I had mapped that landscape . . . what would I have chosen to show, and how would I have shown it? . . . . In making maps of our worlds we each have our own dialect.
>
> —Katharine Harmon, *You Are Here: Personal Geographies and Other Maps of the Imagination*[1]

> I've seen pictures of brain imaging where the brain is coloured turquoise, green and gold. It is like looking at the mind as a wild world . . . . The brain sends rumours through its pheromones, mysteries in the hormones and enigma in its chemistry: *Pssss, pass it on*. The questing mind must be quick to signs, signals and clues, running with, flickering with, lit with wit until paths of the mind work like paths of the land—they lead, they join up things of significance, they lay down patterns, they invite, they hold memory.
>
> —Jay Griffiths, *A Country Called Childhood: Children and the Exuberant World*

---

[1] Harmon's lavishly illustrated book is not about mapping as I discuss it here, although neither is it unrelated to our subject. Her focus is on how individuals, both children and adults, inventively appropriate and transpose the traditional conventions of mapping to illustrate a variety of subjects, such as moods, relationships, experienced and imagined places, and cultural and bodily landscapes.

As discussed here, 'mapping'—or, more precisely, 'experience mapping'—is a technique for exploring an experience or idea, searching for the heart of what needs saying, and suggesting how this might be written as a memoir story or personal essay. Through the mapping process we create a provisional sketch of the landscape of our subject, we name its important elements and qualities, and we begin to see what it is actually about. Although experience mapping can use linear thinking, its real strength is in how it employs non-linear, lateral, *associative* processes of thought. By continuously advancing possibilities, it helps us 'see' elements of an experience or idea that the conscious, logical, practical, and custom-filled mind does not.

The process of exploring an experience or idea continues, importantly so, throughout the writing process, but a useful method for getting it underway is experience mapping.

We will look at how to 'map' in a moment. Let's begin, though, by touching on a few of its benefits for memoir writing. Of course the actual results of experience mapping will vary between individuals and from subject to subject. In general, however, mapping:

- Helps find and recognize important elements of an experience or idea that everyday forms of attention can forget, overlook, or downplay.

- Sets out the context of an experience.

- Helps us become more aware of our material's centres of energy, emotion, interests, tensions, choices, excitement, humour, and other enlivening, dramatic elements.

- Begins to suggest options for how to give our subject a written narrative shape from beginning through middle to end.

- Helps focus our writing: identifies which parts are important, which can be moved through quickly, and which are irrelevant—or need their own story or essay.

- Generates unexpected offspring, such as forgotten experiences and their stories.

- Attunes our thinking to what has inner, creaturely significance, as distinct from what habit, cultural convention, and good manners say are 'significant.'

Overall, mapping counters the tendency among memoir writers to begin with the apparent certainty of *'This* is what happened.' Mapping begins elsewhere. It invites us to explore 'what happened' and ask 'What does it mean?'

Swinging through the trees, or how mapping works

In the context of memoir writing, mapping begins with a subject: an experience, idea, thought or feeling. It then invites the mind to participate in an *unfolding, fluid scan of associated thoughts, feelings, and intuitions*, like the movement of attention in remembering and daydreaming—or, suggestively, like the out-of-the-ordinary 'flowing' of embodied attention found in jazz improvisation. I am thinking here of what Melissa Forbes was told when she asked jazz singers to describe how improvisation works. According to Forbes, the musicians 'likened improvisation to travelling on a journey to a specific location (you have to "let go" and "get into the zone"), and to bodily movement (you "sort of swing through the trees and . . . no-one falls"). One singer described her body as a "vessel" for the music to "flow through." These metaphors,' Forbes comments, 'point towards a deep level of embodiment during improvisation and flow, and further implicate the body in improvisatory ways of knowing.'[2]

Mapping can certainly make logical connections between commonplace things. What makes it unique, though—and especially useful in personal writing—is how it can attune attention to the sensate qualities

---

[2] Forbes, 'The jazz singer's mind shows us how to improvise through life itself,' *Psyche*, August 31, 2020.

of personal experience and use these as conduits to move from one association to another. It invites us to enter the forest of associative feeling-thought and swing through the canopy's branches. Along the way, it can disclose 'nonsensical' but true elements of an experience, and suggest 'illogical' but apt connections within an experience. It helps us cross beyond the borders of 'commonsense,' habit, 'practicalities,' cultural proprieties, and 'normality'—and look back at these anew. It finds the forgotten, the surprising, the unthought, and the unthinkable. Through these movements of attention, mapping begins to suggest what an experience or set of ideas might really mean to us, where their personal significance sits, what they are really *about*, and what needs writing. In the end, mapping can help make our actually lived experience—our creaturely perceptual-emotional history—more accessible to conscious reflection and thus to ourselves as writers.

The basic elements of memoir mapping

Mapping always begins by naming the **subject** that is prompting the map. Let's say our subject is 'memoir mapping.' We begin by writing this subject inside a circle on a blank sheet of paper, as in Figure 1.

Next, let's think of the likely **main elements** of our subject, draw each of these like a branch away from the circle, and name each one. You can also begin a map by naming only one main element, then add others later. Each subject will suggest its own main elements. Figure 1 includes three primary branches or ideas (each underlined) related to memoir mapping.

Now, working from each main element, let's draw and name **offshoot branches** as we think of *associated* details, ideas, and feelings. Continue in this manner until you feel the map is complete. The process is like drawing and naming the branch system of a tree that you have not previously paid full attention to.

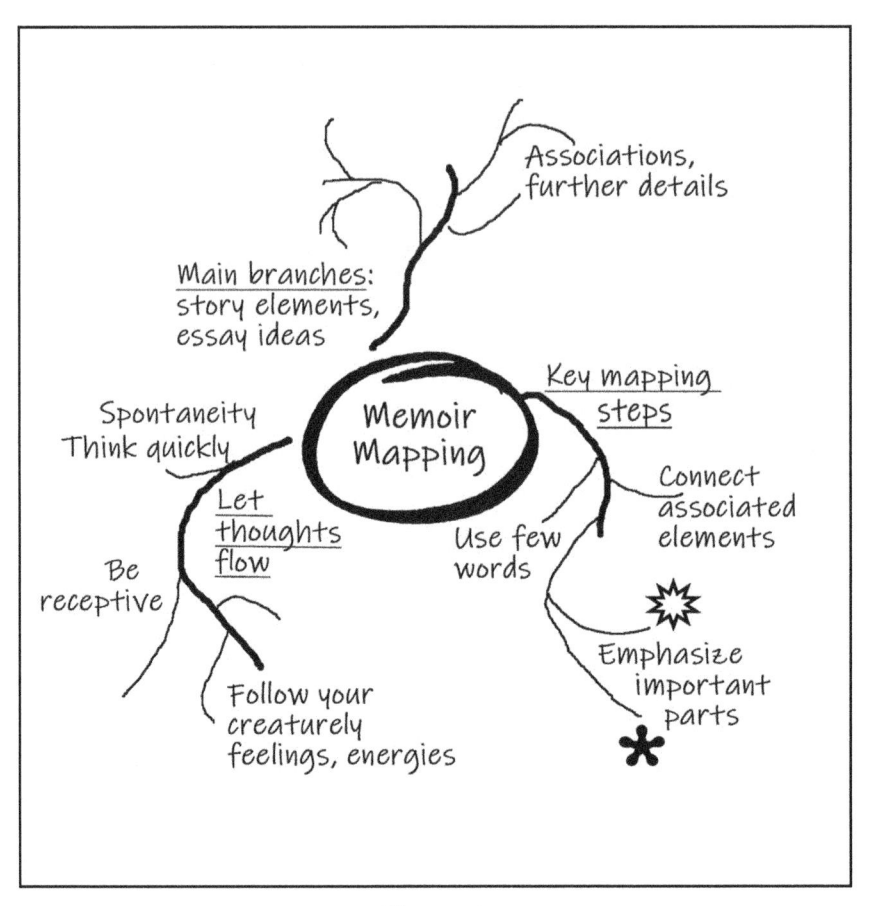

Figure 1

The best memoir maps are drawn quickly and spontaneously. Write what comes to mind, even if silly or improper. Create new offshoots, connect what needs connecting, keep the flow of associations coming. Mapping is best done by hand—and it can look messy. In fact messiness is evidence that the process is working, that you are really exploring your experience. Remember that you are not drawing some familiar package of experience. Instead, you are opening that package and discovering what's inside—which may turn out to have little to do with the original packaging. To map is to explore and discover.

What does the process look like when mapping a personal experience? Exactly as discussed so far. Always begin by naming and circling your initial subject: your childhood home, an embrace, something that vexes or gladdens you, a job, enjoying or creating a song—whatever subject you want to write about. Now draw a branch or branches away from this circle and briefly name each one after a key element of your subject: the rooms in your childhood home; the person, feelings, and context of that 'embrace'; the important steps in creating a song. Alternatively, experiment with drawing six branches and name each after one of the six basic elements of storytelling: who, what, where, when, how, and why. Next, use smaller branches to name the more detailed features and qualities of your subject: characteristics, voices, activities, sounds, smells, textures, emotions, contextual details, points of view, relevant anecdotes. Shut off those voices that ask *Is this correct? Is this logical?* Or whisper *Don't even think that.* For now, completely give way to your intuitive, creaturely self and follow where it leads.

Mapping a summer job

I once used mapping to explore my memories of working with stonemasons on the Stanley Park seawall in Vancouver, Canada, during the summer of 1967. At the time I was a graduate student studying literature at Simon Fraser University. What stands out in my memory of those summer working days? Where are the important personal stories? I began searching for answers by drawing and naming six main branches reaching from my main subject (Figure 2).

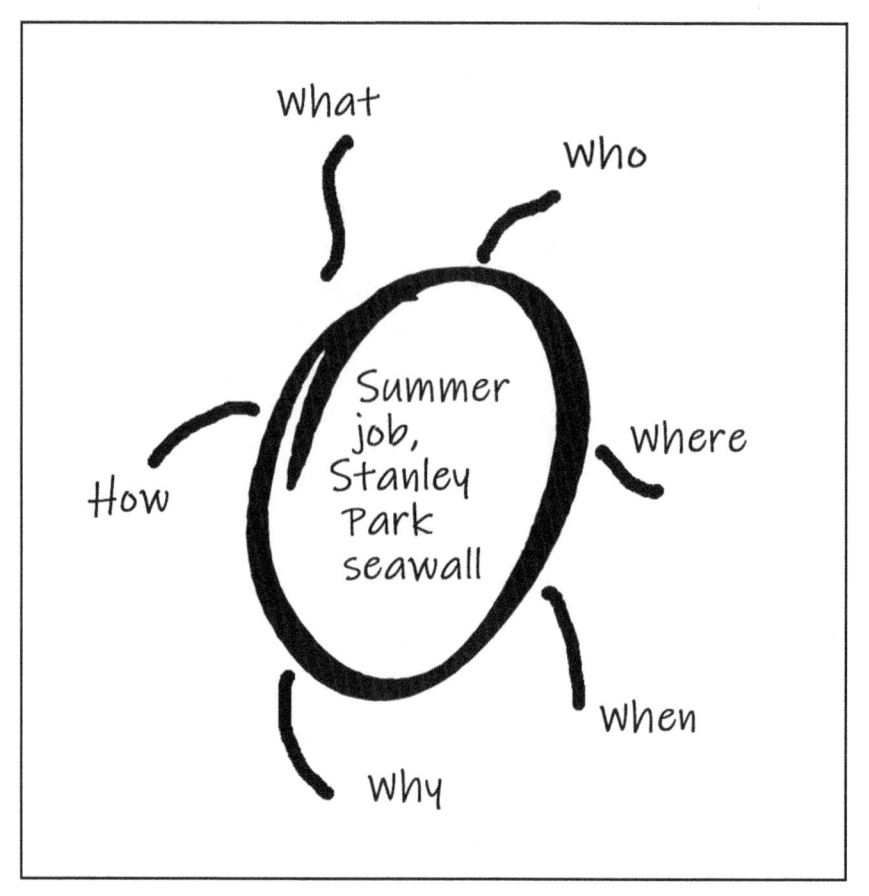

```
         what
              who

How   Summer
      job,      where
      Stanley
      Park
      seawall
              when
         why
```

Figure 2

I wanted to see where these branches would lead, what they might suggest. I then used this initial framework to map a more complete picture of my subject: relevant details, felt energies, evocative or telling anecdotes, how particular parts are connected, what's important and unimportant, significant pieces I was unsure about, elements that needed understanding. Along the way I connected related points, added associated points, and highlighted significant points. Figure 3 shows a mid-map version of this process.

MAPPING OUR EXPERIENCE

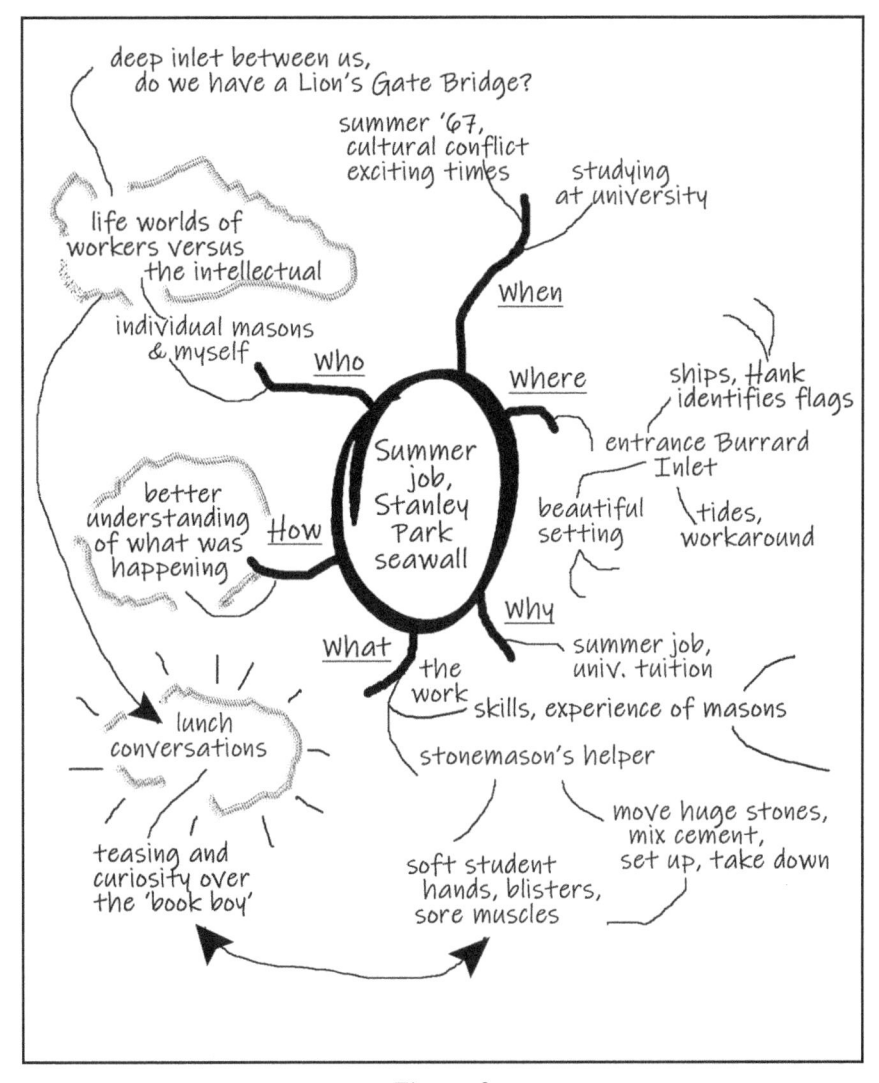

[Figure 3: Hand-drawn mind map centered on "Summer job, Stanley Park seawall" with branches labeled When, Where, Who, How, What, Why]

- When: summer '67, cultural conflict, exciting times; studying at university
- Where: entrance Burrard Inlet; ships, Hank identifies flags; beautiful setting; tides, workaround; deep inlet between us, do we have a Lion's Gate Bridge?
- Who: individual masons & myself; life worlds of workers versus the intellectual
- How: better understanding of what was happening
- What: the work; stonemason's helper; move huge stones, mix cement, set up, take down; soft student hands, blisters, sore muscles; lunch conversations; teasing and curiosity over the 'book boy'
- Why: summer job, univ. tuition; skills, experience of masons

Figure 3

Eventually I let my map speak to me—ask me questions—about how I might turn it into a memoir story. The questions went something like this:

- What is your real, your important subject? Where's the experiential *energy* in this map? What do you really want to write about?

97

- Have you missed important elements? Misnamed any? Misperceived any?

- What is this material's in-built narrative or storytelling shape? Where is the beginning and the ending? What is the main thread of narrative development? Where is the potential for drama?

- What needs emphasis, a quick mention, leaving out?

- What's the mood and the writing tone?

- How to make this subject manageable? How to anchor its telling in 'small,' solid-feeling objects, gestures, anecdotes, moments?

- How to bring this subject alive, make it evocative and engaging?

Mapping my summer job revealed a number of things. First, my original subject was too large; it contained too many possibilities. Second, the process helped me find what I really wanted to write about. Third, it identified a specific scene through which to tell my story. Mapping pulled my attention to a kind of energy field around the apposed life worlds of several individual stonemasons and myself: our differences in life experience, and the points of understanding, empathy, and curiosity between us. This felt important: this was the story I wanted to find a way to tell. The story's focal scene became a single and 'made-up' (composite) lunchtime conversation, and some closely associated experiences, all set against the stunning Burrard Inlet and passing ships. The mapping process had given me something solid and meaningful to work with—and to write about.

A few last points on experiential mapping

- Experiential mapping is a 'letting go,' an uncensored associative flow of attention, the live creature's improvisatory way of knowing. Chase the guard dogs of thought out of the room, enter into a receptive mood, and be led by your inner, spontaneous responses. In other words, enjoy swinging through the trees.

- All good personal writing moves between what exists around us, what we perceive, and how we feel inside ourselves. Allow mapping to ease your movement between these three dimensions: the external, the perceived, and our inner feelings.

- Only later, once your map is done, introduce a fourth dimension: critical self-reflection, using those questions I asked earlier.

- Finally, allow for—and follow—places of tension in your map: areas of transition, differences, uncertainty, choice, conflict, contradiction, crisis, vulnerability, surprises, and other experiential thresholds. These are often sites of energy, meaning, and consequence in our life. Transposed into personal writing, they are sources of narrative drama, character and idea shading, sudden revelation, and gradual insight. As such, they are the building blocks of great storytelling and personal essay writing.

Courtesy © Dominique Fortin, *Vers la vie*. Experientially true-to-life memoirs include stories about facing what everyday consciousness experiences as the strange, fantastic, weird, or wonderful. This is the land of our fears, perhaps, or our sorrows, regrets, and longings. In your own explorations of this land, what stories need telling?

CHAPTER 8

THE MEMOIR WRITER'S DEMONS

Earlier I compared memoir writing to crossing a river stone by stone. I should have said that this river is enchanted, like its ancestor rivers Mnemosyne (Memory) and nearby Lethe (Forgetfulness). The river of memoir writing has its own spirits—mischievous demons that can aid our success but also wreak havoc on our crossing, and even quash our desire to make a beginning. Here I want to introduce a few of these more harmful demons and offer some guidance on how to fend off their powers.[1]

Can I do this? or the demon of self-doubt

The demon of self-doubt has many voices.

My life experiences don't seem important enough to write about. Nothing 'big' ever happened to me. I have nothing really interesting to say.

I don't remember much—or with enough detail or very reliably.

My memories are all jumbled. How do I begin? Where? What to include, what to leave out? How to organize what I write? How will it all come together? Or will it?

---

[1] See Chapter 16 on how to overcome writing blocks when you are midway through your memoir.

Will anyone care about what I have to say? Will I hurt my sister's or friend's feelings, or be accused of Crimes Against the Family Memory?

I'm not 'really' a writer—unlike my brother and my friend Esther who are 'published.' What I'd say will be boring to others.

Let's begin at the beginning: Can I write my memoir? Yes, your wish to write your memoir is entirely reasonable and desirable. Indeed, by having the wish you are giving yourself the right to write. And you can be sure that those who really care about you and your success are cheering you on.

In the memoir writing workshop there is always at least one participant who, although he seems keen to write his life stories, says *Mine is not a particularly interesting life. I don't know what to write—or what's worth writing about.* As proof, he keeps plunking down a binder filled with blank pages at the beginning of each workshop. A few weeks pass. Then one day he sits down, opens his binder, smiles, and announces *I have a story!* His reading captivates us all. Of course he did have 'a story' after all. In fact, like all of us, his life holds many stories.

Whenever a workshop participant says their experiences are 'not really interesting' or 'important enough' to write down, I am reminded of the poem 'Famous' by Naomi Shihab Nye. Nye uses the word 'famous' in the sense of 'important,' 'interesting,' or 'significant,' and she invites us to think anew about why something is 'important.' For her, 'famous' (or 'important') is not cultural: not a matter of renown, not 'anything spectacular,' not what the many might think. Rather, as I read the poem, it is found in 'small,' creaturely moments of mutuality that affirm the delicate magic of life—as when the tear becomes 'famous' to the cheek, and the bent photograph to the one who holds it. As you come to the word 'famous' in Nye's poem, think of how you might sometimes use the words 'important' or 'significant' in regard to your possible life stories.

Famous

The river is famous to the fish.

The loud voice is famous to silence,
which knew it would inherit the earth
before anybody said so.

The cat sleeping on the fence is famous to the birds
watching him from the birdhouse.

The tear is famous, briefly, to the cheek.

The idea you carry close to your bosom
is famous to your bosom.
The boot is famous to the earth,
more famous than the dress shoe,
which is famous only to floors.

The bent photograph is famous to the one who carries it
and not at all famous to the one who is pictured.

I want to be famous to shuffling men
who smile while crossing streets,
sticky children in grocery lines,
famous as the one who smiled back.

I want to be famous in the way a pulley is famous,
or a buttonhole, not because it did anything spectacular,
but because it never forgot what it could do.[2]

The counsel I take from Nye's poem is this: It is enough that you write your stories and essays in a way that they become famous to—are in harmony with and true to—your life experience. Write not with a

---

[2] Naomi Shihab Nye, *Words Under the Words: Selected Poems.*

concern for whether or not your experience is 'spectacular'; write instead because, like the pulley and the buttonhole, you 'never forgot' what needs doing, what needs saying on your own behalf and through your own words.

Writing begins by writing. We begin—and we see what happens.

Write about one specific moment that stands out in your experience. A turning point in your life. That disastrous night with your best friend ever. The first encounter with a lifelong lover. That time when you were forced into silence. The emotion-laden object sitting on your mother's dressing table. The smell of your father. A situation you've 'never understood.' A time of intense pleasure or loneliness. An inner question, irritant, passion, or belief. A childhood secret or a secret place.

Go to those places in memory where you feel your heart pulsing, then begin writing. Quickly jot a few brief notes that name what feels most important about this specific memory, its felt qualities and associations. Or begin 'mapping' the memory (see Chapter 7) and see what else is there. Or write it out in rough form as a story.

Don't be concerned with sensible sentences, or 'finished' or even very intelligible writing. That's not where personal writing begins. Begin by *trying out* words that best express your memory or thoughts. Begin stringing these together into a true-feeling picture of a situation, relationship, scene, or place.

I once met a stone carver in southern India who was turning a rough piece of stone in his hands. When I asked him what he would carve, he replied *I see what happens*. Approach writing about a life experience just like that man approached his piece of rough stone. Begin by giving your memories their felt, true words, and see what happens.

Go to your private creative journal and begin. Make some notes about a memory. No one is saying *You got it wrong*. There's no red ink here. Nothing is incorrect. You are writing for you. Begin with a sentence ...

- 'As a 13-year-old I . . . .'
- 'When I held my baby in my hands for the first time I . . . .'
- 'The last night my father came home drunk . . . .'
- 'When I held her [his] hand I knew . . . .'
- 'The night I stepped onto the tarmac of that new land . . . .'

Tell the story of the experience that flows from your first sentence. Write it out as the words come. There will be time later to rewrite and polish the stories you want to share. Right now, go to your heart and write.

Truth-telling, or the demon of reticence

The demon of reticence whispers: *Don't you dare say that. Let sleeping dogs lie. You know it didn't happen that way.*

Personal writers hear voices—inside and outside the self—that urge us to betray the truths of our actually lived experience. Such voices prey on the limits of memory, on our affections, and on our sense of decency.

There are many reasons to not tell things as we understand them: causing pain or embarrassment to others (or yourself), invading the privacy of others, and 'keeping the peace' are but three that come quickly to mind. As Patti Miller says, truth-telling 'is complex, messy, confronting and fraught with dangers. It is very difficult to avoid upsetting at least one of your readers, if not a community of readers—whether they have read your work of not!' (*Writing True Stories*). I'd go further and say that if your memoir doesn't upset someone on some point, or at least generate disagreement, then you are working too hard at ironing out the wrinkles from real life.

A good place to begin reflecting on truth in memoir writing is to remember that your best reader—thoughtful, empathetic, realistic—wants to hear the genuine you. This means hearing about both your accomplishments and your failures, your strengths and frailty, your challenges and victories, your values and your doubts, your likes and dislikes, your despair and joy. A good reader will appreciate your *effort* to be true to your life—to reach towards the truth.

We will return to the subject of truth-telling in Chapter 21. For the moment, here are a few considerations, adapted from Patti Miller's *Writing True Stories*.

- Check your personal motives. Why are you saying this?

- If the truth will hurt someone or damage a relationship, weigh its importance to your story. It could be expendable, but it could also be essential.

- Find the right approach and tone. Yes, truth matters, but as Annie Dillard says, '[w]riting is an art, not a martial art' ('To Fashion a Text,' in William Zinsser ed., *Inventing The Truth*).

- Truth-telling does not have to be judgemental.

- Remember the fallibility of your memory and perceptions. Allow room for other possibilities besides your 'truth.' Admit that your memoir is your version of events.

- Talk with the people concerned. Consider asking them to comment on a draft text.

- Remember that effective memoir writing is definitely not based on 'being nice.'

- Remember as well that truth-telling can be liberating—to the writer and others.

- Lastly, consider the saving grace of humour.

The demon of egoism

Memoir writers naturally use a personal 'I' voice and perspective. Because of this, the demon of egoism sees an opportunity to take over your story, make it excessively self-preoccupied, and possibly use it as a mouthpiece for unexamined fantasies. Here are a few suggestions for creating an 'I' voice that is true to yourself but is also self-reflective and reaches beyond the self.

- Create a little distance between your narrating self and yourself as a 'persona' or character in your story or essay, then, as needed, have your narrator comment on the views and actions of your persona. Create something of a dialogue between your 'self' as narrator and as persona. Open yourself to thoughtful, critical questioning from within.

- Invite your reader into this dialogue. What do they think? What has been their experience? Would they have done or thought about things differently? Appeal to your reader's comparable experience. Engage them in your work of self-understanding.

- Focus on other people: for example, a person who had deeply influenced you, or some unforgettable person met during your travels. Bring to life these people and how they made an impression on you.

- Set your character or theme in a context that is wider than the self. This 'wider context' could be interactions with and between other people, social-cultural forces, or a landscape.

- Reduce the 'I's' and 'me's.' Instead of 'I loved to retreat into the dark forest surrounding my house,' write 'There was a forest behind our house, thick and dark and secret, with hideaways where no one could find you.' The reader is invited to see through your creaturely self, without 'I' directing everything.

- Follow Annie Dillard's advice and replace an approach that suggests 'I analyze me,' 'I describe me,' 'I discuss me,' where you are the subject and object of the action, with an approach that suggests 'I see this,' 'I did that,' where you are the subject, but the object is out there in the world.[3]

Finally, write against self-preoccupation but don't go missing in your memoir. Remember that your reader wants to know what it means to be you.

The demons of habit and familiarity

Let's say that you have six or seven decades of life experience. Your memory is still working, more or less. You have plenty of ideas about stories that you want to include in your memoir. And you are comfortably retired with time on your hands and the luxury of a computer. What could go wrong? Nothing, necessarily. And yet . . . the very fact of having many years of personal, memory-based storytelling behind us, combined with our sense of being 'comfortable,' thank you very much, can also work against effective memoir writing.

We can repeat oft-told life stories so often that, like certain family photographs, they become substitutes for the original experience, and so obvious in their meaning that they are no longer available to fresh, questioning responses. Habit and familiarity reduce our ability to really notice the distinct qualities—the anomalous, the hidden, the unsaid, and the yet-to-be-understood qualities—of others, our surroundings and ourselves. Familiarity makes the meaning of an experience 'obvious,' not available to curiosity—even when the experience *itself* is puzzling or strange. Habit and familiarity can also make whole dimensions of humanly *made* life appear to be natural (not 'made' at all) and thus not changeable or even worth considering. Familiarity reduces our capacity to wonder, to question, and even to think.

---

[3] Dillard, 'To Fashion a Text,' in William Zinsser ed., *Inventing the Truth*.

It's true that familiarity and routine also make life possible. And yes, genuine peace of mind is an inner state to be desired. But to explore our actually lived life, we need to inquire into the familiar and the habitual, to think *against* their aura of familiarity. We need to question and investigate 'the obvious,' especially in its comforting forms. We need to run our palm over our creaturely life, feel through our hand's nervature our life's wrinkles and frayed edges and tears, sense again the colours and smells and sounds in our creaturely memories. Doing this, we are restoring the sensations of our life experiences, imagining the past afresh, *de-familiarizing* the familiar, remembering our life not as a much-discussed snapshot in a family album but rather as it was still unfolding.

When Galileo turned to his world around 1600, including what was taken for granted as both true and The Truth, he responded with his *own* senses and reason—and found 'the familiar' remarkable and in need of explanation. The best memoirists are like Galileo. They look at their life and find it—including, and perhaps especially, the familiar 'truths' of their life—remarkable. Their writing feels all the more authentic and vital as a result.

The demon of normalization

Each of us experiences some pressure to be like others: to behave like others, to identify with certain ideas and ideals as if they are our own. Being 'normal' has advantages for social creatures like us. It also enables us to lose or 'forget' or avoid our self. Whatever the circumstances, the normalization of the self can easily lead to a mostly unconscious erasing, detachment from, or masking of the self—especially of the independent and actively responsive, feeling, inquiring, wondering, creaturely self.

My interest here is forms of normalizing our life experiences that undermine the exploratory work of memoir writing. In these cases, subjective feelings, impressions, sensations, and spontaneous intersubjective perceptions are tamped down or neutralized in the writing. Conflicts within the self and between self and world are little to be seen; nor are experiences of uncertainty and vulnerability. The self is represented as *too* stable, *too* secure, *too* 'together' and comfortable. The writer gives the impression of living a life 'without ever blinking an eye.' We might hear laughter in the writing, but genuine sadness almost never. Differences, such as quarrels over difference of perspective, get vaporized through avoidance, clichés, and euphemism. The writer needs to be seen as 'a good guy.' Consistent with the broader flight from subjectivity, the normalizing self offers up extended descriptions of external details, which their writing wraps in a pseudo-intimacy. As writers, they focus almost entirely on action, and appear to have little interest in reflection—or they have lost or unlearned the ability to do either. Overall, the voice of the normalizing writer feels like that of a deflecting self: a self that surrounds the actual, changing quickness of feeling of the live creature with a kind of fortress made from meticulously reported facts, meaningless phrases, the evidence of being 'in control' and an 'ordinary' person, and narratives that flatline the wavy rhythms and energy centers of actual experience.[4]

To write our memoir on behalf of the normalized self is to write our *own* self right out of our memoir. We are writing from some made, and perhaps now familiar, now needed, now reassuring self, but not our actually lived, sensate self: that self that lives uneasily *between* culture's normalizing pressures and the needs of the live creature. This is why the self as live creature—life experienced in the single-bodied feeling self—is so critical to meaningful memoir writing. Listening to it acts as a check against the appeals not only of normalization, but how normalization helps us 'forget' its own lifelong work, beginning in childhood. On the other hand, when we remember with the active and emotionally responsive, inquiring, wondering self, we are taking the first step towards writing on our own behalf.

---

[4] See Christopher Bollas, 'Normotic Illness,' in *The Christopher Bollas Reader.*

The demon who says 'I need to see the final result before I begin'

The fortunate ones among us begin their memoir writing with an overall shaping subject. The summer our family moved from Vancouver to the city of Lusaka in Zambia. Our mother's struggles with dementia. The making and unmaking of my faith in God. To these people: go for it!

The rest of us live with half-remembered strings of life stories that might or might not form some nameable whole or Life. Where to begin? And what will it all look like in the end?

Common sense invites us to begin our memoir at the beginning, with our birth or with stories about our parents or ancestors, then move forward to the present. First-time memoir writers often begin by taking this chronological approach. It is easy to follow, and it quickly orders material that can feel unwieldy. A good example is Jill Ker Conway's *The Road From Coorain*. Here chronology works in large part because of Conway's compelling descriptions of childhood places and how she seeks out emotional truths in her experience.

But chronology also has its drawbacks. It can bias attention towards what is culturally (although perhaps not personally) significant, such as years of schooling and work. It can invite heroic 'struggle and success' versions of life. It also imposes something like a conveyor belt determinism over the writing process. We feel we must follow a strict chronological sequence in our week-to-week writing, rather than follow the interests of our heart and body memory.

An alternative, interest-based approach—and the one I recommend—is to turn first to those life experiences that seem to inwardly call out to have their story told, whether as a life story, anecdote, personal essay, or set of reflections. This means going to where you feel the heat of your memories' energies and begin writing. Think of those telling moments that disclose what it was like to be a son or daughter, or mother or father. Those times of new body sensations, of inklings of betrayed hopes, of grief, of unforgettable shaping pleasures. In writing about these experiences, beliefs, and opinions one by one, the connecting materials and key interests will gradually begin to suggest the best overall shape of your memoir.

Think of how a river, like the Fraser in British Columbia, carries sediment from the high Rocky Mountains down twisting and tumbling streams and canyons, at one moment flowing northwest then suddenly turning southwest, eventually amassing its mighty self before changing shape one last time into silt-forming deltas that stretch into the Pacific like the fingers of a drowsy, smiling dreamer. Nothing told the Fraser River to be like this. Rather it created itself out of its elements: ice, snow, water, rock fissures, fault lines, the play of rushing water and silt on the earth. Like the Fraser, the shape of your memoir—its key themes, its sounds and colours, the ebb and flow of its energies, its overall direction, its beginning and ending—will emerge from the telling of your life experiences. We begin with life itself, then reflect, explore, and write. Gradually the overall form of your memoir begins to emerge. Maybe that 'form' will focus on 'departures' or 'loves of my life.' Maybe it will be shaped out of 'my many careers,' 'my life in 20 recipes,' a life-defining journey. Possibly—given your life or your approach to telling it—your memoir's overall form will have several key themes, moving forward, like the Fraser, in more than one direction. Whatever form begins to emerge—and watch for signs of it along the way—keep your attention on the writing's forward-moving, changing, and direction-carving energies. The river will gradually create itself.

For more advice on shaping your memoir, see Chapters 17. On forming or structuring an individual story or essay see Chapters 9, 10, and 12.

The demon of the quick fix

First-time memoir writers often write as thoughts and details 'come to mind.' Then they do some rewriting and 'fixing up'—more adjectives or adverbs here and there, replace this sentence, add another, check spelling—until they feel they are done. This stage of writing is often seen as fussy and tiring, the sooner completed the better. The result, including the minor revisions, is writing that typically includes irrelevant digressions and unnecessary words; doesn't take advantage of its inherent drama or line of inquiry; has an unvarying rhythm, tone, and energy; and lacks focus. The reader is left asking: What is this really, essentially, about? What is really important here?

By contrast, more effective writing results from an intentional re-drafting, shaping, and refining process. Writers use writing and rewriting, including complete overhauls of a piece of writing, to discover what they want to say—then, finding what really needs saying, they write again. They gradually order their material into a dramatically unfolding sequence of events, anecdotes, or arguments. Each word, phrase, sentence, and image has its own place in this order—and each matters. A more fully realized piece of memoir writing makes the reader feel and really attend to its sense of importance in the writer's life.

Look at the successful personal writer's initial working manuscripts. They are often a scribbled mess. Why? Because the writer is actively using language—trying out words and phrases, scratching them out, discovering associations, calling up new elements, playing with possibilities—towards finding and giving expressive shape to their real subject. Call it scribbling with a purpose.

A story or personal essay's final 'shape' is always the result of creative activity: trying things out, and gradually ordering experience into its true, expressive, dramatic verbal form. Little of this is straightforward, no more than the Fraser River. The effective writer moves ahead zigzag fashion, synchronously, thoughtfully, creatively feeling her way until she arrives at what I call the 'good enough' expression of her subject (see Chapter 15).

In sharing their experiences, the memoir writer creates a circle of companionship within which we, as listeners and readers, come to feel the warmth of their presence. Here we sit—with our mother, our grandfather, our sister, a friend, or a stranger—in the twilight world of life's stories, ready to be taken on expeditions, to hear the rustling and laughter and sighs that speak of creaturely life, to lift that loose floorboard, to surmise meaning, to unknowingly store away for some later time what the story counsels. *Let me tell you*, the rememberer begins, *although about what I don't exactly know. We will find out, together.* Photograph courtesy Alex Green (pexels.com).

CHAPTER 9

STORYTELLING IN A MEMOIR

> *Zurrumurru*—whisper, in the Basque language—*hush!* Step from the ordinary noise of the tilled fields or the busy streets into the quiet of the woods. Step across the boundary and the trespass of story will begin.
>
> —Jay Griffiths, *A Country Called Childhood*

> Traces of the storyteller cling to the story the way the handprints of the potter cling to the clay vessel.
>
> —Walter Benjamin, *The Storyteller*

In this chapter we begin by looking at what storytelling is as an experience—what makes a good story and how stories work—with particular reference to autobiographical or memoir stories. The chapter ends with a descriptive glossary of key terms for understanding story writing as a craft. Most of these terms are discussed in greater detail in later chapters. Storytelling is one main form of writing used in memoirs. The other, the personal essay, is discussed in the next chapter.

What is a story, like this one about the Queen of the Dumpster Divers?

'Did I ever tell you about the time I used to dumpster dive, just down this street actually?'

Dusk had arrived among our small circle of neighbours. The crickets had just begun their chirp-chirping. Deep in the shadows, the speaker was already a mere voice, a woman's youthful-seeming voice now emerging from a band of faintly glimmering white hair.

In those days, the woman continued, this whole area was nothing but a newly bulldozed forest, a few water-filled foundations, and the beginnings of a row of freshly-bricked houses—a construction site for our new 'adult community,' which is a pleasant way to refer to a place where older folks get older.

All around this site were dumpsters, each one filled with what the local do-in-yourselfers described as perfectly good pieces of lumber, carpet, pipe, wire, drywall and other odds and ends. Each evening the men would gather around one of the dumpsters and talk about how wonderful it would be if they could get their hands on the treasures inside. But to do that you had to climb up six feet or so to the lip of the bin, then drop down into its dusty innards—a jumble of boards and nails, globs of mysterious black stuff, wire, pop cans. A garbage dump really. Who among the men, with their thinning hair, had the dexterity to climb into these dumpsters? And besides, who among them was going to set aside their dignity to gain the riches inside? None, apparently. And so there the coveted throwaways sat until they were trucked away.

These evening gatherings continued for many weeks. That is, until one day, I don't remember exactly when. I was returning home from work—I was known as 'the young working woman' at the time—and the men had gathered as usual, trading stories about the amazing things they would build if only. 'So what's happening?' I asked them, as I often did. And again I was told about the unreachable prize materials inside the dumpsters. Many of these men, all of them new homeowners, were capable carpenters, and I knew these bins were filled with really good stuff. What happened next I can't really explain. No sooner did the men begin describing, in a sad chorus, what they would build IF ONLY, when some voice from somewhere—my voice, as it turned out—said 'Well that shouldn't be a problem. I'll just climb in and get what you want.' And up and in I went!

You're probably wondering how I managed to do it. It wasn't that hard actually. There was always a boulder or pile of roots or bricks nearby. The real trick was deciding where to jump once you got to the top, or whether to jump at all, and once you landed, how to move. I often found myself standing neck deep in boards bristling with nails, drywall pieces, and scraps of sharp-edged sheet metal. I can still smell the egg sandwiches, and remember slipping on tomatoes and watermelon rinds. It was a real snack bar down there.

If you had passed by on the evening I'm talking about, or the many similar evenings to follow, you would have heard me calling out 'How's this one?' as I raised a two-by-four into sight, like a periscope. 'Nope, too many nails,' a voice might answer. 'What about this?' I'd ask again, raising another board. 'Oh ya, peeerrfect' one of the men would say, reaching up and adding the plank to his growing pile.

Look around the neighbourhood today and you'll find that there's more than one basement finished with the scraps we pulled from those dumpsters. Best of all, the men also built me stuff, like my workbench, from the pieces I scavenged. They called me the Queen of the Dumpster Divers, and some still do, at least the ones who can remember and are still alive. That was some time ago.

The voice from the dark now went silent, leaving us to our own thoughts and the crickets' song.

We recognize that what we just read is a story. But why? What makes it a story? First, it announces itself as a reminiscence told as a story: 'Did I ever tell you?' We know that we are entering a second world, similar to our everyday world but bracketed off, having a certain shape, and inviting close attention. This story world immediately introduces a point of tension (a problem, a dilemma, a wish) that needs working through and, possibly, resolving. It now moves forward, creating a continuous—a narrative—thread of unfolding and often intensifying action. Along the way, this narrative thread develops and elaborates the initial problem, the characters involved, and a sense of a specific, concrete setting for the action. From the outset the story prompts curiosity and anticipation. It involves us, it invites us to participate in its drama. We want to see if and how things work out. Lastly, there is a closing to this story, a resolving of the initial problem, a sense that all's well that ends well.

To be sure, not all stories include all these characteristics, nor do all stories take the form of the Dumpster Queen story. For example, some stories do not end clearly or well. Still, when we sense that we are hearing a story, it is because we are being tuned in to many of the characteristics I have just named.

A story as an experience

Think of a story that has really engaged you, one that has moved and possibly changed you. Now ask yourself why and how this story has worked its magic. In your experience, what makes a good story?

Consider the many stories you have heard, created, and told. Those stories from your childhood and youth, the ones you were read and the ones you exchanged with friends and told yourself. The stories heard around a campfire or kitchen table. The countless stories told and listened to amidst everyday conversations. All the stories you have experienced in written and unwritten forms: novels, short stories and letters, but also through theatre, paintings, dance, song, mime, carvings, and sculpture. What is this thing we call 'storytelling'? Why stories? What is it about stories—the *experience* of creating, telling, hearing, feeling, reading stories—that is so attractive to humans?

> Take some time to reflect on your own answers to these questions. Talk to others about their experience.

When I wonder about my personal experiences with stories and storytelling, one place I go to is a recurrent scene in my childhood. It's evening, a time of half light and shadows, hushed calm. The only thing that exists is my mother's natural storytelling voice, her soft, safe warmth, and the unfolding, feeling-charged events brought alive through her words. Three-quarters of a century later, every story I read sits inside the aura of those first storytellings. How the owl and the pussycat sailed away for a year and a day 'to the land where the bong-tree grows.' The *clang, clang, clang!* and *Wheeeeeee!* of the five little firemen's truck, how they rescue the Hurricane Jones family from certain death, the jolly fat cook hollering *Jee-wollapers* as she slides to safety, how my mouth and ears can't get enough of that word. *Jee-wollapers!* Feeling the wrong of Black Beauty's pain on being whipped and worked to exhaustion. The anguish of Dumbo's separation from his mother, then her imprisonment, those tears, the power of friendship, Dumbo's final victory. Shipwrecked like the Robinson family, living in a tree house atop a giant banyan tree, and riding ostriches. Ostriches! The eerie midnight *tap-tap-tapping* of Long John Silver's peg leg, the mysteries of 'Doctor is all swabs', 'dead men don't bite', 'daddle 'em again' and a place called 'Offe Caraccas'. And, near the beginning of time, that 'sound so quiet it was like snow melting, like a flower growing, quiet as an egg, quiet as a bee swallowing honey from an apple blossom.' As the poet Eavan Boland writes in 'Nights of Childhood,' there are stories 'lucid as a nursery rhyme and as hard to fathom / revealed in rhythm, belied by theme, never forgotten / in those nights of childhood.'

Enchantment. Adventure. Beauty. Foreboding. Laughter and silliness. Complete contentment. Misunderstandings. Injustice. Vindication. The victory of truth. Stories speak to—and allow an inner voice for—powerful sensations of danger and safety, injustice and restitution, loss and attachment, adventure and wonder, frustration and fulfillment. They acknowledge—name and make more intelligible—our inner, actually felt life.

By beginning to tell as a story my memory of being read stories as a child, I relive the experience's drama and emotional qualities. I find its words and make it solid. I give it a narrative shape. I express it, claim it as my experience. And by doing this, I make an important part of my life more conscious, and thereby more accessible to reflection and understanding.

Stories—certainly childhood, folk, and myth stories—take us to the *primal scenes* of human experience: mother/father/child, life/death, lost/found, hunger/satiation, passion/revulsion, love/hate, right/wrong, power/vulnerability, what exists/what can be imagined.

Whether we are writing or reading them, stories can *move* us and leave us different beings. Because they are, or can be, permissive, they invite us to become promiscuous. They can remind us, for instance, of unfulfilled longings. They help us claim our right to beauty in life. They create occasions to laugh at indifferent power. They enable us to relinquish those inwardly cherished parts of ourselves that make us dumb and irresponsible. And they can deliver an axe blow against those frozen seas of normalcy, rage, and guilt within us.[1]

Stories can also offer counsel. They do so not by telling us what to do or think, but rather in a more liberating sense: they *act out*—release onto the page or stage or painting—our wishes, fears, guilt, anger, anxiety, joy, and longing, and in doing so, in our responses to their *storyness*, they invite us to feel and reflect anew, for ourselves, even if only half-consciously, on what it means, and could mean, to be alive.

Margaret Atwood has written that '[i]n Paradise there are no stories, because there are no journeys. It's loss and regret and misery and yearning that drive the story forward, along its twisted road' (*The Blind*

---

[1] In a letter to a friend, the storyteller Franz Kafka writes: 'If the book we're reading doesn't wake us up with a blow to the head, what are we reading for? So that it will make us happy . . . ? Good Lord, we would be happy precisely if we had no books, and the kind of books that make us happy are the kind we could write ourselves if we had to. But we need books that affect us like a disaster, that grieve us deeply, like the death of someone we loved more than ourselves, like being banished into forests far from everyone, like a suicide. A book must be the axe for the frozen sea within us' (*Letters to Friends, Family and Editors*).

Assassin). We tell stories, she suggests, out of the felt urgency of time's quick passing, of endings and loss (the loss of loving attachments, say), of a wish to redeem past stupidities and wrongs. Where everything is known and complete there is no need to go on a 'journey.' In this sense, humans create stories because time is running out and there are some things we must find the key for: remember, relive, explore, 'figure out,' amend, and reimagine.

Many stories, particularly memoir stories, seem to be prompted by a situation that we need to give words to, *express* (get out of ourselves), and better understand—and then share with others who in turn experience something of the need that originally occasioned the story. Do we become attached to certain stories for similar reasons? Do personally important stories finally express, and thereby permit the recognition of, something we *know* as our experience but haven't been able to fully say, perhaps haven't even been able to think? If this is true, then memoir stories that merely repeat the already well-known have hardly begun their work. Autobiographical storytelling more fully realized is like a true travel experience: we explore and are explored by where we are. And we come away changed.[2]

---

[2] The Latin and ancient Greek roots of the word 'story' can be found in *storia* (the shortened Latin *historia*: history, account, tale, or story), the Latin *narrare* (to tell) and *narrativus* (suitable for telling), as well as the Greek *historia* or learning by inquiry. These roots suggest an integrated view of human experience that is quite alien to the modern human sciences. *Narrare* and *narrativus* are themselves associated with the Latin *gnarus* (knowing). While modern English distinguishes between 'story' and 'history,' the Old French *estorie*, derived from *historia*, still combines the two. The word 'story' is also associated with the Greek *histōr*, the person who knows or witnesses, and Greek *historeo*, 'I inquire.' In ancient Greece, storytelling was associated with the goddess Mnemosyne, the rememberer and mother to the Nine Muses, among them Clio (history), Calliope (epic poetry), Erato (lyric poetry), Melpomene (tragedy), Terpsichore (dance) and Thalia (comedy). Storytellers were thought to receive their powers of authoritative speech from their possession of memory and their special relationship with the Muses.

The work of inner storytelling

One aspect of autobiographical storytelling becomes clearer when we consider how children use stories. Not only do children hear stories from the start of life and learn to tell stories to others, they soon begin telling stories to themselves. This inner storytelling is a form of playing with and testing reality and the self, in large part an attempt to influence, even assert the self's power over reality. For example, a child—feeling 'small,' vulnerable, perhaps humiliated—may create imagined adventure stories in which he must face, again and again, the repeated aggressions of various giants and monsters over which, again and again, he is victorious. He is telling a story about his experience to himself as a *listener,* a story in the form of a wishful experiential experiment. He may even repeat forms of this story many times because in actual life he remains 'small,' and he enjoys the moment of victory. He is using fantasy stories to grapple with, endure, become wise to, and 'get on' amidst the forces of living. By doing so, the child's self reshapes his experience, and therein 'corrects' life (storytelling as revenge, restitution, making amends, longing), or it tries to make sense, tries out imagined possibilities, or searches for reassurance that 'things will work out.' Variations of this primal inner storytelling work continue throughout life, surely influencing who we are and the stories we tell.

The storyteller's invitation

The good storyteller's invitation is always the same. *Stop, rest awhile and have a listen. Let me tell you about the time . . . .*

We may sense, beneath consciousness, that we are being invited into something like a close darkened room, at the front of which is a small stage lit by flickering candles, where some drama, some enacted 'slice of life' meant especially for us is about to begin. *A hush came over the audience.* The storyteller's invitation makes us curious, expectant. It concentrates and opens us at the same time. We may have left the actual street, but we are about to hear something about life on the street, even from inside the soul of a person walking the street. This 'something' has been bracketed out, made into a story, and thereby given an aura of importance, something that will make us feel the 'handprints' of the storyteller pressing on—stirring, shaking, tickling, unsettling—our creaturely self.

Afterwards we might say *Now that was a real story!* What do we mean? At the least we are confessing to having been *moved* and thereby somehow changed, even if we cannot say precisely in what way. Now the storyteller's work continues—taking on a kind of afterlife inside the listener or reader as their own experience, somewhere whispering *Moved where? Changed how?*

Even though that small lit stage is out there, beyond us, a successful story's engaging *storyness* releases itself inside us, makes us accomplices, invites us to compare felt experiences, makes us feel exposed, invites us to ask questions and make judgements, moves us, maybe shakes us . . . and leaves us wondering.

Stories versus 'information'

A good deal of writing in today's world can be thought of as 'information.' Stories are something else entirely. The distinction helps clarify how storytelling works.

Let me use a personal example: being taught to make bread by my mother-in-law, Clara. I can describe how to make bread: the ingredients, the steps, and dos and don'ts. This is *information*. Alternatively, I can tell you the *lived story* of how Clara taught me to make bread in 1972 in Lusaka, Zambia, along with the continuing pleasure, fifty years on, of making and sharing bread—a pleasure, not incidentally, inseparable from Clara's presence. (Clara is no longer alive, which makes me wonder whether we also tell stories in order to feel the warmth of the ghosts of our life?)

As I've said, bread recipes and instructions are information, indeed useful information. They describe with precision established and necessary details. Information is concerned with the matter-of-fact and the self-evident; it doesn't want the listener/reader to wonder, feel, reflect, or interpret. On the contrary, it expects immediate verifiability and assent. By contrast, stories are suggestive; they invite questions, conjecture, wonder. Yes, stories include information. Indeed, they are more effective by attending to the precise *solidity* of things. But they leaven solid things with the story itself. Stories make 'details' speak beyond their preciseness; they make 'information' evocative. Rather than telling us what we must think and do, stories use their materials to *release* meaning inside our experience.

My story about bread making is a narrative about the teaching and practice of a craft. But it is also about human relationships, about attachments and care, and about labour, memory, the passing of time, changing circumstances, and mortality—all rendered as the lived experience of specific individuals. When he is ready, the bread-making storyteller sits us down in the story's specific room in a particular house and place and time, then he invites us *to listen in on* two people making bread: one adept, the other being taught. The story allows us to experience (overhear, feel, piece together, guess at) who these individuals are, their relationship, this to-and-fro of making, their success and sharing, what else is 'going on,' the meaning and meaningfulness of it all. This is not information. Not: *This is how to make bread—follow these instructions.* Instead, it is something the story *enacts* for us as a drama about life, however 'small' and 'ordinary' on the surface. And it is something *experienced*—lived, felt, thought about, and interpreted: all the brokers of changing awareness—by the reader's inner life-world. In the experience of reading a good story we might be 'told' next to nothing, yet we are being *changed* by how this concentrated, unfolding, enacting of life *works*—like a further leavening—in our affections, thoughts, and yearnings.[3]

---

[3] This is why advertisers, who are very clever storytellers, are actually anti-storytellers in the sense that they see any independent experiential breathing

Memoir stories as non-fiction and fiction

'Memoir stories are non-fiction.' This is an oft-repeated maxim, although like many maxims it is naïve and simplistic. It's true that we don't expect our cousin—the one who grew up in Toronto's Bridle Path and inherited his parents' billions—to write a rags-to-riches memoir. That is, we don't expect memoirists to openly flout the non-fiction rule. Beyond that, however, things are more complicated.

As the memoir's bestseller lists demonstrate, there are many readers who enjoy being entertained, or peeping in on or identifying with the rich and famous, truth-to-life be damned. Middle-class readers ate up the vividly rendered misery, misery, misery in Frank McCourt's *Angela's Ashes*, spurning the many reports that it was filled with melodramatic exaggerations and that McCourt's mother famously called the book 'a pack of lies.' The modern marketplace invites memoirists to lace their 'non-fiction' with appealing fictions—lurid, glittering, affable, and otherwise—and there are always memoirists willing to oblige.

McCourt has since described his book as 'a memoir, not an exact history,'[4] despite making repeated claims for its exactness. This playing both sides of the street suggests a further characteristic of memoir readers, and a few memoir writers as well: when it comes to being true to life, they want their memoirs to *feel* convincing, even if they are the product of self-serving fancy and market forces. It is unlikely that we would apply the same standard to a memoir written by a person we actually know. We expect something else: if not 'exactness,' then at least the writer's sincere effort to be true to their experience. It's this 'effort,' I believe, that moves us closer to how true memoir storytelling actually works.

---

    space in their viewers/listeners as anathema. They tell stories, but expect one and only one type of response.
[4] http://gerryhannanthetruth.blogspot.com/2009/07/yet-another-article-relating-to-gerry.html

When McCourt distinguished 'memoir' and 'exact history,' he is simply agreeing to the obvious: that all memoir stories are fictions. I mean by this that every memoir is the result of a kind of construction and shaping work that uses selected materials from our experience. When I say 'materials' I mean that whirlpool of memories, emotions, perceptions, interests, wishes, real-life circumstances, and cultural rules, fashions, and ideals that churns at the wellsprings of autobiographical writing. In memoir writing, there is no knowable 'exact' personal history. Rather, there is living personal history, something we stand inside, something moving and changing and mostly unseen, like an iceberg; and something that, at best, we can make an honest try at exploring and understanding. It's from here, standing inside our life, trying to get at the truths of our actually lived experience, that memoir stories emerge.

'Getting at the truths of our experience.' This sometimes necessitates invention, as we will see in later discussions on re-creating the past (Chapter 18) and truth in memoir (Chapter 21). The issue is not whether elements of a memoir story are invented or otherwise 'made up.' What matters is whether these inventions help to explore and name the memoirist's actually lived experience, or whether they bolster fixed and usually reassuring ideas the memoirist holds about himself and his experience—as well as ideas about how he wants to be seen by his readers.

In the best memoir storytelling, there is no 'exact history,' only an exacting search for and disclosing of actually-lived personal history and its consequences.

Storytelling as a craft: a writer's glossary

Here we take brief looks at the elements of a *well-crafted* story, with special attention to memoir stories. I am describing writing conventions, like the seventh inning stretch in baseball. Storytelling, however, is not baseball. That's because the first interest of a true storyteller is to find the right way to express their story, regardless of convention. In good memoir writing, experience always guides how conventions are adapted and ignored. So: be familiar with the conventions but tell your stories in ways your material suggests. You can find more detailed discussions of storytelling's craft elements in Part II.

What is a memoir story? So far we have considered what stories, storytelling and story listening/reading can mean as *experiences*. Here is a more formal definition of a memoir story: the memoirist's telling of a connected sequence of true, personal life events, relationships, thoughts, and other experiences, with the aim of exploring and better understanding these experiences and sharing them with others.

Narrative development. All stories have a narrative form: the more or less continuous, unfolding, dramatic development of events, situations, or descriptions from beginning through middle to end. A story's main narrative is sometimes called its 'through line' or 'red thread' along which its meaning and meaningfulness are released. Narrative development gives a story its sense of inner coherence, continuous forward 'pull,' and direction. It helps the reader know that wherever a story might take them, they are always inside its distinct experiential world. Memoir stories typically begin with some problem, puzzle, or point of tension or transition that needs working through. They then develop this initial situation through the introduction of new circumstances, characters, events, information, perspectives, and responses. Narrative development creates anticipation and curiosity, suggests cause and effect, adds real-life shadings to the story's human drama, opens up the possibility of new perspectives and understandings, and brings the narrative to an end.

One oft-cited form of narrative development is the 'narrative arc.' The story's drama unfolds through 'rising' tensions and complexity, reaches some crisis or turning point, then 'descends' towards resolution or closure. In practice, narratives take many forms, depending on the story you want to tell and how best to tell it. You might narrate a story called 'Reflections on My Travels in Turkey' through a series of loosely connected anecdotes or scenes that hold together because of their common theme. Compared to a single narrative thread, this approach allows you to concentrate on specific experiences, include a variety of experiences, juxtapose different experiences to get at some truth, and not worry about linking the parts together.

Another approach to narrative, a kind of lyrical hovering, can be seen in Annie Dillard's *Pilgrim at Tinker Creek*. Very little happens in Dillard's book: no action, adventure, or conventional forward movement. Yet her memoir successfully absorbs the reader. It does so through its firsthand, beautifully woven, and thoughtful observations on the natural environment of a lowly creek. In this case, Dillard's narrative follows the movements of her creaturely attention. Different again is Dylan Thomas's 'A Child's Christmas in Wales,' which begins at a high point and descends into humorous disarray. A narrative might also be maze-like, a collage or montage, braided with two related stories, or like an unclosed circle.

'Endings' vary as well. Some offer a clear sense of closure, some are ambiguous, and others resemble an unhealed wound. In every case, a story's narrative development emerges from your material: from both your understanding of your material's significance and your decisions about how to release—breathe life into—this significance in a narrative or storytelling form.

Drama. A story's narrative drama is built out of experiential tension. Tension might result from such things as opposing views or forces, making a decision, being in an in-between or threshold place, a challenge, the unknown, some quandary, the unexpected, heightened pleasure, or some other instance of indeterminate experience that a story's characters will live through. In actual life these are places of possibility, the yet-to-be-decided, and among the most important sources of memoir storytelling. Each story has its own in-built dramatic situation that is explored through a series of dramatic scenes. To take one very effective example, Carol Guess introduces the drama of her story 'Evelyn' by juxtaposing the 'facts' and the 'mystery' of this woman and setting in motion a narrative that wonders which is which. The story begins: 'Her name is Evelyn. She's lived in her house since 1960.

She was born in 1915 or 1916, near the Nooksack River, which still floods its banks. These are the facts. This is the mystery: a 91-year-old woman and me. She can't hear me, but I talk with my hands.'[5]

Engage your reader. Effective stories invite their reader to move closer. They arouse curiosity and anticipation. *What is really happening here? What will happen next? How will this work out?* We want to know more, we want to see what happens. Good memoir storytellers make their reader complicit in their story's situation, dilemma, puzzlement, emotions, regrets, or yearnings—as if these could be the reader's own. Invite your reader to think and feel with you. Stories 'work' by having the reader imaginatively live through a shared experiential journey.

Beginnings. Effective beginnings help locate and anchor a story's experiential world. They introduce what Mary Karr calls the 'emotional stakes' of a story (*The Art of Memoir*). They are also written, or at least finalized, last, once you know your story. Beginnings can be observational ('What is past is not dead; it is not even past,' from Christa Wolf's *Patterns of Childhood*), but they are more often situational, specific, and concrete, as in Brenda Miller's story 'Ordinary Shoes': 'I'm not a graceful child. I bump into furniture, spill drinks, wake with bruises for no discernible reason at all. I trip over carpets, stain my shirts the minute I walk out the door, and my lank hair slithers free of any barrette. But when I put on my roller skates, I turn into a different person, a person who can skim lightly above the surface. I'm going so fast—the world is a blur—but I know how to stop. I can execute the perfect turn that will keep me from spilling off the curb.'[6]

Storytelling time. Conventional stories follow a narrative or dramatic forward movement from beginning through middle to end. But good storytellers know that stories can also begin at their end or in their middle, and move forward through tangents. There are storytelling reasons for this. While actual lived events can be said to take place in conventional linear time and be recalled and told this way, storytelling

---

[5] Posted in *Brevity*, September 10, 2010.
[6] Posted in *Brevity*, September 18, 2014.

or narrative 'time' serves the interests of the teller's sense of what they are telling, and even its imagined affect on a reader. Stories can use conventional time to heighten drama. But a story's narrative unfolding—how it begins, and how one part builds on another, prepares for the next part, refers back, and creates anticipation for parts to come—all this is determined by what best serves the experiential interests of the story. Storytelling time can move any which way, as long as it does not abandon the story's deep narrative thread, confuse the reader, or feel contrived or manipulative.

Narrative summary versus dramatic scenes. Stories move forward through a series of 'dramatic scenes' (the narrative slows, intensifies, deepens) and 'narrative summaries' (briefly described shifts in time, place, and situation). This technique focuses a story on what matters most, it varies the story's rhythm, and it permits quick switches in narrative movement across time and space—linking, say, an experience when you are fifty years old to another when you were five years old. This is discussed in more detail in Chapter 12.

Narrator and persona. In memoir writing the narrator is the personal voice of the writer telling the story. Memoir writers will sometimes make a distinction between their narrator's voice and their self as a character or 'persona' within a story. This allows the writer/narrator to observe and to reflect on their own actions and thoughts.

Voice and tone. 'Voice' is *what* a narrator and story character says and thinks. Memoir stories can have many voices: the writer's and narrator's, the voices of the writer's persona at various stages of their life, the voices of other characters, inner thought voices, and outwardly expressed voices. An important aspect of voice is 'tone' or *how* a narrator or character sounds: their attitude, manner, mood, or point of view. Tone is expressed by how a person speaks and their associated gestures. It influences how we 'hear' the emotional and attitudinal inferences of words and phrasings. Narrative tone can cast an atmospheric veil or mood over a whole story. A tone might be sad, joyful, humorous, curious, skeptical, reflective, lyrical, or hypocritical. Voices and their tones breathe emotional life into characters and stories. See Chapter 13.

Character. 'Character' refers to who the story is about, including the narrator's persona. Character is revealed in at least two ways. The first is through characteristic attributes, mannerisms and gestures, speech and its tone, activities, emotional life, and expressed versus inner thoughts. The second occurs as the narrative unfolds. In this case we experience how a character changes (or not) in response to, for example, changing circumstances, their questions and uncertainty, and the discrepancies between what they say and think and between their feelings and thoughts.

Context. 'Context' is the assembly of details that locate a story in time and place or that establish facts such as age or how people are related. 'Context' is also the more decisive circumstances of a story: its field of interests, influences, beliefs, values, background, and history as well as its overall tone and mood. Contexts have consequences: they delimit how you explore your experience and influence your reader's responses and understanding. Although they are usually presented as entirely natural, all contexts are constructions: a particular selection, arranging, and weighing of story elements. Good memoir writers will question their story's contextual elements, and will invite readers to do the same.

Solid things. Stories come more alive and engaging by conveying the solid, singular, felt realness of things, people, places, and situations. Storytellers suggest solidity through sensate qualities—weight, mass, smell, touch, sound, texture, colour, movement, taste—and by using all the senses. Even experiences of the ethereal and the abstract can be made more real by suggesting how they *press on* or *make an impression in* the inner feeling-thinking life of a character.

Show and tell. Stories combine 'showing' and 'telling,' although in different measures. Let's begin with the technique of showing. If you write 'My mother was a strong, kind woman,' I might respond: *So what? Many women are strong and kind.* Alternatively, if you write, 'My mother carried fifty pounds of mail on her back, yet she had a shy smile for each of her neighbours as she laboured up the hill,' you have breathed life into this *particular* woman. You are *showing* her moving, struggling yet smiling, in her characteristic way. You give her solidity and make her *enact* herself to us as readers.[7] By using solid things, sensate qualities, and actions, showing dramatizes or demonstrates a character, a situation, and even a place. 'Telling' is different. It provides needed information, sets a story's context, establishes its narrative direction, and summarizes what has happened. Telling also refers to those moments when a storyteller reflects on—questions, analyzes, wonders about, interprets, evaluates—certain elements of their own story. *What do I make of this?* As Philip Lopate puts it, the memoirist is thinking on the page: evaluating her experience and her way of recounting and understanding this experience (*To Show and To Tell*). In memoir writing, showing brings alive a story's characters, objects, situations, and places. Telling explores what these mean for the writer. See Chapter 12 for further discussion.

What's in, what's out. Joyce Carol Oates writes, 'Storytelling is shaped by two contrary, yet complementary, impulses—one toward brevity, compactness, artful omission; the other toward expansion, amplification, enrichment.'[8] This is especially true of short memoir stories. 'What's in, what's out' only begins to be clear after your have written your story at least once. Only then can you sense its essential *aboutness*. Once you find this, tell your story *complete*, ensure your reader has what he needs, and mercilessly cut everything that does not contribute to your essential purpose.

Let your story speak for itself. I mean this in a variety of ways. Sooner or later you are not going to be around to respond to questions about your stories. While you have the chance, give your reader everything they need to *enable* their own experience of your story. Don't frustrate them with omitted or inconsistent details or a confusing narrative. At the same time, do not *explain* your story, and do not

---

[7] I have taken this example from Tristine Rainer's *Your Life as Story*.
[8] Oates, 'Characters Dangerously Like Us,' *New York Times*, September 14, 1986.

make connections that your story, as a story, can suggest on its own. A well-told story 'explains' itself by creating a rich, fully told, engaging, generous experiential and interpretive space for its responsive reader. Always write to this reader. The best stories attest to their reason for being told through their actual telling. Hannah Arendt: 'Storytelling reveals meaning without committing the error of defining it.'[9] When a memoir story begins with an experience that needs 'working out' or 'working through,' it is precisely its *storyness*—its string of events, its unfolding drama, conversations, the inner and outer lives of its characters, questions asked and implied, changes in circumstance and awareness, contradictions, ironies, its inner causes and effects—it is precisely this *storyness* that suggests answers to the question of why is was important to tell in the first place. The best memoir stories enact their significance. They speak for themselves.

Leave yourself and your reader something to think about. By the time a story has run its course, things are not as they were at the outset. Something has been passed through, changing everything in its wake. Inside the story, circumstances have changed, and characters as well, whether their situation or their awareness. In addition, the process of personal storytelling, especially understood as exploration, changes the writer—and their reader. By touching and stirring our inner self and its store of ideas and feelings, life stories—whether ever so subtly or dramatically—invite us to see things differently, prompt new questions, make us laugh in illicit ways, complicate what we already 'know,' and surprise us with memories and longings and feelings we didn't know we had. We can resist these *stirrings*—pretend we didn't laugh, or that our thoughts are not 'really' illicit—but the story has already begun its work inside us, indifferent to what some inner voice says 'should' be our response.

The best stories leave us with something new and challenging to think about, often in spite of ourselves.

But that is another story.

---

[9] Arendt, *Men In Dark Times*.

In their afterlife in memory, the physical buildings in which we have lived, even if long demolished, can come to be storehouses of charged experience. A door slightly ajar or always closed, voices down a hallway, a dank basement or dusty attic, hideaways and play spaces, smothering and chilling places, lovemaking places, mealtime and goodnight places, reassuring places, daydreaming places. What do you hear or smell or find yourself wanting to touch when you enter, then wander the hallways and rooms of an important dwelling in your life? © Lucy Jones, *Stockbridge Colonies Steps*. Courtesy the artist at lucyjonesart.com.

CHAPTER 10

THE PERSONAL ESSAY: INVESTIGATIONS OF MY SELF IN THE WORLD

> [The personal essay captures] how the world comes at another person, the irritations, jubilations, aches and pains, humorous flashes.... We learn the rhythm by which the essayist receives, digests, and spits out the world, and we learn the shape of his or her privacy.
>
> —Phillip Lopate, *To Show and To Tell*

> I like to circle around the idea, stretch it out, wriggle it about, snap it back, tease it out again and give it a good shake. That is why the endless elastic form of the personal essay is perfect.
>
> —Patti Miller, *Writing True Stories*

The personal essay is the second common expressive form used by memoir writers, along with autobiographical stories. In general, life experiences are best told in the form of stories while personal viewpoints and other reflections are best expressed through essays. Having said this, essays are brought alive through stories and anecdotes, and memoir stories can become more discerning through essay-like reflections.

'Trying out' or 'making an attempt at' one's subject

The personal essay—sometimes called the 'exploratory,' 'familiar,' or 'informal' essay—uses a personal 'I' voice to investigate any subject of interest to the writer. Beyond this, the personal essay's elastic form allows for many tones of voice and investigative approaches and is capable of taking up a multitude of subjects.[1]

The modern-era personal essay was launched by the sixteenth-century French writer Michel de Montaigne. It was he who coined the French word *essai*, from *essayer*, meaning to try, to prod, to attempt, to make a run at something. This sense of *making an attempt* at one's subject has remained at the heart of the personal essay to our own day. Montaigne wrote short, nonfiction prose pieces whose aim was to investigate his self and his relation to the world. He gave his essays the motto *Que sais-je?*—'What do I know?'—a telling choice, as we will see.[2]

Montaigne was not the first person to write personal essays. The early Romans Seneca and Plutarch had used the form, as had Sei Shonagon in tenth-century Japan, Ou-Yang Hsiu in China ('let his brush write what it would,' he said), and the fourteenth-century Japanese writer Kenkō, whose title 'The Tsurezuregusa' derives from the expression 'with nothing better to do.' Historically, the personal essay is associated with prose meditations, orations, *moralia* ('matters related to customs'), and epistles. It also has roots in the custom of

---

[1] The best collection of personal essays, edited and with a fine introduction by Phillip Lopate, is *The Art of the Personal Essay*. In this chapter, all quotations from Lopate are from this introduction, unless noted otherwise. Good current examples of the personal essay appear in the *Globe and Mail*'s 'First Person' feature, the *New York Times* online 'Lives' (examples of the 'Best of Lives' are online, while the feature itself has been replaced by similar columns), and websites such as brevitymag.com and creativenonfiction.org. In what follows, I borrow extensively from Lopate's introduction as well as from his book *To Show and To Tell: The Craft of Literary Nonfiction* and Patti Miller's chapter 'Random Provocations—The Personal Essay' in her *Writing True Stories*—each of which I recommend reading in the original.

[2] All passages from Montaigne's work are taken from Montaigne, *The Complete Works*, trans. Donald M. Frame.

keeping personal 'commonplace books': catch-all scrapbooks filled with quotations, recipes, letters, proverbs, prayers, legal formulas, personal memory notes and more. Commonplace books in turn are related to the fifteenth-century Italian *zibaldone* or 'hodgepodge book', or as one writer called his own, a 'salad of many herbs.' A tossed salad: the name certainly suits many personal essays today.

What makes Montaigne a historical original is how he combined a thoroughly personal, scrupulously investigative, skeptical, secular, and physicalist approach to writing. About the time that Galileo turned his telescope on the far outer world, Montaigne was using inner, personal inquiry to explore what it meant to be human in his time. His was an open-minded, opinionated sensibility, all the more remarkable when we remember that he wrote during a period of war, dogmatism, and uncertainty—not unlike our own era. Montaigne's approach was later popularized by the spread of a vernacular and secular literacy and other democratizing social-cultural forces. The *essai* voice he helped create has since been a key part of the critical, humane counter-tradition of individual observation, reflection, and writing that has come to stand against the 'productive,' administrative voices of the modern era's dominant culture.[3]

The informal personal essay versus the formal essay

The *informal* personal essay is quite unlike the schooled world's *formal* essay and its formula of topic sentence/thesis, several paragraphs of exposition, and conclusion. Writing influenced by the formal essay—that is, the approach to writing used in modern administration, academic culture, business, science, medicine, and technology—has a number of characteristics. It typically uses a cool, impersonal voice; favours the readily describable; sets out to 'demonstrate' or to 'prove' this or that;

---

[3] The broad tradition described here, focused on human experience as mediated by the individual, is now being set alongside alternative traditions with at least as deep historical-cultural roots—for instance, the 'collective' and 'shared' expressive forms found in Aboriginal cultures. See Susanne Conklin Akbari's 'Can the Essay Still Surprise Us?,' *Literary Hub*, August 14, 2020.

moves efficiently along a more or less straight line of deductive and inductive reasoning; aims to be as argument-proof as possible; is results-driven within the world as it is; dreams of mastering one's subject and arriving at final principles; and, perhaps of greatest consequence, adapts and enlists human 'reason' to serve existing institutions and their supporting systems of beliefs and values. This paragraph, and in many respects this book, follow the formal style, although one of my goals is to question and oppose this style (and the arrangements of life it voices) by exploring and encouraging the use of its counterpart.

This counterpart, the informal personal essay, is rooted in the writer's personal experience, reflections, and investigations. It is curiosity-driven, and can be chatty, playful, self-deprecating, colloquial, intimate, and confiding in approach. Its structure is based on the writer's movement of attention through wonderings, digression, uncertainty, contradiction, ambivalence, and open-ended endings. Its writer is sensitive to the finiteness and shared precariousness of life. 'I paint transience,' wrote Montaigne. 'I do not depict being, I depict passage.' As a historical form, the personal essay is bound up with cultural processes associated with the individualization of the person, with skepticism, and with open dialogue and independent thought. The personal essayist assesses the claims of cultural tradition, convention, fashion, or 'things as they are' not on their own terms but rather in terms of one's actually lived and critically considered personal experience.

The personal essay is not 'productive' or 'useful' in ways that serve the world as it is. As Phillip Lopate recommends, replace the word 'idler' with 'essayist' in the following passage from Robert Louis Stevenson's essay 'An Apology for Idlers' and you have a catalogue of the form's virtues.

> 'Extreme busyness . . . is a symptom of deficient vitality; and a faculty for idleness implies a catholic appetite and a strong sense of personal identity. There is a sort of dead-alive, hackneyed people about, who are scarcely conscious of living except in the exercise of some conventional occupation.

> Bring these fellows into the country . . . and you will see how they pine for their desk or their study. They have no curiosity; they cannot give themselves over to random provocations; they do not take pleasure in the exercise of their faculties for its own sake . . . they cannot be idle, their nature is not generous enough; and they pass those hours in a sort of coma, which are not dedicated to furious moiling in the gold-mill. When they do not require to go to the office, when they are not hungry and have no mind to drink, the whole breathing world is a blank to them.'[4]

A catholic appetite. A strong sense of personal identity. Moved by curiosity. Given over to random provocations. Able to recognize absent inner nature, pleasure, and vitality. Taking pleasure in thought for its own sake. Disaffected questioning and negation of the status quo. These are the fingerprints of many personal essayists.

The personal essay comes not from places of established power and confident know-how but from the ground up and the grimy rear stairwell. Let's return to Montaigne. He felt the need for a form of writing that kept speaking on behalf of dimensions of human experience that had been banished by the writing-thinking needs of the Church as well as by the emerging forms of modern science, business, and state. He dreamed of 'reserving a back shop [*arrière-boutique*] all our own, entirely free, in which to establish our real liberty and our principal retreat and solitude.' According to Montaigne, most of his contemporaries enlisted thought and writing to advance themselves, their careers, and the business of the existing world. They think and write, that is, in the front of the shop. But what about, Montaigne wonders, all those regions of human experience and activity that the public domain (the front shop) declares unproductive or does not even recognize? It is here, in personal experience's 'back shop,' that Montaigne devised his alternative approach that he called 'essaying.'

---

[4] 'An Apology for Idlers' is included in Phillip Lopate (ed.), *The Art of the Personal Essay*.

The essayist's method

Personal essayists wonder about things, they are curious, they ask questions. They are not content with the claimed obviousness of 'the obvious'; they need to investigate for themselves. What sets many personal essayists apart, however, is how they carry out these investigations. They observe their subject as if turning it in their fingers. They do some research, they ask questions. They try out samples on the tongue of their creaturely self—the Italian 'essay' is *saggio*, with the same root as *assaggiore*, to sample, taste, or nibble food—and in doing so they ask themselves *What and why is this, and what does it mean?* The result—the personal essay itself—is a public record of these investigations carried out by the creaturely self.

Essaying follows the writer's movement of attention in response to a particular subject. When Phillip Lopate describes the essayist's method, he imagines the flight of a preying hawk. The essayist, he writes, 'surround[s] a something—a subject, a mood, a problematic irritation—by coming at it from all angles, wheeling and diving like a hawk, each seemingly digressive spiral actually taking us closer to the heart of the matter . . . . In a well-wrought essay, while the search seems to be widening, even losing its way, it is actually eliminating false hypotheses, narrowing its emotional target and zeroing in on it.'[5]

When asked about the movements of his attention as he wrote *The Rings of Saturn*, W.G. Sebald, in inveterate walker, responded as both walker and essayist:

> I can't quite remember how it worked. I had the idea of writing a few short pieces . . . in order to pay for this extravagance of a fortnight's rambling tour. That was the plan. But then as you walk along, you find things. I think that's the advantage of walking . . . . You find things by the wayside or you buy a brochure written by a local historian . . . and in that way you find odd details which

---

[5] Lopate, 'Introduction' to *The Art of the Personal Essay*.

lead you somewhere else, and so it's a form of unsystematic searching.... And the more I got on, the more I felt that, really, one can find something only in that way, i.e., in the same way in which, say, a dog runs through a field. If you look at a dog following the advice of his nose, he traverses a patch of land in a completely unplottable manner. And he invariably finds what he is looking for. I think that, as I've always had dogs, I learned from them how to do this.[6]

Following the advice of one's nose. The essayist sniffs around, fingers and weighs the evidence, wonders, asks questions, researches, encounters new materials and thoughts, pursues associations and coincidences, abandons one path only to have another suddenly appear, moves 'forward' through juxtapositions, contrasts, speculation, contradictions, digressions, ambivalence, and paradoxes, all the while exploring, encountering, *finding*, and 'coming upon' their subject by a continuous, even if tangled, unplottable path. The structure of an essay emerges not from some already-known 'plot.' It is prompted, rather, by some personal question, vexation, mood, or fascination that the essayist's process of creaturely 'finding' (or 'essaying') seeks to better understand. You begin with a few solid landmarks but set out as if into a dark wood, following your creaturely nose.[7]

---

[6] 'A Conversation with W.G. Sebald' by Joseph Cuomo, in Lynne Sharon Schwartz (ed.), *The Emergence of Memory: Conversations with W.G. Sebald*. Some in Sebald's audience laughed when he compared his method to a dog's explorations, but perhaps they didn't fully grasp what his intuitions were telling him. I think what Sebald is noticing, at least in part, is what E.V. Walter calls 'primordial haptic perception.' Walter adapts this concept from the psychologist James Gibson. Gibson developed the concept of 'haptic perception' (from *haptien*: to lay hold of something, to touch, to fasten, to latch on to) to describe the embodied perceptual system by which *both* animals and humans 'are literally in touch with their environment' in what Gibson calls an 'active exploratory touch [that] permits both the grasping of an object and a grasp of its meaning.' Gibson and haptic perception are discussed in Walter's *Placeways: A Theory of the Human Environment*.

[7] Many personal essayists have been ardent walkers—from Jean Jacques Rousseau ('My mind only works with my legs.') to Hazlitt, Virginia Woolf, Thoreau, Bruce Chatwin, Sebald, Robert Macfarlane, and Rebeccca Solnit. They describe how the movements of their attention are stimulated by and somehow mimic

What do personal essayists write about?

A sampling of titles, mostly from English-language writers, suggests the experiential landscape of the personal essayist: Charles Lamb's 'A Chapter on Ears,' William Hazlitt's 'On the Pleasure of Hating,' Robert Louis Stevenson's 'An Apology for Idlers,' Virginia Woolf's 'The Death of the Moth,' Walter Benjamin's 'Unpacking My Library,' Mary McCarthy's 'My Confession,' Joan Didion's 'In Bed,' Jorge Luis Borges's 'Blindness,' Wole Soyinka's 'Why Do I Fast?,' Natalia Ginzburg's 'He and I,' George Steiner's 'Ten (Possible) Reasons for the Sadness of Thought,' Edward Hoagland's 'The Courage of Turtles,' and Phillip Lopate's 'Against Joie de Vivre.'

Personal essayists take up many subjects. Friendship, solitude, childhood, family ties, love, sexuality, marriage, social manners, walking, idleness, busyness, travel, a place, hobbies, public spectacles, books, art, film, theatre, politics, race, ethnicity, beliefs, ideas, values, favourite foods, cooking, appetite, décor, illness, aging, disability, death, war as individually lived, city or country life, nature. Add to these possibilities your own delights, obsessions, doubts, best-loved places, things hated, flaws, and vulnerabilities. Personal essayists know that there are many worthy subjects in the perplexing, vexing, uncanny, charming, luminous, and mysterious moments of 'ordinary' daily existence.

'Voice' in the personal essay

In general, the personal essayist uses an 'I' narrating voice—or what Elizabeth Hardwick calls 'the soloist's personal signature flowing

---

the rhythms of their foot fall on the slowly but ever-changing earth, and how thoughts gradually untangle and become conscious to the beats of these rhythms. A number of studies suggest how walking, at least outside the noise of modernity, aids reflection, remembering and creativity. There are many good online essays on the subject, plus these books, among others: Rebecca Solnit's *Wanderlust: a History of Walking*, Frédéric Gros' *A Philosophy of Walking*, Bruce Chatwin's *The Songlines*, Robert Macfarlane's *The Old Ways*, and E.V. Walter in his *Placeways: A Theory of the Human Environment*.

through the text.'[8] Because of this the mood is often intimate, confiding, and conversational, with the essayist seeming to speak directly into our ear. Lopate says essayists 'converse with the reader because they are already having dialogues and disputes with themselves.' Although they use 'I,' they often write in a way that suggests 'you and me'—as if writer and reader are sitting as interested companions on a front porch late in the afternoon having a relaxed, engrossing chat. Layered over this basic quality of conversational intimacy, an individual essayist's voice can be tender, melancholic, playful, self-effacing, humorous, ironic, world-weary, discontent, acerbic, horror-struck, cheeky, or serious—anything really, as long as it is not pontificating, overly earnest, or mean-spirited.

The best personal essays are narrated by an 'I' with attitude, or at least a distinct and complex 'personality.' They combine idiosyncratic characteristics of their narrator—anxiety, romanticism, hopelessness at managing the practical details of life, a determination to 'be positive,' and other follies, faults, and yearnings—with the narrator's explorations of the subject at hand. The essayist's voice feels honest and vulnerable—although he is not without a self-effacing humour. As Lopate puts it: 'Honest to the world of facts outside ourselves, honest in reporting what we actually felt and did, and, finally, honest about our own confusion and doubts.' This honesty of voice takes courage. As Patricia Hampl says of Augustine and his *Confessions*, the essayist is willing to 'risk being a fool for the truth' (*I Could Tell You Stories*).

The essayist uses their voice to involve us, as readers, in following the twists and turns of their curiosity and wacky opinions, observations, and reflections; to participate in their untangling of some problem or observation. As readers we are actively drawn into considering things we haven't thought of, doubting things we have never questioned, or thinking things we haven't yet voiced or 'could never imagine.' The best essayists help us hear, and take seriously, new voices—from outside and within ourselves.

---

[8] Hardwick, 'Its Only Defense: Intelligence and Sparkle,' *New York Times*, September 14, 1986.

Conversations with the self and the world

The questioning of the personal essayist includes a self-questioning: of perceptions, biases, prejudices, and interests. Their investigations implicate themselves—as when the 'left'-sympathetic George Orwell admits his murderous feelings as a colonial official towards 'subject' peoples, or when he criticizes fascism while acknowledging the proper little fascist somewhere inside himself. Good essayists question the self's affections, evasions, falseness, flattery, or priggishness—any kind of dishonesty regarding self and world. Patti Miller calls the personal essay 'the child of uncomfortable truth, an expression of the urge to note as honestly as possible the gap between the dream we have of ourselves and what we actually are.' This sincere struggle towards truth is one of the shaping forces of many personal essays, whether it concerns matters of the self, the world, or self–world relations.[9]

To adapt a point from Lopate, the personal essay can be seen as an enactment of the creation of the self in the actually lived world. This is what we witness in some of Orwell's work, in James Baldwin's 'Notes of a Native Son,' and in many other essays. The personal essayist argues with himself and with the world through different selves. He says what he isn't sure of, voices feelings he wants to find the originals of, and interrogates his ignorance. It is these argumentative dialogues, held amidst the contradictions in the world itself, that give the essay its distinctive 'polyphonic' or multi-voiced, dissentient quality, as T.W. Adorno describes it,[10] and that draw the reader into conversations whose insights we—essayist and reader—will find together, although for ourselves.

---

[9] See Chapter 21 for a more detailed discussion of 'being true' in memoir writing. On self-questioning and the examined life, see Chapter 20.
[10] Adorno, 'The Essay as Form.'

Learning through your essay's persona

One way personal essayists create a dialogue with themselves is by creating a 'persona' within their essay. The writer is present through their narrating voice as well as in the form of a character or personality or persona. Sometimes the narrator identifies fully with this persona, sometimes they stand at some distance, observing, questioning, and commenting on themselves as represented in their persona. The power of this 'distance' is in how it enables the personal writer to take up repugnant or otherwise displeasing aspects of the self, as we saw in Orwell, or consider aspects and possibilities of the self that internal censors or habits of thought usually keep silent.

A true-to-life persona reveals the actual human complexity of the self: its contradictions, quirks, ambivalence, uncertainty, idiosyncrasies, limits, and longings as well as the discrepancies between thoughts and actions. It breathes life into your presence in your writing and gives you depth and solidity as nothing else will. Be true to yourself through your persona. Then use your narrating self to question this persona, sympathize with it, cheer it on, mock it, think against it, and thereby learn from it.

Some qualities of effective personal essays

Tension. Create tension, and a related sense of drama, by posing some question, by introducing a point of perplexity, by contrasting opinions, through narrator–persona differences, or through contrasts between past and present ideas, thoughts and actions, and ideals and practice.

The small, the concrete. Whatever your 'larger' subject and however unfamiliar your point of view, follow the lead of good storytellers and anchor your essay in the small and concrete. If your subject is peace, set your writing down among a group of people who are creating PEACE placards for the next demonstration. Listen to them talk, show what they are doing—and why. Bring the 'big' subject alive through the 'small.'

Show and tell. Essays explore their subject and engage their readers in two ways. They **show**: enact or demonstrate particular points by taking advantage of the evocative, solid, sensate qualities of a person, or a mannerism, action, situation, place, or object. And they **tell**: set the context, stand aside and reflect, question, offer new perspectives, and summarize points of view. See the discussion of show and tell in Chapter 12.

Vary how you express your material. For example, through observation, information-giving, feeling, reasoning, reflection, storytelling, research, analysis, argument, speculation, and wisdom.

Use an informal style. As we have already seen, the personal essayist often seems to be speaking directly to their reader, sometimes addressing them as 'you.' Make your reader experience your warm presence in your writing. Use real-life stories and anecdotes to illustrate a point. Acknowledge questions and doubts your reader might have. And find the grammar of your own writing voice without sacrificing clarity. For example, use incomplete sentences or ones beginning with 'And' and 'But,' one-sentence paragraphs to stress specific statements, or occasional emotional interjections such as 'Ouch' or 'Phew.'

Use storytelling techniques. These include anecdotes, direct speech, characters and their voices, dialogue, setting, scene, tension, dramatic development.

Go to subjects that rouse you. Why I can't bear city life. The allure of the colour blue. My distaste for chit-chat. The importance of indolence. Turn to something perplexing, something that vexes, something that enthralls.

Give your essay context. Take into account relevant points in your background and social identity: race, ethnicity, gender, religion, class, where you grew up and have lived, political views, other beliefs and interests, personal challenges. Although you are not reducible to contextual influences, include meditations on such influences and the ways in which they have or have not helped formed you. Lopate: '[T]he personal writer must be like a journalist, who respects the obligation to get in the basic orienting facts—who, what, where, when, and why—as close to the top of every story as possible.'

Give your character something to do. Explore layers of yourself by comparing *thoughts* with *actions* and actual experience. Sure, your persona thinks or says such and such, but what does he really think or actually do, how does he actually respond? 'Show' your character squeezed between beliefs and reality, as when George Orwell's 'progressive' self admits, in *The Road to Wigan Pier*, that he finds the coal miners' smell repellent.

Question your certainties. The known is always context-specific, changing, and provisional for the personal essayist. There can be no refuge from uncertainty and the need to question. If you are self-satisfied and sure about your subject, you will not make an interesting essayist. The whole point of the form is to *try out*: to acknowledge and be curious about what you don't know, to go in search of it, to investigate, and make a try at a fresh understanding.

Be meddlesome, be contrary. Good personal essayists are like the stranger arriving from afar who pesters us with questions about things we have come to take for granted, even champion. They ask because they don't know or because they are not convinced by what passes for accepted understandings and existing arrangements. This questioning of the 'obvious' is what Lopate describes as the essayist's 'meddlesome contrariness,' what Robert Louis Stevenson called the essay's 'random provocations,' and why T.W. Adorno writes of the 'heretical' and 'anti-systematic' sensibility at work inside many essays. The most interesting essayists look skeptically at everything given, everything 'commonsensical,' everything 'streamlined,' everything seen to 'fit.'[11]

Finally: Use your essaying voice to give your reader something unexpected to take away and think about.

---

[11] Adorno, 'The Essay as Form,' and Stevenson, 'An Apology for Idlers.'

Types of personal essays

The personal essay comes in four main types, with essayists often working in one type but borrowing features from the others. What type or hybrid of types you choose depends on your subject and purpose.

- **Narrative essays** use storytelling techniques to write about a real-life experience. Travel writing, for example, often uses this form.

- **Descriptive essays** paint a picture of, say, a person, place, object, or set of associated memories.

- **Lyric essays and reveries** trace the affective and reflective dimensions of an experience, such as an eclipse, a night walk in the city, or the shadow worlds of traditional Japanese houses—all subjects taken up by lyrical essayists.

- **Expository essays**, in the context of memoir writing, use firsthand experience, research, and examples to explore a personal opinion, a belief, or some common experience.

Structure, or how the essayist represents their movement of attention

I have said that *essaying* as an activity follows the writer's movements of attention, and I've pointed to analogies with the flight of a hawk, sampling foods, and how a dog searches a patch of land in its 'unplottable manner.' 'Structure' refers to how the essayist organizes, develops, and represents their movement of attention in a coherent, cohesive, fluent, and engaging form. Listed here are a few typical structures that essayists use, adapt, or combine. Choose among these approaches in your own writing, experiment with them, and develop your own variations.[12]

---

[12] The personal essays referred to in this section can be found in either Lopate (ed.), *The Art of the Personal Essay*, or online. I have borrowed here from Lopate's

Argument or exploration by indirection. Explore or 'make a case' through examples, tangents, associations, contradictions, speculation. This approach is widely used by many essayists, from Montaigne to the present.

The walk. The walk or stroll or even journey provides a structuring path along which all sorts of things can happen: conversations with characters, surprising encounters, or moments of reflection and reverie. Virginia Woolf's 'Street Haunting' in one noteworthy example. Travel writers make frequent use of this approach.

Structuring occasions, places, things. A walk is not alone in suggesting its own structure. A meal, with its social rituals and courses, can play the same role, as can moving from room to room in a house, or the topic of 'living in my body,' examined part by part.

A structuring metaphor. In this case, a word such as 'journey' is used metaphorically, as in 'My Journey to Buddhism.' Structuring metaphors abound: a patchwork quilt, unpacking (one's books, an idea), blind alleys, tree branches and roots. The only condition is that the metaphor effectively organize, develop, and express your material.

Journey combined with inner excursions in thought. By way of example, here is Tim Bascom's discussion of 'excursions' in Wendell Berry's essay 'An Entrance to the Woods.' 'In the middle of a quiet description of an overnight camping trip,' Bascom writes, 'Berry notices the distant roar of cars on a highway, and the "out-of-place" sound leads him on a long tangent. He describes how the "great ocean of silence" has been replaced by an ocean of engine noise, in which silence occurs only sporadically and at wide intervals. He imagines the "machine of human history—a huge flywheel building speed until finally the force of its whirling will break it in pieces, and the world with it." And the reader realizes that what appeared to be an odd tangent is actually an essential descent into the well of meaning. The

---

discussion of the essay's form in his 'Introduction' to *The Art of the Personal Essay* and his *To Show and To Tell*.

essay is not about camping at all, but about the fragile nature of nature. In fact, Berry uses several of these loops of reflective commentary, and though they seem to be digressions, temporarily pulling the reader away from the forward flow of the plot, they develop an essential second layer to the essay.'[13]

Hovering, whorling. Rather than moving directly to one's subject, the writer wrests meaning through a process of reflective hovering and circling—as Adrienne Rich does in 'Split at the Root,' where she examines her ambivalence about being a Jew, or half-Jew, and a woman. Annie Dillard uses a somewhat similar approach in 'Total Eclipse,' where her responses to a solar eclipse in Washington State include meditations on human connectedness, remembering, and 'waking up' to our natural world.

Braiding. The essayist begins with one subject, sets up a counter-theme, and gradually braids the two. In her essay 'Meatless Days,' Sara Suleri begins with her humorous disgust with various organ meats, then 'braids' this theme with the related themes of her family history, cultural displacement, generational conflict, gender, and grief.

Pairing and contrasting. Among the best examples is Natalia Ginzburg's 'He and I,' in which she pairs and contrasts aspects of her husband and herself in order to evoke two individual personalities, as well as what Lopate calls 'the seesaw of companionship and love' (*The Art of the Personal Essay*).

Fleshing out. Begin with a specific subject, like Charles Lamb's 'A Chapter on Ears,' and elaborate it through associated examples, lists, similes, exaggeration, or quibbles.

Opening out from the centre. Junichiro Tanizaki's 'In Praise of Shadows' begins as a limited meditation on the Japanese house, but opens outward, segment by segment, to consider the connections

---

[13] Tim Bascom, 'Picturing the Personal Essay: A Visual Guide,' in *Creative NonFiction*, Issue 49, Summer 2013.

between interiority, space, architectural shadow play, tradition and modernity, ethnicity, the body, and eroticism.

Collage, montage, assemblage. Use a form of associated but discrete written fragments or sections separated by simply identified visual breaks. The breaks permit jumps between, for example, related subjects, the particular and the general, the concrete and conceptual, the personal and cultural, and the incidental and essential. Examples include Walter Benjamin's *One-Way Street* and *Berlin Childhood Around 1900* and T.W. Adorno's *Minima Moralia*, subtitled *Reflections on a Damaged Life*.

Remember that your essay's structure is the cohesive, fluent, and engaging expression of your *essaying* process: how you-in-the-world and the-world-in-you receive, gather, and move your attention. Focus on how to best organize this process in a written form. In doing so, your essaying will, as is said, 'take shape.'

Essay beginnings

'I want to see where this goes': this is what you want your reader to feel on beginning to read your essay. Beginnings attract your reader's interest, suggest key elements of your subject matter, and give a sense of why it is important to continue reading on. Beginnings are often written or at least finalized last, after you know what your essay is about. Let's look at three examples of beginnings.

Here is how Phillip Lopate begins 'Against Joie de Vivre': 'Over the years I have developed a distaste for the spectacle of *joie de vivre*, the knack of knowing how to live. Not that I disapprove of all hearty enjoyment of life. A flushed sense of happiness can overtake a person anywhere, and one is no more to blame for it than the Asiatic flu or a sudden benevolent change in the weather (which is often joy's immediate cause). No, what rankles me is the stylization of this private condition into a bullying social ritual.'[14] Lopate introduces an argument that likely rubs against the grain of the reader's assumptions. He then qualifies his argument ('*not that I*'), showing himself to be human like us. He elaborates this qualification with humour, sharpens the reasons for his opening 'distaste' ('what rankles'), and then narrows the object of his complaint ('bullying social ritual'). Lopate's reader, perhaps dismissive at first, is being encouraged to become an interested accomplice in these explorations of his distaste.

Jay Griffiths begins her essay 'Daily Grace' in this way: 'Any tiddly doorway [to a Balinese family compound] might have an offering . . . a shrine. At a waterfall, the spray is incense-scented, and a banyan tree is garlanded with flowers. The Balinese year is drunk with feast-days (more than 60 in a year), yet every morning women also make up to 50 small offerings. Each is made of a base of coconut palm containing petals, often of hibiscus, hydrangea and marigold, a few drops of water from a frangipani flower, and a whisper of a prayer. The offerings, called *canang sari*, can carry a little metonymic prayer too: a bus ticket to ask for safety on a journey, some small change representing the hope for a little more money, or a condom, suggesting, I was told: "More sex; less children." They are a kind of gossip to god, a hint let slip.' [15] Griffiths immediately immerses us in a world of solid sensate things, voices, intriguing activities, each of which demonstrates and sets in motion curiosity about her larger subject: ceremonies of grace. She is saying: This is what rituals of grace look and feel like in practice, they are moving, I was moved, I want to better understand what is happening here, come along . . . .

Edward Abbey begins his 'Shadows from the Big Woods' with these words: 'The idea of wilderness needs no defense. It only needs more defenders. In childhood the wilds seemed infinite. Along Crooked Creek in the Allegheny Mountains of western Pennsylvania there was a trace of forest we call the Big Woods. The hemlock, beech, poplar, red oak, white oak, maple, and shagbark hickory grew on slopes so

---

[14] From Phillip Lopate (ed.), *The Art of the Personal Essay*.
[15] From the online magazine *Aeon*, January 31, 2019.

steep they had never been logged. Vines of wild grape trailed from the limbs of ancient druidical oaks—dark glens of mystery and shamanism. My brothers and I, simple-minded farmboys, knew nothing of such mythologies, but we were aware, all the same, of the magic residing among and within those trees.'[16] Abbey begins with a declaration of his key idea, then immerses the reader in a specific childhood 'woods' that is closely remembered. This is a place of magic, affection, and deep time. The essay, an argument built over an experience and a love, will go on to trace other shadows: the 'earth mover' destruction of this and all woods, a culture of mastery over the natural world, and the shadows cast across personal memory and imagination.

Beginnings can take many forms, but each is a promise of interesting things to come.

Essay endings

Given that the personal essay follows the path of one's thoughtful investigations and is not dependent on any predetermined structure, what is to say that it cannot continue without end? How to bring a personal essay to a close?

Sometimes one's subject offers up a natural ending: the close of a day, the end of a journey, death, the end of a story that has been serving as an experiential anchor for your essay. You can also end by summarizing and revising a previous idea that stems from the essay itself. Another approach resembles the pulling-up-and-away, panning shot used by filmmakers—in effect taking a broader, longer-term, reflective view.

What about a subject that resists closure, as many *essaying* subjects do? Its subject matter is intrinsically unresolvable or pulls the writer in contrary directions? James Baldwin arrives at just such a point in 'Notes of a Native Son,' an exploration of conflict between son and father, and between Black and white society. Here is Baldwin's final paragraph:

---

[16] In Edward Abbey, *The Journey Home*.

> It began to seem that one would have to hold in the mind forever two ideas which seemed to be in opposition. The first idea was acceptance, the acceptance, totally without rancor, of life as it is, and men as they are: in the light of this idea, it goes without saying that injustice is a commonplace. But this did not mean that one could be complacent, for the second idea was of equal power: that one must never, in one's own life, accept these injustices as commonplace but must fight them with all one's strength. This fight begins, however, in the heart and it now had been laid to my charge to keep my own heart free of hatred and despair. This intimation made my heart heavy and, now that my father was irrecoverable, I wished that he had been beside me so that I could have searched his face for the answers which only the future would give me now.[17]

Baldwin holds pairs of opposed feelings, ideas, and truths suspended in his and our thoughts. He refuses false resolutions, instead realizing that he must live with multiple, conflicting truths: he must acknowledge ('acceptance') injustice as a commonplace, he must oppose (refuse to 'accept') injustice 'with all one's strength,' he must continue the 'fight' against injustice (*feel* its wrongfulness), and he must carry on this 'fight' with a heart free from hatred and despair. Baldwin's situation, and his honest response, is a reminder that there can be actually lived forces in life that do not lend themselves to clean, smooth, 'cleared-up' endings. Indeed, to impose such endings would be to deny our experience.

Keep your reader with you

Given the personal essayist's dog-like 'unsystematic searching,' it's not surprising that some essays risk losing all sense of cohering structure—such as the 'nonchalance bordering on formlessness' that Lopate finds in the work of the essayist Lu Hsun.

How then ensure that your reader keeps footing it with your wandering self?

---

[17] This is one of ten essays published as *Notes of a Native Son*.

Three things are helpful here. First, establish your primary subject, then maintain its omnipresence in the background. Second, establish a distinctive narrative voice and persona. Third, use your writing to make your reader feel like an interested, engaged accomplice in your thought excursions. Converse with them, get them wondering with you. You are going for a walk with Sebald's 'dog'—a real walk and a thought-walk. Invite your reader along. And take your cue, both of you, from how the dog moves to and fro over a patch of land, unsystematically it seems, but following its nose, and all the time 'grasping' the meaning of where it is.

It's said that we humans need both bread and circuses. What are your remembered places—circuses or not—of wonder, of shameless wildness, tingling thrills, enchantment, the ludicrous, the fantastic? Those unfenced places in your experience and your imagination? Images from pexels.com, isorepublic.com, and unsplash.com.

PART II

STRENGTHENING YOUR WRITING

CHAPTER 11

WONDER

Some years ago I lay on the Nullarbor Plain under a dazzling midnight sky. Everywhere I looked were glimmering specks of gold, green, white, orange, and red in an inky canopy of infinite depth—far more stars than I had ever seen. The cosmic bios: animated, vibrant. Scorpius. Argo. A V-shaped Hyades cluster. The eagle's foot of the Southern Cross. The Milky Way's great celestial Emu high overhead, *Gugurmin* in the Wiradjuri language, a time for the Wiradjuri to collect emu eggs. The storied sky of Aboriginal peoples. How Crow's error let wind blow Bungil and his people into the sky. How the sacred places on earth fell out of the Milky Way. How Orion and the Pleiades became story rocks. Guiding stars, too, for Aboriginal walkers, and for Torres Strait Islander and Polynesian paddlers. The sky as home to ancestors who have ascended ladders stretching from earth to the eternally abundant upper world. The wisdom place for traditional healers who climb ropes of hair, lightning, trees, flames, rainbows. The eloquent wayfinding, season-telling, story-filled sky that tonight reverberates with a soft, keening murmur. My mind begins to slow and thin into gossamer, then vanishes. I am floating inside the glimmering, indigo deep, solid but weightless, hovering, rolling, wavering this way and that, surrounded by stardust . . . sensations of harmony, wholeness, completion, and, most of all, wonder.

Remembering that night now, I find myself wondering about the place of wonder in personal writing.

Let's begin at the beginning: What is it, anyway, this thing we call *wonder?*

Something marvellous, to be sure.

A kind of attention to things that elicits their marvellousness. The surprising in things, the amazing.

To be surprised. To be astonished.

Emotions inspired by the surprising, the unknown, the unfamiliar, especially things experienced as beautiful.

To experience the unfamiliar in the familiar.

To be curious, to feel puzzled, uncertain, to doubt—and thus to question.

To wish to learn more, to explore, to know.

Is not the best memoir writing prompted by these senses of wonder, by experience sprinkled with stardust?

⁂

The Nullarbor night sky is a deep, wonder-filled, expressive place layered in drama, feeling, and meaning.[1] It only waits to be *noticed*, to

---

[1] When traveling the Nullarbor I was reading Dianne Johnson's recently published *Night Skies of Aboriginal Australia* (1998), a 'composite,' as Johnson writes, 'of non-Aboriginal versions of Aboriginal astronomical ideas.' Today, Australian Aboriginal peoples, who have always studied the stars, are key astronomical-cultural researchers and teachers. See, for example, the website aboriginalastronomy.com.au. As Kirsten Banks, a Wiradjuri woman, writes, 'Aboriginal star stories are not just stories, they are lessons that educate us about the relationship between the sky and the land, as well as how the universe functions around us. This knowledge has existed for more than 65,000 years.

be *attended to*, to have its expressiveness made eloquent through human experience and in human terms. Do not all personally significant experiences—involving people or objects or places, from the touch of a lover's earlobe on the lips, to the flames of Nepal's Pashupatinath funeral pyres, to the 'feel' of a screwdriver used over a lifetime—contain their own wondrous expressiveness which, with loving attention, the writer can make personally eloquent?

The sources of wonder need not be like a starlit sky, itself something of a cliché of the wondrous, although still a thing of wonder. Much of what is 'ordinary' in the made world was once extraordinary: the steam locomotive and the telephone, tea drinking (to Europeans), cities and factories (to rural people). No doubt familiarity, things made 'ordinary,' even natural-seeming, can kill wonder. But cannot the 'obvious' and 'ordinary' still be made subjects of wonder? Only consider Virginia Woolf's evening walk in search of a lead pencil ('Street Haunting'), Robert Macfarlane's walk across the muddy tidal waters of the Broomway (in *The Old Ways*), and Walter Benjamin's remembered childhood fascinations with his pillow or market women (*Berlin Childhood Around 1900*).

What these writers share is an engaged, creaturely attentiveness to the world. Their writing is grounded in a caring, careful, empathic curiosity. They move amidst the familiar as knowledgeable but wondering, questioning strangers. They are open to the world, letting it come at and in their creaturely bodies as felt experience. Theirs is a grounded inquisitiveness and intelligence. They *grasp* the world on their bodies for themselves, including the creaturely self's sensations of shock in response to the frantic *overwhelmlitude* of entirely ordinary contemporary city life.[2]

Today, in modern Australia, we are working to learn more and revive the knowledge of Indigenous Australian astronomy' (*The Guardian*, May 21, 2018).

[2] I borrow the term 'overwhelmlitude' from Jerry Zaslove's 'Decamouflaging Memory, or, How We Are Undergoing "Trial By Space" While Utopian Communities Are Restoring the Powers of Recall,' *West Coast Line* #34 (Spring 2001). This essay and others by Zaslove are important sources for my own

How does—how might—'wonder' influence memoir writing?

- Wonder begins by allowing our creaturely, sensate self to be exposed to and curious about the world. To wonder is to explore our live creatureliness and its experience—and make these eloquent.

- As young children we naturally lived in a state of wonder—a *Wow!* world. Do you remember what it was like? Do you remember the mysteries of a crack in the sidewalk or the wet darkness beneath a drain grate? The distant lands you travelled to in bedtime stories, the ghosts in your fluttering bedroom curtains. Awaking to snow-covered trees. Peering into the pawnbroker's or toy shop's window. Sailing your pirate ship beneath the dining room table. Soap bubbles. How the façade of a neighbourhood house was both house and demon giant. The contents of a sewing or button box. How a train's day car metamorphosed into a 'sleeper' with its velvety, snug warmth.

- To wonder is to shake our surround or ourselves, like one of those snow globes of childhood, and to delight in the unfolding effect.

- Just as glacial landforms include cirques, nunataks, arêtes, kettles, and till and flour, so the land of 'wonder' has its own natural characteristics to which it invites us to pay special attention: imagination, déjà vu, correspondences, coincidence, transformation, ambivalence, contradiction, anticipation, the unknown, hopefulness, shadows, longing, the foreign, the exotic, dreaming, and those liminal places of morning/waking and evening/drowsiness.

---

thinking about modernity, its experientially overwhelming forms, and human struggles toward more autonomous forms of remembering and creation. I return to the subject of modernity, childhood, and remembering in Chapter 18.

- To wonder is to be released into a field of the present, of remembering and of longing—running back and forth like an excited dog, sniffing, digging, exploring, investigating, discovering the possibilities of where it is.

- If wonder means to become more consciously, curiously attentive, it can also mean losing yourself, becoming self-forgetful in order to remember.

- To wonder is to wander. These two shadow-words, although having no literal connection, still feel connected. Arabic uses the word *sarha*, originally meaning to let the cattle wander freely in the pasture, and later humanized to suggest the movement of a walker energized by the delight of escape, of improvising, of *sauntering,* itself a word from the French *sans terre*, a contraction of *à la Sainte Terre*, meaning Holy Land.[3] To wonder is to loll about in our thoughts and feelings, to experience delight in both the wandering mind and the places through which it tramps.

- To wonder is to experience total delight in a place, as I did on the Nullarbor Plain. The poet Gary Snyder is writing of this form of 'wonder' when he gives a naturalistic meaning to the Sanskrit term *darśana* or *darshan*: 'It's a gift; it's like there's a moment in which the thing is ready to let you see it. In India,

---

[3] The example is from Robert MacFarlane's *The Old Ways*. As we saw in the discussion of the personal essay (Chapter 10), essaying has a long association with walking, in the form of sauntering, as well as with wondering. The Spanish language also differentiates between walking with a purpose (*caminar*) and strolling, ambling, sauntering (*pasear*). In his essay 'Walking,' Henry David Thoreau writes: 'I have met with but one or two persons in the course of my life who understood the art of Walking, that is, of taking walks, who had a genius, so to speak, for sauntering; which word is beautifully derived "from idle people who roved about the country, in the Middle Ages, and asked charity, under pretence of going à la Sainte Terre"—to the Holy Land, till the children exclaimed, 'There goes a *Sainte-Terrer*,' a saunterer—'a Holy-Lander . . . . Some, however, would derive the word from *sans terre*, without land or a home, which, therefore, in the good sense, will mean, having no particular home, but equally at home everywhere.'

this is called *darshan*. Darshan means getting a view, and if the clouds blow away, as they did once for me, and you get a view of the Himalayas from the foothills, an Indian person would say, "Ah, the Himalayas are giving you their darshana"; they're letting you have their view. This comfortable, really deep way of getting a sense of something takes time. It doesn't show itself to you right away. It isn't even necessary to know the names of things the way a botanist would. It's more important to be aware of the "suchness" of the thing; it's a reality. It's also a source of a certain kind of inspiration for creativity."[4]

- Wonder emerges from listening to our creaturely self noticing—and being surprised, startled, or astonished by—the familiar and routine. To wonder is to notice the perplexing in what we thought we understood, to respond not from our certainties but from our uncertainty and doubts. To wonder is to move beyond the neatly landscaped into its weedy fringes, or over the fence into the woods—to explore beyond the orderly made world, the agreed upon and the 'sensible.'

- To wonder is to ask—especially to question the authoritative 'obvious' and 'of course.' Wonder oils the rusted, immovable hinges of 'experience.'

- Wonder is a way to discover what needs finding, not to simply find what you have set out looking for.

- Just as the process of catabolism involves the breaking down of molecules to create energy, so wonder, as curiosity, breaks down or breaks into the taken-for-granted—the routine, habit, repetition, the readymade—and thereby releases otherwise hidden potentialities and re-energized wonder.

---

[4] From Jonathan White (ed.), *Talking on the Water: Conversations about Nature and Creativity.*

- To wonder is the beginning of critical understanding: both a demystifying of life-denying illusions, and a listening for and investigation of those creaturely yearnings that modern culture often dismisses as naive 'illusions.'

- 'Wonder puts aside the known and accepted, along with sophistication, and instead serves up an intelligent naïveté.'[5]

- Wonder invites us to look into the forbidden, like opening the door of that usually locked cabinet, or retrieving a book kept out of reach.

- Wonder is what the logical mind experiences as the surprising correspondences, similarities, and coincidences that spring from a suddenly remembered taste, touch or sound. Wonder suggests nothing is forgotten, especially by the body.

- There is wonder in acts of transformation. Walter Benjamin recalls the childhood pleasure of reaching inside a pair of his socks—neatly turned inside out into a pocket—and pulling the inside out until the little bundle became the socks themselves. In the memory stories of *Berlin Childhood Around 1900*, he reminds us many times of the element of wonder in the power to conjure, to bring about, to imagine and create.

- The converse is also true: there is an element of wonder in being transformed *by* the conjuring-like work of many experiences—sexuality, for example, or loving or loathing a place, a teacher, a book, or ideas.

- Like Benjamin's socks, wonder sits waiting to be found in ambiguity, ambivalence, doubleness, transmutation, masks and masking (pretending, trying on, duplicity), paradox, slips of speech, 'impudent' speech, jokes, dreams, blushes, and the telling and holding of secrets. According to wonder there is

---

[5] Charles Baxter, *Burning Down the House*.

much in life that resembles the fisher's oar, which is an oar at the seaside, but becomes a winnowing shovel in the wheat field, a table on which to set lunch in the local tavern, a marker planted into the sailor's burial mound, and, when planted into a heap of grain, a sign that the harvest is done.[6]

- Wonder makes its appearance at thresholds, crossroads, boundaries, beginnings, endings—and it leads us to such places as well. Paul Valery: 'The bottom of the mind is paved with crossroads.'[7] Both 'the bottom of the mind' and physical life. Here sits the heightened, energized world of choice, uncertainty, guesswork, speculation, anticipation, expectation, foreboding, hope. It's here, too—as we reflect on what exists and where we have come from and what could be—that we might ask: *Am I happy? Am I satisfied? Is this what life is about? Or could be about? What is possible? What do I want from life, really?*

- To wonder includes asking the fundamental questions of memoir writing: *Who am I? Where have I come from? Where am I going? Why am I here?*

༒

What does 'wonder' sound like in writing? Here, from among its many voices, are several examples.

The first two passages are excerpts from Walter Benjamin's *Berlin Childhood Around 1900*.[8]

From 'The Carousel':

The revolving deck with its obliging animals skims the surface of the ground. It is at the height best suited to dreams of flying. Music rings out—and with a jolt, the child rolls

---

[6] The example of the oar is taken from Hyde's *Trickster Makes the World*.
[7] Quoted in Lewis Hyde's *Trickster Makes This World*.
[8] I use a translation from the German by Howard Eiland.

away from his mother. At first, he is afraid to leave her. But then he notices how he himself is faithful. He is enthroned, as faithful monarch, above a world that belongs to him. Trees and natives line the borders at intervals. Suddenly, his mother reappears in an Orient. Then, from some primeval forest, comes a treetop—one such as the child has seen already thousands of years ago, such as he has seen just now, for the first time, on the carousel. His mount is devoted to him: like a mute Arion, he rides his mute fish; a wooden Zeus-bull carries him off as immaculate Europa. The eternal return of all things has long since become childhood wisdom, and life an ancient intoxication of sovereignty, with the booming orchestrion as crown jewel at the center. Now the music is slowly winding down; space begins to stutter, and the trees start coming to their senses. The carousel becomes uncertain ground. And his mother rises up before him—the firmly fixed mooring post around which the landing child wraps the line of his glances.

From 'Winter Morning':

The fairy in whose presence we are granted a wish is there for each of us. But few of us know how to remember the wish we have made; and so, few of us recognize its fulfillment later in our lives. I know the wish of mine that was fulfilled, and I will not say that it was any more clever than the wishes children make in fairy tales. It took shape in me with the approach of the lamp, which, early on a winter morning, at half past six, would cast the shadow of my nursemaid on the covers of my bed. In the stove a fire was lighted. Soon the flame—as though shut up in a drawer that was much too small, where it barely had room to move because of the coal—was peeping out at me. Smaller even than I was, it nevertheless was something mighty that began to establish itself there, at my very elbow—something to which the maid had to stoop down even lower than to me. When it was ready, she would put a little apple in the oven to bake. Before long, the grating of the burner door was outlined in a red flickering on the floor. And it seemed, to my weariness, that this image was enough for one day. It was always so at this hour; only the voice of the nursemaid disturbed the solemnity with which the winter morning used to give me up into the keeping of the things in my room. The shutters were not yet open as I slid aside the bolt of the oven door for the first time, to examine the apple cooking inside. Sometimes, its aroma would scarcely have changed. And then I would wait patiently until I thought I could detect the fine bubbly fragrance that came from a deeper and more secretive cell of the winter's day than even the fragrance of the fir trees on Christmas eve. There lay the apple, the dark, warm fruit that—familiar and yet transformed, like a good friend back from a journey—now awaited me. It was the journey through the dark land of the oven's heat, from which it had extracted the aromas of all the things the day held in store for me. So it was not surprising that, whenever I warmed my hands on its shining cheeks, I would always hesitate to bite in. I sensed that the fugitive knowledge contained in its smell could all too easily escape me on the way to my tongue. That knowledge which sometimes was so heartening that it stayed to comfort me on my trek to school. Of course, no sooner had I arrived than, at the touch of my bench, all the weariness that at first seemed dispelled returned with a vengeance. And with it this wish: to be able to sleep my fill.

The beginning and ending of Adrienne Rich's world-questioning and self-questioning 'Split At the Root: An Essay On Jewish Identity'[9]:

Beginning of 'Split At the Root':

For about fifteen minutes I have been sitting chin in hand in front of the typewriter, staring out at the snow. Trying to be honest with myself, trying to figure out why writing this seems to be so dangerous an act, filled with fear and shame,

---

[9] Adrienne Rich, *Essential Essays*.

and why it seems so necessary. It comes to me that in order to write this I have to be willing to do two things: I have to claim my father, for I have my Jewishness from him and not from my gentile mother; and I have to break his silence, his taboos; in order to claim him I have in a sense to expose him.

And there is, of course, the third thing: I have to face the sources and the flickering presence of my own ambivalence as a Jew; the daily, mundane anti-Semitisms of my entire life.

These are stories I have never tried to tell before. Why now? Why, I asked myself sometime last year, does this question of Jewish identity float so impalpably, so ungraspably around me, a cloud I can't quite see the outlines of, which feels to me to be without definition?

And yet I've been on the track of this longer than I think.

Ending of 'Split At the Root':

Sometimes I feel I have seen too long from too many disconnected angles: white, Jewish, anti-Semite, racist, anti-racist, once-married, lesbian, middle-class, feminist, exmatriate Southerner, *split at the root*: that I will never bring them whole. I would have liked, in this essay, to bring together the meanings of anti-Semitism and racism as I have experienced them and as I believe they intersect in the world beyond my life. But I'm not able to do this yet. I feel the tension as I think, make notes: *if you really look at the one reality, the other will waver and disperse* . . . . Nothing has trained me for this. And sometimes I feel inadequate to make any statement as a Jew; I feel the history of denial within me like an injury, a scar. For assimilation has affected my perceptions; those early lapses in meaning, those blanks, are with me still. My ignorance can be dangerous to me and to others.

Yet we can't wait for the undamaged to make our connections for us; we can't wait to speak until we are perfectly clear and righteous. There is no purity and, in our lifetimes, no end to this process.

This essay, then, has no conclusions: it is another beginning for me. Not just a way of saying, in 1982 Right Wing America, *I too, will wear the yellow star*. It's a moving into accountability, enlarging the range of accountability. I know that in the rest of my life, the next half century or so, every aspect of my identity will have to be engaged. The middleclass white girl taught to trade obedience for privilege. The Jewish lesbian raised to be a heterosexual gentile. The woman who first heard oppression named and analyzed in the Black Civil Rights struggle. The woman with three sons, the feminist who hates male violence. The woman limping with a cane, the woman who has stopped bleeding, are also accountable. The poet who knows that beautiful language can lie, that the oppressor's language sometimes sounds beautiful. The woman trying, as part of her resistance, to clean up her act.

The opening paragraph of 'The Knife,' an essay by the surgeon Richard Selzer:

One holds the knife as one holds the bow of a cello or a tulip by the stem. Not palmed nor gripped nor grasped, but lightly, with the tips of the fingers. The knife is not for pressing. It is for drawing across the field of skin. Like a slender fish, it waits, at the ready, then, go! It darts, followed by a fine wake of red. The flesh parts, falling away to yellow globules of fat. Even now, after so many times, I still marvel at its power—cold, gleaming, silent. More, I am still struck with a kind of dread that it is I in whose hand the blade travels, that my hand is its vehicle, that yet again this terrible steel-bellied thing and I have conspired for a most unnatural purpose, the laying open of the body of a human being.[10]

⁂

From Junichiro Tanizaki's 'In Praise of Shadows':

And so it has come to be that the beauty of a Japanese room depends on a variation of shadows, heavy shadows against light shadows—it has nothing else. Westerners are amazed at the simplicity of Japanese rooms, perceiving in them no more than ashen walls bereft of ornament. Their reaction is understandable, but it betrays a failure to comprehend the mystery of shadows. Out beyond the sitting room, which the rays of the sun can at best but barely reach, we extend the eaves or build on a veranda, putting the sunlight at still greater a remove. The light from the garden steals in but dimly through paper-paneled doors, and it is precisely this indirect light that makes for us the charm of a room. We do our walls in neutral colors so that the sad, fragile, dying rays can sink into absolute repose . . . [T]he walls of the sitting room will almost always be of clay textured with fine sand. A luster here would destroy the soft fragile beauty of the feeble light. We delight in the mere sight of the delicate glow of fading rays clinging to the surface of a dusky wall, there to live out what little life remains to them . . . .

We have all had the experience, on a visit to one of the great temples of Kyoto or Nara, of being shown a scroll, one of the temple's treasures, hanging in a large, deeply recessed alcove. So dark are these alcoves, even in bright daylight, that we can hardly discern the outlines of the work; all we can do is listen to the explanation of the guide, follow as best we can the all-but-invisible brush strokes, and tell ourselves how magnificent a painting it must be. Yet the combination

---

[10] From Selzer, *Mortal Lessons: Notes on the Art of Surgery*. The essay is also available online.

of that blurred old painting and the dark alcove is one of absolute harmony. The lack of clarity, far from disturbing us, seems rather to suit the painting perfectly. For the painting here is nothing more than another delicate surface upon which the faint, frail light can play; it performs precisely the same function as the sand-textured wall . . . .

A Japanese room might be likened to an inkwash painting, the paper-paneled shoji being the expanse where the ink is thinnest, and the alcove where it is the darkest. Whenever I see the alcove of a tastefully built Japanese room, I marvel at our comprehension of the secrets of shadows, our sensitive use of shadow and light. For the beauty of the alcove is not the work of some clever device. An empty space is marked off with plain wood and plain walls, so that the light drawn into it forms dim shadows within emptiness. There is nothing more. And yet, when we gaze into the darkness that gathers behind the crossbeam, around the flower vase, beneath the shelves, though we know perfectly well it is mere shadow, we are overcome with the feeling that in this small corner of the atmosphere there reigns complete and utter silence; that here in the darkness immutable tranquility holds sway. The "mysterious Orient" of which Westerners speak probably refers to the uncanny silence of these dark places. And even we as children would feel an inexpressible chill as we peered into the depths of an alcove to which the sunlight had never penetrated. Where lies the key to this mystery? Ultimately it is the magic of shadows. Were the shadows to be banished from its corners, the alcove would in that instant revert to mere void.

Do you remember the crazy exciting wonder of youthful love? Photographer unknown (brightside.me).

CHAPTER 12

BRINGING YOUR EXPERIENCE ALIVE

In this and the next several chapters we look at a variety of techniques, stylistic elements, and other considerations that can increase the effectiveness of your memoir writing.

To show and to tell

Whether you 'show' or 'tell' in your writing depends on what you want to accomplish. Each has its uses and each complements the other.

Telling has three meanings and uses.

First, to tell is to name something directly, such as a date or place, how something works, or how tall or thin a character is. Telling sets out the necessary facts—what, where, when, who—and helps express the particularity of a character, scene, setting, or place. Telling also adds context, such as details related to gender, ethnicity, race, class, beliefs, geography and the historical surround. Contextual telling names social-cultural influences; delimits a character, setting or situation; qualifies and challenges exaggerations, such as an individual's claim to being self-made; and helps make your writing feel less self-preoccupied.

Second, telling has narrative uses. It efficiently moves a story or essay from situation to situation, scene to scene, idea to idea, and one timeframe to another. You can also use telling to review and summarize events or ideas. We will return to these uses of telling in a moment when discussing 'narrative bridges and summaries.'

Telling in its third sense refers to those times when a writer-narrator wants to reflect on, analyse, interpret, and express opinions about anything done, thought, or said in their writing. The writer steps a little aside from their story, takes a reflective, critical look at what has been said, and offers their assessment, opinions, and other thoughts. They are not telling the reader what to think; they are showing themselves thinking. They are, as Phillip Lopate says, 'thinking on the page.' By this Lopate means:

> to question all that might have transpired inside and outside [the writer's self] at the time, and to catch the hunches, doubts, and digressive associations that dart through [the writer] . . . . In attempting any autobiographical prose, the writer knows what has happened . . . but not necessarily what to make of it. It is like being handed a text in cuneiform: you have to translate, at first awkwardly, inexpertly, slowly, and uncertainly. (*To Show and to Tell*)

In effect the writer asks: *What do I make of this experience? What does it seem to be telling me? What am I learning here?* The writer is exploring and elucidating their experience—although not only their experience. Their telling is also an implied invitation to their reader. *Come closer,* the writer seems to be saying, *compare my experience with your own, and judge the sense I have made of it against your own thoughts.* By reflecting on their own life experiences, the writer is facilitating the reader's own reflective activity.

Showing enacts or dramatizes a character (or place or situation) in such a way that your reader doesn't simply read *about* the character but *experiences them inside themselves,* like a fully alive inner echo. To 'show,' as the Russian writer Anton Chekhov once described it, is to 'seize on small details, grouping them so that when the reader closes his eyes he gets a picture. For instance, you'll have a moonlit night if you write that on the mill dam a piece of glass from a broken bottle glittered like a bright little star . . . .'[1]

When Tristine Rainer replaces 'My mother was a strong, kind woman' with 'My mother carried fifty pounds of mail on her back, yet she had a shy smile for each of her neighbours as she laboured up the hill' (*Your Life as Story*), the rewritten version helps us inwardly perceive the woman's weight and volume, the strain in her movement, her strength, her inner character, her solid creaturely presence. It *shows* us the woman. More than that, we *feel* the woman's presence, sympathetically. We care about her: the origins of her determination, that shy smile, her own caring, her fate. She suddenly interests us. Paradoxical as it may seem, by showing the living particularity of someone or something, writers create a deeply sharable experience. Suddenly your reader is not merely reading as an observer; they are connecting with your writing from within themselves.

Here are a number of techniques for showing:

- Enact human activity, including direct speech and dialogue, how a person talks, their gestures, the reactions of others. (All the points in this list take advantage of the qualities of what I call 'realia,' a term discussed later in this chapter.)

- Use strong, specific verbs. Don't use 'walk' if you mean saunter, strut, or trudge.

- Use specific, concrete nouns and adjectives. Resist ready-at-hand adjectives such as 'sad,' 'beautiful,' and 'wonderful.'

- Use evocative objects: not the usual tears at a funeral, but the wet tissue clenched in a shaking hand.

- Include selected, sensory details of, say, a person's clothing or appearance, or a setting. Rather than referring to a 'memorable

---

[1] From a letter to his brother, in Avrahm Yarmolinsky (ed.), *The Unknown Chekhov*.

room,' write how the stained, web-filled lampshades filled the oak-panelled room with a soft amber glow.

- Use language that *demonstrates* how someone or something sees, smells, sounds, tastes, and feels. Use and appeal to all the senses.

- Use figures of speech. Well imagined, they show like nothing else can—see Chapter 14.

How do you *show* a birth, death, or funeral in your memoir? Everyone has some experience of such events. But your memoir is not the experience of some 'everyone.' It is your own. It is your record of how life came at *you* and how *you* responded. As your reader, I want to know how this experience, a funeral for example, moved you. Don't tell me 'it was sad.' *Show* me how sadness looks on you and others, show me how it is actually lived inside. In *The Memoir Project*, Marion Roach Smith recalls dressing for a funeral where she used clothing as a way of wishing power over death. It is not until later, in the process of slowly undressing, that Smith experiences waves of memories of the deceased suddenly, involuntarily flowing through her. It is here—not at the funeral, but at this moment—that, as she says, she feels the sharp anguish of mortality, the surprise of grief. It is in this private, unanticipated moment that her actually felt grief, and its implacability, finally shows itself to Smith, and gives her the occasion to show it to her reader.

Smith tells another story, this time about a student who hated and yet adored her drunken, brawling father. Again and again the student wrote about how she despised and loved her father—but she never showed this as her own distinct experience. Then one day in conversation with Smith, the student angrily described how, every Father's Day, she went to a card shop and came home empty-handed. With another Father's Day coming up, Smith asked her to again go to the card shop, this time with notebook in hand, and write about her experience. She returned, Smith says, with a marvellously personal story that no one else could have written. She was finally able to show—write the enacting of—her love-hate as actually lived experience.

I began by saying that showing *enacts* a character, place, or situation in the sense of bringing it alive as an experience in our reader. Now we see, in the two examples from Smith's work, how this *enacting* can also include the *expressing* of—the releasing out of ourselves into words—emotionally true moments in our creaturely life.

Dramatic scenes and narrative bridges and summaries

Beginning memoir writers often write as if every episode, character, gesture, and piece of information has equal significance. The narrative's energies and rhythms don't line up with or express the experiential content. One incident follows another without let-up: this happened, and-then-this-and-then-this-and-then-this to the end. The reader is left wondering: Where is this really going and what's important?

```
Narrative without dramatic scenes
  ~~~~~~~~~~~~~~~
This and then this and then this . . .
```

Used together, 'narrative bridges and summaries' and 'dramatic scenes' match narrative energies with experiential content, they focus your writing on the most significant parts of your material, they vary the rhythm of your narrative, and they efficiently manage its forward motion.

```
    Scene  →  Scene  →  Scene
      1         2         3

         Narrative bridges and summaries
```

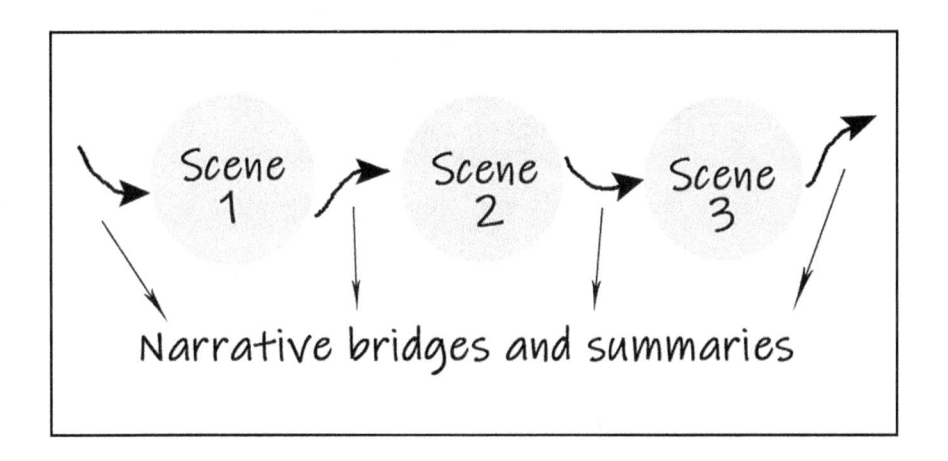

Dramatic scenes are the zoom lenses of writing. They pause a narrative's forward motion, focus on experiential moments of consequence, and give volume, weight, depth, and subtlety to these moments. Dramatic scenes are often places of disclosure, discovery, and revelation. As such, they complicate and change the reader's understanding. Whatever their subject—a granddaughter opening, then reading her grandmother's journal; the slow unfolding marvel of a sunset across the Kakadu floodplain; siblings discussing their mother's affairs; or the moments before one's first parachute jump—a dramatic scene whispers: *This is important, slow down, pay attention.*[2]

As the name suggests, **narrative bridges** act as bridges between dramatic scenes ('By then I had moved from Ocean Park to . . .'), they shift the narrative between different time frames ('Ten years earlier . . .'), and they move a narrative forward ('As I was thinking of the previous evening's conversation with Gabriel, I heard . . .'). They can also be used to set the context of a scene or a whole piece of writing, e.g., they name where and when.

Writers use **narrative summaries** to recapitulate, reflect on, interpret, question, speculate about, and offer alternate views and opinions on what has occurred, whether in a memoir story or an essay. Summaries introduce a 'conversational' dimension to personal writing, what I

---

[2] See the discussion in Chapter 19 of the 'dramatic scene' from Maya Angelou's memoir *I Know Why the Caged Bird Sings*.

referred to earlier, using Lopate's language, as 'thinking on the page.' The writer is both telling a story (or arguing a point of view in a personal essay) and commenting on and assessing what is being said.

Dramatic scenes tend to rely on 'showing,' narrative bridges and summaries on 'telling.'

Realia

'Realia,' a term used by educators, are actual, tactile objects used to illustrate and teach vocabulary, especially to foreign-language learners. For example, the word 'pen' is this actual pen that I am holding in my hand. In philosophy, realia are used to distinguish real things from theories about them. Realia is a plural formation, just as 'memorabilia' refers to 'memorable things.' In the context of memoir writing, realia help us remember, and they bring our memories alive in our writing,

Realia often house memories and act like hubs between which exist webs of charged associations. Consider, for example, the difference for memory of having seen a flashcard with an image of a pineapple, as opposed to holding, then eating a pineapple whose juicy sugars make you *Mmmm* with pleasure and suddenly return you to an evening stroll you took 30 years earlier amidst the drifts of saris on Dar es Salaam's harbour promenade. Or how a remnant of wallpaper can return you to a scene 60 years ago . . . a farmhouse, upstairs, a rocking chair, you are enfolded snug in your grandmother's lap, she murmuring her pleasure at the view out the window, those golden fields fringed in green hedging, a car, dust, granddad returning home, 'and about time' you can hear her saying. It's not surprising that educators use realia to reinforce the remembered associations between words (which are inherently abstract) and the physical sense qualities of objects and activities.

Even certain words and word clusters in themselves, when charged with felt associations within an individual's life experience, can act like realia. *Grandma|silverware|sugar donuts*, to use a personal example. Or: *Moon|China Sea|mist. Soir de Paris|blue|mother.* Sonorous phrases from childhood books: *Above and beyond the stars.* Words like *grisly* or *whip-poor-will.* Realia are like returning ghosts who transport us to the dramatic scenes and dream sites of our life.

Besides aiding memory, realia are the solid, sensate, evocative phenomena that make our writing feel real. This applies whether our subject is a character (a characteristic mannerism, or an experienced quality: *Hugging Aunt Mae was like embracing a sack of scrap metal.*), an object (a keepsake, photo, book), a place, a situation, or a set of activities. Here is how Frank Conroy uses realia to bring back to life who he was as an adolescent: 'Eyes closed, head back, I drank directly from the carton of milk, taking long gulps while cold air from the refrigerator spilled out onto my bare feet. Leaving an inch for [my stepfather's] coffee, I replaced the carton and pushed the fat door shut. End of breakfast' (Conroy, *Stop-Time*).

The value of realia becomes strikingly apparent when words fail to express the reality of an experience. Compare, for example, the felt experience of grief with the amorphousness of the word 'grief.' Realia can help bring grief alive, as an actually lived experience, through its physical evidence: the sensation in one's hands of the absolute coldness of a headstone, the delicate handwriting in a Book of Remembrance, the indifference to our wishes of that hole in the earth.

Lisa Ohlen Harris tells a story about how grief—the realness of it and the words for this realness—finally came to her. As a 20-year-old volunteer in a youth outreach program, she had read textbooks on grief, but had had no experience with death. Suddenly she found herself trying to console a 15-year-old boy whose father had just died. The boy's mother appeared calm, the boy himself 'seemed the same as ever.... Nothing was as I'd expected'—until, that is, Harris noticed a wastebasket overflowing with crumpled tissues, 'and for the first time, I felt another's grief.' Harris continues: 'It wasn't words that pierced me. I was moved by the physical remnants of invisible grief. Attempts to describe grief may focus on abstract descriptions: pain, sorrow, ache, hopelessness, tears. The description only starts to have some heat when we pull it down into the realm of the concrete. The sorrow comes in waves, I might say. I am overtaken by weeping. These descriptions may well be clichés, but they are less abstract because they incorporate evocative, active, physical phrases . . . . When you sit down to write about deep emotions, make sure to ground those emotions in the physical world. Go ahead, describe, if you can, the swirling haze of denial, the sharpness of despair, the impossible vacuum of loneliness . . . [But] look closer. Pay attention to . . . what's in the wastebasket . . . . Take the abstraction of grief and pull it down into the physical world of the concrete.'[3]

Like the basket of crumpled tissues, realia can be thought of as the sensate, solid *evidence* of actually lived life, whether this evidence is an object, or an enactment, such as the woman carrying the mail, or a physical feeling. As such, realia 'show,' and in showing then help enact our writing inside our reader, offering them the solid materials for their own experience.

Chronological, experiential, and narrative time

Here we touch briefly on handling narrative time within a story and personal essay.[4]

Many beginning memoir writers construct narratives based on conventional chronological time. This is the most familiar and easiest approach to handling time, but it is also predictable and inflexible. And it cannot fully render actually lived or experiential time, as when we say 'Time is standing still' or 'I feel like I've been here before.' Chronological time and temporal accuracy do matter in personal writing. After all, you were born in a certain year, and you visited East Berlin before and not after the collapse of the wall. Treatments of narrative time in personal writing need to take such facts into account.

---

[3] Harris, 'Writing the Sharp Edges of Grief,' *Brevity*, September 2015.
[4] On memory time, see Chapter 18. On handling time in the context of organizing your whole memoir, see Chapter 17.

How you construct *narrative* and *experiential* time, however, is more often based on other factors, such as how a narrator's or a character's attention moves within a temporal world, and your decisions as a writer about which narrative approach to time most effectively breathes life into your stories and essays. In other words, your material and its presentation, not a reflexive following of chronological time, needs to determine how you work with time. Given these considerations, here are a few techniques for experimenting with time:

- **Flashbacks.** A 55-year-old suddenly recalls a moment in childhood that illuminates some life question at 55.

- **Flashforward.** You foresee from age 35 a related experience at 65 that you now know about because you are 75.

- **Bookends.** Your story or essay line ends by returning to its beginning.

- Use 'scenes' to **s-t-r-e-t-c-h out** and **deepen** important experiential moments. Use 'narrative bridges' to move efficiently between scenes and different time frames.

- **Foreshadowing.** Your story begins with your end-scene, then shows the reader how you got there. You set clues for what is to come, you create anticipation.

- **Circling.** Move your attention around a specific theme or experience, seeing it from varied angles that build one on the others. Circling resembles a forward-moving narrative spiralling.

A caution: Don't play with time simply for effect. Take advantage of the conventions of chronological time where needed: 'He died on August 8, 1962, three days before I was born.' Be true to the workings of inner experiential and memory time. Use narrative time to create curiosity and anticipation. Let your material and purpose determine your treatment of time.

Forming your experience into a story or essay

We are always carrying out some forming or shaping work on our experiences, even if much of this is improvised and unconscious. Writing continues this work, but does so with more conscious intent. The process of forming an experience through writing helps establish what is really meaningful about the experience. To form an experience in writing means constructing and organizing it in a way that makes it cohesive, coherent, fluent, and engaging—and, most importantly, brings the experience alive.[5]

Think of sculpting a figure from a piece of rough stone. Faced with a block of marble, the Renaissance artist Michelangelo said that he began each sculpture by trusting that the form of the figure was already in the stone. He was not alone in thinking this way, as interviews with Inuit and other stone carvers suggest. Something like this is true of our significant-feeling personal experiences. Their meaningfulness lives within us as a feeling or intuition or thought, like the unique texture and lines in a piece of raw stone. To grasp, then voice this meaningfulness, we need to articulate—to more clearly set forth: organize, shape, or sculpt, compose, give expressive form to—what we only incompletely 'see.' Just as the carver *closely attends* to their piece of stone, the personal writer *closely listens* to their experience, chipping off unneeded pieces here and there, and *giving form* to what remains. They are gradually releasing the inherent significance of their raw experience into its appropriate form.

In the context of autobiographical writing, my sculpting analogy should not be taken to mean that the form of what we create is always 'pleasing' or 'entertaining.' Experience determines form. If a lived experience is unpleasing—it may be painful, or it may be objectively incoherent—then this needs casting in its true expressive form. In such cases the structure of the writing may feel fragmentary, like shards of shattered glass, or it may not appear to 'get anywhere,' or end

---

[5] See Chapter 17 on approaches to organizing or forming your whole memoir.

inconclusively. Indeed qualities such as these describe the form of a good deal of personal writing over the modern era.[6]

How to give form to your experience through the writing process? Begin with your first rough draft. Express the vitality and flow of what needs saying. No conscious 'processing,' no rationalizing, no 'should' qualifications. Don't bleach out the colours of your experience. Just tell what needs telling. Consider this draft a proto-experiment in letting your material disclose its content and form. Now ask yourself these questions: What is really important here? What's this really *about*? What needs saying and *how* best to say it? Use your answers to begin rewriting and shaping your text to give greater fluency to your purpose.

Every element of a story or essay—discussed in this chapter and throughout this book—contributes to its form: subject matter, word choices, an organizing metaphor (such as a journey), narrative voice, atmosphere, imagery, narrative development, and more. These elements work together *through the writing itself*, creating something like a painting wash, with its distinct pigment and binder. The writing coheres, becomes fluent and expressive. It 'takes shape'—which is to say that it realizes the meaning and meaningfulness of the experience that needed telling.

I feel, I think: write from the permanent construction site of your life

> Whenever a writer gets reflective about how she feels or complains or celebrates or plots or judges, she moves inside herself to where things matter and mean.
> —Mary Karr, *The Art of Memoir*

Many people new to personal writing write as if they are observing and reporting on their experiences. They mainly *describe* well-known

---

[6] Examples include the work of Christa Wolf, Imre Kertész, W.G. Sebald, Jenny Offill, and Jordan Abel.

activities, characters, or objects, and suggest in every sentence that there's nothing more to be 'seen' or wondered about. Other than a few questions about details, their writing doesn't invite curiosity. As readers we might think *Well, that was interesting*, or *That was entertaining*, but then we find little more to say. The writer hasn't really engaged, let alone challenged us as readers, perhaps because they haven't challenged themselves. There is little evidence of the tension, the ambiguity, the puzzling, and the quality of the yet-to-be-determined that is part of actually lived experience. There is little about how the world and the writer's changing self interact; or how, within the self, one experience reverberates in another over time, forever altering the self. Absent are those consequential spaces *between* world and inner self, as well as *inside* our single-bodied life. We sense the writer saying *I observe—and I see everything I need to see*. What we don't sense is a writer saying *I feel, I think, I wonder, I reflect, I am uncertain, I question, I seek*. What is missing is the more complete 'I'—curious, motile, unsteady, mutable—that animates good personal writing.

Memoir writers are not reporters, not even simply observers. We are *participant* observers. We are inside our experiences and our remembering. The best memoir writing is rooted in the inner workings of the desire to know—that alert, humming world where felt interests, perceptions, hunches, memories, longings, and surprise brawl and embrace, and give birth to the new. Personal writers are always *becoming*. When they stop tuning in to their always-becoming creaturely 'I,' the writing itself begins to feel too easy, too complete, too 'packaged,' a little too pleased with itself, like a newly-finished building with a large ribbon on its door.

The best personal writers don't stand at this door; they write from the permanent construction site of their life. Sometimes this site is at rest, although even then something is happening: a dream flutters out of a shadow, somewhere there's a sigh. More often, though, our self-in-the-world is a noisy, working place. The 'noise' is our interaction with the world. But it is also the sound of how these interactions take on a life *inside* us—that changing concoction of demands, necessity, uncertainty, fears, self-betrayals, wishfulness, contradictions, inhibitions, loneliness, vulnerability, pain, joy, astonishment, regrets, worries, values, beliefs, longings, hopes, and wonder that we might call our *becoming-self-in-the-world*. Memoir writing was never the stories or essays of some finished self or a fully grasped experience. Quite the contrary, in fact. It has always been driven by a curiosity about the 'noise' of an experience-in-the-making and of the self's becoming—in other words, the life of one's inner life.

Writers who attend to their inner life reveal changes in their awareness over time. They develop new understandings, including ones that can suddenly launch them in new directions. They follow the tangled roots of memory towards some lost aspect of their past. They reveal differences between two people's understandings of the same event: 'Even though I felt my recovery had now passed through several trying years, my doctor referred to it as "uneventful."' Only the inner life holds the story of a self divided by and overcoming the hard facts of circumstance: the son who, growing up in an emotionally dead family, begins to compose songs 'in his head,' and emerges from years of inner pain towards a satisfying life as a folksinger. Without attention to our inner life, we can't begin to acknowledge the contradictions between our inner thoughts and our expressed speech and actions; the outward face of willed 'resilience' versus our inner disinterest, despair or rage; the discrepancies between personal practice and professed ideals; and those inner self-betrayals driven by the allure of social acceptance and advancement.

Human life broken down into personal stories is rarely the tidy, clear, complete thing suggested by many beginning personal writers—unless you have worked a miracle and made a perfect accommodation with life. For most of us, actually lived life unfolds in the dissonance created in the fraught spaces between the forces of the external world and our inner life. Good memoir writers have the courage to hear this dissonance and 'show' how it sounds inside the self. As Mary Karr writes, 'In almost every . . . memoir I know it's the internal struggle providing the engine of the tale' (*The Art of Memoir*).

By way of an example, let's look at a passage from George Orwell's essay 'Shooting An Elephant.' Orwell is remembering his younger, 'sub-divisional police officer' self in colonial Burma, and, in particular, one 'tiny' but life-changing experience: the day he was expected to kill a working elephant that had come loose and was 'ravaging' a local bazaar.

> [I]t was at this moment, as I stood there with the rifle in my hands, that I first grasped the hollowness, the futility of the white man's dominion in the East. Here was I, the white man with his gun, standing in front of the unarmed native crowd—seemingly the leading actor of the piece; but in reality I was only an absurd puppet pushed to and fro by the will of those yellow faces behind. I perceived in this moment that when the white man turns tyrant it is his own freedom that he destroys. He becomes a sort of hollow, posing dummy, the conventionalized figure of a sahib. For it is the condition of his rule that he shall spend his life in trying to impress the 'natives,' and so in every crisis he has got to do what the 'natives' expect of him. He wears a mask, and his face grows to fit it. I had got to shoot the elephant. I had committed myself to doing it when I sent for the rifle. A sahib has got to act like a sahib; he has got to appear resolute, to know his own mind and do definite things. To come all that way, rifle in hand, with two thousand people marching at my heels, and then to trail feebly away, having done nothing—no, that was impossible. The crowd would laugh at me. And my whole life, every white man's life in the East, was one long struggle not to be laughed at.

Only by attending to his inner life in this situation is Orwell able to begin exposing the price the cultural self exacts from the creaturely self. And what is this 'price'? It is the 'mask' he became as an Imperial functionary, as distinct from his individual 'face' before it grew to fit the mask. It is also his inwardly loathed 'job'—'doing the dirty work of Empire'—which he does nevertheless. Orwell lets us hear the 'noise' of his historical situation, his inner divided, betrayed self, and his self *working towards* greater self-understanding. This is not the personal writer merely describing his observed experience, as if what is literally visible is the sum of the scene's meanings and significance. Rather, this is a writer engaged in a complex, painful inner conversation between his masked, 'dummy' self and his creaturely 'I.' He is critically interrogating his experience and the historical surround—exploring them both—on behalf of his *own* 'face,' or what I would call his creaturely self. Orwell's is an inquisitive, impertinent writing self—questioning, thinking, and still *becoming*. Like all good memoirists, there he is at his writing desk, each covered in grime, in the construction site of his life.

Humour

'Levity is the opposite of gravity,' as Eric Idle writes in *The Road to Mars*. Seeing the humour in things is among the most potent means of exploration and truth-telling in personal writing. Humour, writes Tristine Rainer, helps the memoirist 'strip away façades and expose the imperfect bare-assed truth beneath. It's an antidote to bragging; a light that illuminates the ugly and subhuman; a salve for corrosive anger; a remedy for the lasting pain of embarrassment' (*Your Life As Story*). Humour gives us an inner license, as well as the means, to feel, think, and say what other voices say we shouldn't.

Humour is the Road Runner repeatedly outwitting and making a fool of the know-it-all, self-preoccupied Wile E. Coyote. Humour expresses the forbidden, especially in the face of power, including inner, psychological power. It can unclothe the masters of fear. As satire, humour can reveal stupidity, pretense, and the punishing things people do to themselves and others. It reveals the unforeseen, the accidental, the unplanned—the banana peels—in life. Humour plays with and suggestively re-imagines things as they are, from wordplay, such as puns, to imagining life's possibilities. Far from least of all, humour is comic in the ancient sense of being redemptive. It enables us to wrest meaning from mortal and often chaotic life.

In sum, humour is the voice of the unpredictable, unpretentious, imaginative, mortal, and seditious in life. Listening for this voice can reduce anxiety in the writing process, humanize you as a writer, ignite your writing, and deepen your connection with your reader.

Here are a few tips on using humour in memoir writing:

- Ask what kinds of humour make you laugh, and translate this into your writing. Express humour naturally in your own voice.

- Use humour intentionally. Make it serve your story or essay.

- Be wise. Wise people realize that the more they know, the less they know. Shakespeare: 'The wise man knows himself to be a fool.'

- Be self-deprecating. Oscar Wilde: 'It is a curious fact that people are never so trivial as when they take themselves seriously.' Include moments when you are the subject of humour: that time when you tried so hard but fell flat on your face.

- Introduce a touch of irony, although avoid a 'cool,' superior ironic tone. Irony plays with the difference between what is said and the intended meaning. Irony is to call your Great Dane 'Tiny', or to see a photo of a car smashed into a restaurant and think 'Wow, now that's a drive-through.'

- Play with experience by playing with words, like calling your battery-run bicycle a Hardly-Davidson.

- Don't use humour to insult others. Avoid sarcasm.

- Use humour to gain power over 'dark' experiences, or at least make them more bearable and understandable. Remember that 'humor,' as Mel Brooks apparently quipped, 'is just another defense against the universe.'

Your hands and the hands of those close to you. Who and what have they held? What have they laboured at? What created? What emotions have they expressed, what feelings have they received? What stories do they hold? Source: Author's collection.

CHAPTER 13

'VOICE' IN MEMOIR WRITING: FINDING THE SOUND OF WHO I AM

I'm writing a story in my journal, and I'm searching for a true voice. I make my way through layer of acquired voices, silly voices, sententious voices, voices that are too cool and too overheated. They then all quiet down, and I reach what I'm searching for: silence. I hold still to steady myself in it. This is the white blank center, the level ground before Babel was built, that is always there before the Babel of our multiple selves is constructed. From this white plenitude a voice begins to emerge: it's an even voice, and it's capable of saying things straight, without exaggeration or triviality. As the story progresses, the voice grows and diverges into different tonalities and timbres; sometimes, spontaneously, the force of feeling or of thought compresses language into metaphor, or an image, in which words and consciousness are magically fused.... This is the point to which I have tried to triangulate, this private place, this unassimilable part of myself. We all need to find this place in order to know that we exist not only within culture but also outside it.... It's only after I've taken in disparate bits of cultural matter, after I've accepted its seductions and snares, that I can make my way through the medium of language to distill my own meanings; and it's only coming from the ground up that I can hit the tenor of my own sensibility, hit home.

—Eva Hoffman, *Lost in Translation*

What is 'voice' in memoir writing?

'Voice' is how our writing expresses—presses out and represents—our characteristic way of taking in and responding to the world. Voice is the expression of our self on the page, *inside* our writing: in our subject matter, in our approach to our material, and in the expressive rhythms, intonations, pacing, and images of our language. Voice cues our reader to our points of view, our moods, and our felt responses to specific experiences. Voice is that something our reader experiences when they say: 'That sounds just like you.'[1]

Our voice changes as we respond to life's stages and our unfolding experiences. We also switch voices from moment to moment, depending on mood, who we are speaking with, and whether we are speaking, thinking, or feeling, even in response to the same situation. Indeed, it's reasonable to ask whether we have a single 'characteristic' voice at all. Perhaps it is more helpful to say that we have two related kinds of voices: those voices that are responsive to immediate situations, and another more constant, habituated, deeper, and 'characteristic' expressive manner—the 'sounds just like you' voice—that gradually develops over time, like the age lines, scars, and other telltale markings on our hands.

Like our hands, our voice has a bodily history, as voice coaches know. Evidence of this can be found in our body's musculature (lungs and chest, larynx, and the many parts of the mouth), as well as in the characteristic expressive tone and rhythms of our speech, and in the interactions of our voice, mind, emotions, and self. When we say 'That sounds just like you,' we are hearing more than what is called 'personality.' We are hearing the bodily–emotional history of the live creature's 'voice' and its relation to the self. Memoirists know this well, or at least they sense it. Only consider how often they reflect on the experiential history of their voice, understood literally: those occasions, for example, when the self was silenced or when words were put into its mouth; how it learned to 'choose its words' and 'measure' and pace its speech; the availability and absence of words; and the development

---

[1] See the examples of 'voice' in personal writing at the end of this chapter.

of its inner speech. In order to be true to their *own* life, memoirists know that they need to better understand the creaturely making of their voice—and what is and is not their voice.

This questioning of one's voice is unusual. Wouldn't most of us say that our voice is our own and leave the matter there? But is this actually the case? Probably not. Unlike other species, humans undergo a prolonged childhood that ensures that our shared mother tongue—its language, speech patterns, and expressive–interactive norms, and how these shape our world—is deeply internalized at an early age. Later, from childhood through adulthood, we use words, phrasings, meanings, pacings, and idioms that have insinuated themselves into 'our' voice—what Hoffman calls the 'Babel' of the many voices not really our own. These cultural elements of 'voice' come to *seem* to be 'our own,' and even *appear* to 'make sense' because they 'work,' sometimes more, sometimes less, in the world as it is. This is not to say that individuals don't have a characteristic voice. Rather—and this is what Hoffman is drawing attention to in that opening passage—we can't assume that all the elements of our 'voice' are our own, and therefore adequate for finding and expressing who we are.

This is something else that good memoir writers understand: that the mere ability to think and speak doesn't mean that we are speaking (or writing) *out of* and *for* our Self. Rather, our *personal* writing voice is something that needs to be found and developed. This calls for two kinds of activity: first, becoming sensitive to what in 'our voice' is not really *our* voice; and second, *listening* to how our single-bodied creaturely self takes in, feels, ponders, and responds to the world, then using this to develop a voice that is true to our experience. It's only by recognizing the 'seductions and snares' of culture and its language that we can find a language to distill our own meanings and, in Hoffman's words, 'hit the tenor of [our] own sensibility, hit home.'

This 'home' voice sounds necessary, precise, distinct, and authentic. It's the sound of experience from inside the skin of your single-bodied, grounded 'I.'

Voice in writing and speaking

Another way of thinking about 'voice' in writing is to compare writing and speaking. Conversation—what I say and how my listener experiences and interprets what I say—comprises far more than words. Conversation depends on an array of vocalized, non-verbal cues, such as pitch, pacing, volume, and intonation, as well as physical cues, such as the speaker's 'look' and eye contact, their hand gestures, and their posture and other body movements. Without these expressive cues, conversational understanding is hit-and-miss at best. By contrast, writing has no vocal pitch, literally understood, nor eyes that shy away nor a body that stiffens while speaking. The writer has only their words on the page. This is less of a limitation in technical writing, with its rule of a flat, cool, impersonal voice. In personal writing, however, mere words—understood as information—are insufficient, precisely because the whole point is to render and experience the viewpoints, the warmth, the moods, and the expressive presence or *voice* of this embodied live creature. In this sense, 'voice' in personal writing is the translation into words on the page of the non-verbal and physically expressive cues of speech. Only when we experience the play of voices in a piece of personal writing, including the writer's own voice, can we really begin to appreciate and make sense of what we are reading.

Developing your own voice

How do we find and develop our personal writing voice—the expression of ourselves on the page? I discuss ways of thinking about this question throughout this book. Here we review a number of key considerations.

Listen to and express your heart, your gut, your authentic creaturely self, as well as your *own* thoughtful, reasoning, self-reflective intelligence. Speak for yourself, not for others, and not on behalf of cultural conventions and proprieties. Voice in your own words and images what you personally feel, remember, and know.

Acknowledge the voices of your complicated self: your flaws, changeableness, passions, anxieties, and uncertainties—your contradictory selves. Don't iron out the wrinkles of your actual self.

Listen to your past and unvoiced voices. Distinguish your 'today voice' from your earlier voices—say from childhood or adolescence—and allow those earlier voices their own say. We'll return to this idea later in the chapter.

Be critically self-reflective. Voice your experience directly, *in itself*, but also use a second personal voice that reflects on and helps you learn from your experience.

Take advantage of writing as a process. When writing your first, quick, rough draft, *feel* your actually lived experience—don't simply report it. Attend sympathetically to its emotional qualities and energies, and to its containers of feeling: specific people, voices, silences, objects, gestures, 'looks.' Try imagining that you are writing to a trusted friend, someone who accepts you as you are, including your sometimes sputtering, oddball efforts to find and voice your becoming. Set your rough draft aside for a week or so, then read it aloud, or have a good reader do so. Listen to the energies in its words and phrasings, how it creates emphasis, its tone and rhythms and pacing. Are the words, phrases, and rhythms your own? Is this *your* experience speaking in its own voice?

Do more than describe. As mentioned earlier, many beginning personal writers take a 'just the facts, ma'am' approach to their life experiences. They report the observed trappings of an experience—where they went, what they saw—rather than their *living* of the experience. The result is personal writing without the flesh and blood of the personal. Take a different approach. Step inside the skin of your actually lived experience. Listen to your heart's tremourings amidst all those 'facts.' Listen, listen, listen to the live creature within—then 'voice' what you hear through your writing's language, images, tone, and rhythms.

Check your expressive tone. Tone suggests a writer's relation to what they are writing. A tone might be serious or humorous, intimate or more detached, formal or casual, self-conscious, meditative, wistful, ironic, whimsical, or cynical. Tone offers cues that help the reader understand the narrator's viewpoint and the narrative's direction. A story might call for tonal shifts from, say, concern to relief to humour. An essay might feature two disputing voices, each with their own expressive tone. Having said this, each story or essay will likely have a consistent overall narrative tone.

Use the informal voice. On a continuum of writing styles between formal and informal, the voice of memoir writing is usually informal and conversational. Formal: 'It is believed that the health effects of . . . .' Informal: 'I believe the health effects of . . . .' Loosen your writing from the rules of schooled writing. What matters are vividness, clarity, and honesty.

Decide when to be 'close' and when to be 'distant.' Distance and closeness in voice convey differences in perspective combined with their affective qualities, such as coolness and warmth, attachment and detachment. Among humourists, for example, one exposes the self's foibles through confession (closeness), another through irony (distance). Some writers characteristically write close to their emotions, others take a more reflective, even analytic approach. Personal writers often use two voices: one that speaks from *inside* their experience and another that reflects on their experience, as if from *outside*. More generally, a narrative voice can make a writer and reader feel close to (living firsthand) or distant from (observing) an experience. The following examples suggest how this works, and something of what you gain and lose with each perspective. Close: 'I felt I had been sailing on a stormy sea after my overnight bus ride through the mountains.' Close and distant: 'Hearing the others' groans and retching, you knew you were among kindred spirits.' Distant: 'As the passengers stepped from the overnight bus, they staggered towards the restrooms like drunks.'

Make your sentences sing. Write for the most part in an 'active' voice. Emphasize what is significant by placing it at the beginning or end of sentences and paragraphs. Create emphasis through contrast ('Unlike most babies, Susan could talk as soon as she was born.'), repetition ('She looked to the left, she looked to the right, she looked straight ahead.'), and italics (use sometimes), all caps (use rarely), and exclamation marks (use sparingly). Vary the cadence and rhythm of your voice by mixing sentence structures, as Gary Provost demonstrates in this passage: 'This sentence has five words. Here are five more words. Five-word sentences are fine. But several together become monotonous. Listen to what is happening. The writing is getting boring. The sound of it drones. It's like a stuck record. The ear demands some variety. Now listen. I vary the sentence length, and I create music. Music. The writing sings. It has a pleasant rhythm, a lilt, a harmony. I use short sentences. And I use sentences of medium length. And sometimes, when I am certain the reader is rested, I will engage him with a sentence of considerable length, a sentence that burns with energy and builds with all the impetus of a crescendo, the roll of the drums, the crash of the cymbals–sounds that say listen to this, it is important.'[2]

Finally, listen to the written voices you enjoy. What makes them work? Can you use any of their techniques and qualities to express your own voice?

Memoir writing's many voices

Memoir writers become adept at listening for, speaking, and writing in many tongues. Here is a brief survey of some of memoir writing's possible voices.

The writer's 'I' voice. This is the primary expressive voice of memoir writing. The writer determines what is said, how it is expressed, and how the action is commented on.

---

[2] Gary Provost, *100 Ways to Improve Your Writing*.

The narrator's voice: the voice of the person living, telling, or thinking out a personal story or essay. This and the writer's voice can be the same, as is often the case with beginning memoir writers. More practiced writers use a narrator *persona* in order to more candidly represent and comment on themselves.[3] For example, Deborah Levy writes of 'creating a persona that was braver than I actually felt . . . . It is so hard to claim our desires and so much more relaxing to mock them' (*The Cost of Living*).

Some other narrative voices. A number of contemporary hybrid memoir-novels are narrated through an at least partially fictionalized 'I.' Examples include W.G. Sebald's *The Rings of Saturn*, Christa Wolf's *Accident: A Day's News,* and Édouard Louis's *History of Violence: A Novel*. In Sebald's case, each work typically has an 'I' narrator–experiencer and combines elements of memoir, biography, history, travelogue, and fiction—a style he referred to as 'documentary fiction.' Although these three books are referred to as novels—that is: fiction—their 'I' also feels deeply personal, historical, real, and existential all at once. Another narrative approach is evident in Annie Ernaux's *The Years*, a generational–historical memoir told in a choral 'we' voice which sometimes shifts into the third person, with the author appearing as 'she.' Ernaux writes both personally and collectively, setting her own story within the wider story of her generation of the 1940s to 2006. 'There is no "I"', she writes, 'there is only "one" and "we."'

The voices of your characters. Few things more immediately breathe life into a character than hearing their voice, whether expressed, thought, or felt. Imagine a Christmas dinner. Tell the story of this dinner in your own voice, as you experienced it. But better still, let your reader hear selected, telling snippets of the voices of the dinner guests in conversation. Directly expressed voices create situational immediacy, they enact human relationships, they articulate differing perspectives, and they take attention off yourself as narrator. They also draw your reader closer to the dinner table, turning them into engaged

---

[3] Narrative voice is discussed in Chapters 9 and 10.

participant–listeners. One more point: remember to help your reader interpret what a character says by including clues to how they say it. For example, you can write '"Help me," she said' or you can write '"Help me!" she exclaimed' or '"Help me," she said, as tears came to her eyes.'

Inner and expressed voices. One of the best ways to suggest the complex lived reality of a situation or character is to juxtapose *outwardly* expressed voices and *inner*, reflective, feeling voices: what is said and what is thought and felt. Take a family funeral, for example. Funerals are inherently serious occasions, places of loss and grief, even when cast as 'celebrations' of a life. But what if a personal memory of the now dead person makes you want to laugh out loud? Or what if, in order to tell the truth about this funeral, you need to show the irony of feuding family members professing their mutual affection, knowing they will be at each other's throats again tomorrow? Sure, voice the tone of the external, shared situation. But voice as well the inner life of this same situation. Account as well for situations where a person is saying a lot through their silence, or through what they are saying entirely within themselves, including how they name their feelings.

Are there voices that are best avoided?

Yes, definitely. Among these are the self-conscious wit, the pedant, and the person who needs to be admired. Avoid as well the defensive voice that over-argues or over-explains, trusting neither his writing nor his reader. Shun the voices of the clever, know-it-all narrator who is surprised by nothing in life, as well as his ironic, sardonic, or indifferent brothers who are above caring about anything or anyone.

Express rage, but not with the voice of contempt or a voice that only lives off old grievances. Even if life sometimes hands you a disagreeable voice, that doesn't mean you should make a virtue of it in your writing. The best personal writing comes from our sympathetic centres, especially when these are attuned to the often fumbling, vulnerable, creaturely lives of our self and others.

There is one more voice, or rather a type of voice, to avoid: the cliché. *My heart sank. The next thing I knew. Twinkling eyes. I blushed crimson. My soul lifted. My head swam. Every cloud has a silver lining. Only time will tell.* The lazy parts of our brain are full of clichés: widely exchanged packets of language that appear to declare some indisputable truth while arising from and speaking to no one's experience. Nothing succeeds better than a cliché to undercut the personal voice of memoir writing. Unless you have some reason to use one—to make a point, say, about a person who uses clichés—remember to kick them out of your writing and find the language of your own experience.

Finding the voices of our earlier experiences

Our 'I' may be a six-year-old engulfed in a fiery nightmare. Or a hormonally hopped-up 13-year-old. Or an adventurous, devil-may-care 20-something heading across country or around the world. Or a first-time mother or father with a newborn nestled against our body. We memoir writers naturally re-create experiences from earlier stages of our life. But we must do this while standing in the here and now of our life. In this section we look at how to most effectively voice our earlier life experiences.

One approach, common among beginning memoir writers, especially those older than 50 or so, is to view the past almost entirely through the lens of their current sensibility and values. The significance in one's life of childhood, youth, fantasy, wonder, adventurous play, and sexuality is diminished (patronized, sentimentalized, made subjects of nostalgia, written about as 'a stage one grows out of'), while more 'adult' matters, such as careers and family, are given priority, and even used as demonstration pieces for how one's life has 'come together.' More than this: past experiences are subjected to editorial commentaries written by the present self, as in 'Of course I should have known better.'

I recommend taking a very different approach: one that is truer to life and that results in a far more interesting memoir. In this case the memoirist listens—in a mood of curious, fully empathetic, appreciative care—for the distinctive 'voices' *inherent* in their earlier experiences. They listen, that is:

- For what was said and heard.

- For what was not said but thought or felt.

- For the feeling-laden, living realia of specific voices, gestures, sensations, objects, and place.

- For the emotional tenor and other qualities of each significant experience that once had, and still requires, its own voice.

To the extent possible, they let the past speak for itself, even if this means through mere slivers of remembered details supplemented by the work of memory's sympathetic imagining.

This is not me now, the memoirist begins. There he sits, that other he, that other me curled up crying beneath that blanket . . . or alone at that train station or slamming the door or seeing ghosts or about to die of unsated lust. The memoirist befriends the *otherness* of their other self beneath that blanket or alone in that room or slamming that door or being visited by a dead parent or dying with desire. They feel—they hear the voice of—that other self's warmth, its loneliness, its puzzlement, its unadult cartwheels of thought, its fury and fear, its pounding creaturely heart . . . and they write what they hear.[4]

Comment on the past however you like—but save this for later. Always begin by allowing the past to speak for itself, as well as it can. The best memoirists work at re-experiencing, through their creaturely or sensate memories, the actually lived What and How of things achieved and forsaken in life, its delights and funks and scars. In doing so, they create possibilities for new personal understandings of their past, and thereby new perspectives on their present and future. Befriend your creaturely past selves, let them speak, then decide what else needs saying.

---

[4] See the example by Díaz at the end of this chapter.

Using voice to redeem the past

There are occasions when we are made speechless or denied a voice. That time in our childhood or youth when our parents announced 'arrangements' for the next few years of our life, then asked 'What do you think?' Or that other time when our partner shouts and raises his fist to our face. Or those public events that are so appalling that any words feel insufficient or indecent. Or when some know-it-all denies a place in conversation for any voice but his own. Or how groups, group-think, and established cultural conventions make genuinely independent responses appear so outlandish that one hardly dares voice them at all.

Among the most wondrous gifts of memoir writing is the opportunity to return to these scenes of speechlessness and to have a second chance to voice what once needed saying. Our own *voicing* can serve as redress for those times when someone, or circumstance itself, throttled our voice.[5] Voicing through memoir writing can finally loosen that muscular stiffening in our throat and shoulders that results from silence, self-betrayal, or regret. It can unburden the self from the weight of secrets and guilt. It can redeem the past by finally voicing ire or love. And it can help us find our *own* words, as a form of witnessing, to name the effects of the unjust and monstrous.[6] Finally, the deeply personal, creaturely voicing inherent in memoir writing is an invitation to us

---

[5] One example of finding one's voice, stolen in childhood, is Kate Shayler's *The Long Way Home*. Jeanette Winterson, in *Why Be Happy When You Could Be Normal?*, says this about the loss and regaining of one's voice: 'Do you remember the story of Philomel who is raped and then has her tongue ripped out by the rapist so that she can never tell? I believe in fiction and the power of stories because that way we speak in tongues. We are not silenced. All of us, when in deep trauma, find we hesitate, we stammer; there are long pauses in our speech. The thing is stuck. We get our language back through the language of others. We can turn to the poem. We can open the book. Somebody has been there for us and deep-dived the words. I needed words because unhappy families are conspiracies of silence. The one who breaks the silence is never forgiven. He or she has to learn to forgive him or herself.'

[6] The Hungarian writer Imre Kertész says he wrote *Dossier K.* and his other memoir-like novels in order to reclaim his life: 'the expropriation, nationalisation

to express thoughts that the group mind calls 'unrealistic.' Voicing in this sense is to crack open the frozen sea of 'things as they are,' to create breathing holes for the 'unrealism' of our hopes. We are finally accepting into consciousness the truer voices of our experience, then telling their stories.

Some examples of voice

It is foolhardy to include, as I do here, three examples of voice in memoir writing—varied examples to be sure, but still a mere three, and the briefest excerpts at that! If there is an excuse for doing this, it is to demonstrate some of the ways that these particular writers use language to create a sense of voice, and then use this voice to breathe life into their stories and personal essays.[7]

From Phillip Lopate's 'Against Joie de Vivre'

> I am invited periodically to dinner parties and brunches—and I go, because I like to be with people and oblige them, even if I secretly cannot share their optimism about these events. I go, not believing that I will have fun, but with the intent of observing people who think a dinner party a good time. I eat their fancy food, drink the wine, make my share of entertaining conversation, and often leave having had a pleasant evening. Which does not prevent me from anticipating the next invitation with the same bleak lack of hope. To put it in a nutshell, I am an ingrate . . . .
>
> . . . As everyone should know, the ritual of the dinner party begins away from the table. Usually in the living room, hors d'oeuvres and walnuts are set out, to start the digestive juices flowing. Here introductions between strangers are also made. Most dinner parties contain at least a few guests who have

---

of one's own fate . . . which I had to take back from "History" . . . because it was mine and mine alone' (from *Dossier K.*).

[7] Other examples of voice can be found throughout this book, including the end of Chapter 11.

been unknown to each other before that evening, but whom the host and/or hostess envision would enjoy meeting. These novel pairings and their interactions add spice to the post-mortem: who got along with whom? . . . . Although an after-work "leisure activity," the dinner party is in fact a celebration of professional identity. Each of the guests has been pre-selected as in a floral bouquet; and in certain developed forms of this ritual there is usually a cunning mix of professions. Yet the point is finally not so much diversity as commonality; what remarkably shared attitudes and interests these people from different vocations demonstrate by conversing intelligently, or at least glibly, on the topics that arise . . . .

. . . I don't expect the reader to agree with me. That's not the point. Unlike the behavior called for at a dinner party, I am not obliged, sitting at my typewriter, to help procure consensus every moment. So I am at liberty to declare, to the friend who once told me that dinner parties were one of the only opportunities for intelligently convivial conversation to take place in this cold, fragmented city, that she is crazy.

From Jaquira Díaz's 'Beach City'[8]

We were the ones who knew what it meant to belong here, to be made whole during full moon drum circles, dancing, drinking, smoking it up with our homeboys. We knew what it meant to bloody our knuckles here, to break teeth here, to live and breathe these streets day in, day out, the glow of the neon hotel signs on the waterfront, the salt and sweat of this beach city.

One night we parked Brown's Mustang behind the skating rink on Collins, hoofed it to the beach. We took our bottles of Olde English and Mad Dog 20/20, the six of us passing a blunt and listening to 2Pac's 'Hit Em Up' blaring from somebody's radio, and every time they sang, 'Grab your Glocks when you see 2Pac, the boys grabbed their dicks, and we all laughed our asses off. Brown danced, stripping off his

---

[8] Online at *Brevity* #52, 2016.

clothes while we cheered him on, me and A.J. keeling over, slapping our knees. Flaca, China, and Cisco climbed to the top of the lifeguard stand, singing, 'Go Brown! Go Brown!' When he was down to just boxers, Brown gave up, and we booed him, threw our balled-up socks and sneakers at him.

Me and A.J. were out behind the lifeguard stand, sand between our toes, feeling for each other in the dark. We ran around laughing and laughing, and I took his hand, danced circles around him in slow motion.

I don't remember when A.J. first told me he loved me, or even if he told me, but I knew. I felt it every time he came around, every time our thighs touched while sitting together on China's couch, or when the six of us had to squeeze into Brown's Mustang and I sat sideways on his lap, my lip brushing against his ear, his arms around my waist . . . . A.J. looking at me under the moonlight, a cloud of smoke all around us, I wrapped my arms around him and said, "Don't let me go."

We were laughing, hitting the blunt. We were the faraway waves breaking, the music and the ocean and the heat rising rising rising, like a fever. We were bodies made of smoke and water.

From Virginia Woolf's 'Street Haunting: A London Adventure'

No one perhaps has ever felt passionately towards a lead pencil. But there are circumstances in which it can become supremely desirable to possess one; moments when we are set upon having an object, an excuse for walking half across London between tea and dinner. As the foxhunter hunts in order to preserve the breed of foxes, and the golfer plays in order that open spaces may be preserved from the builders, so when the desire comes upon us to go street rambling the pencil does for a pretext, and getting up we say: 'Really I must buy a pencil,' as if under cover of this excuse we could indulge safely in the greatest pleasure of town life in winter—rambling the streets of London.

The hour should be the evening and the season winter, for in winter the champagne brightness of the air and the sociability of the streets are grateful. We are not then taunted as in the summer by the longing for shade and solitude and sweet airs from the hayfields. The evening hour, too, gives us the irresponsibility which darkness and lamplight bestow. We are no longer quite ourselves. As we step out of the house on a fine evening between four and six, we shed the self our friends know us by and become part of that vast republican army of anonymous trampers, whose society is so agreeable after the solitude of one's own room . . . .

. . . . Passing, glimpsing, everything seems accidentally but miraculously sprinkled with beauty, as if the tide of trade which deposits its burden so punctually and prosaically upon the shores of Oxford Street had this night cast up nothing but treasure. With no thought of buying, the eye is sportive and generous; it creates; it adorns; it enhances. Standing out in the street, one may build up all the chambers of an imaginary house and furnish them at one's will with sofa, table, carpet. That rug will do for the hall. That alabaster bowl shall stand on a carved table in the window. Our merrymaking shall be reflected in that thick round mirror. But, having built and furnished the house, one is happily under no obligation to possess it; one can dismantle it in the twinkling of an eye, and build and furnish another house with other chairs and other glasses. Or let us indulge ourselves at the antique jewelers, among the trays of rings and the hanging necklaces. Let us choose those pearls, for example, and then imagine how, if we put them on, life would be changed. It becomes instantly between two and three in the morning; the lamps are burning very white in the deserted streets of Mayfair. Only motor-cars are abroad at this hour, and one has a sense of emptiness, of airiness, of secluded gaiety. Wearing pearls, wearing silk, one steps out on to a balcony which overlooks the gardens of sleeping Mayfair. There are a few lights in the bedrooms of great peers returned from Court, of silk-stockinged footmen, of dowagers who have pressed the hands of statesmen. A cat creeps along the garden wall.

Love-making is going on sibilantly, seductively in the darker places of the room behind thick green curtains. Strolling sedately as if he were promenading a terrace beneath which the shires and counties of England lie sun-bathed, the aged Prime Minister recounts to Lady So-and-So with the curls and the emeralds the true history of some great crisis in the affairs of the land. We seem to be riding on the top of the highest mast of the tallest ship; and yet at the same time we know that nothing of this sort matters; love is not proved thus, nor great achievements completed thus; so that we sport with the moment and preen our feathers in it lightly, as we stand on the balcony watching the moonlit cat creep along Princess Mary's garden wall.

But what could be more absurd? It is, in fact, on the stroke of six; it is a winter's evening; we are walking to the Strand to buy a pencil. How, then, are we also on a balcony, wearing pearls in June? What could be more absurd? Yet it is nature's folly, not ours. When she set about her chief masterpiece, the making of man, she should have thought of one thing only. Instead, turning her head, looking over her shoulder, into each one of us she let creep instincts and desires which are utterly at variance with his main being, so that we are streaked, variegated, all of a mixture; the colours have run. Is the true self this which stands on the pavement in January, or that which bends over the balcony in June? Am I here, or am I there? Or is the true self neither this nor that, neither here nor there, but something so varied and wandering that it is only when we give the rein to its wishes and let it take its way unimpeded that we are indeed ourselves? Circumstances compel unity; for convenience' sake a man must be a whole. The good citizen when he opens his door in the evening must be banker, golfer, husband, father; not a nomad wandering the desert, a mystic staring at the sky, a debauchee in the slums of San Francisco, a soldier heading a revolution, a pariah howling with skepticism and solitude. When he opens his door, he must run his fingers through his hair and put his umbrella in the stand like the rest.

Recall the death of a person you cared about deeply. How did this death affect you? Did it help you discover something new about yourself or your relationship with the deceased person? Over time, what did you learn from this death? Does this experience need to be part of your life story? About the image show here, Anji Johnston writes: 'I composed this piece, *The Lights Are On But No One's Home*, after my sister and nephew both passed away on the same day. After arranging the funerals in another country, I returned to an empty house and found the only way to express my sadness was through my artwork.' Courtesy © Anji Johnston.

CHAPTER 14

BATS IN THE BELFRY: FIGURATIVE LANGUAGE AND ITS USES

Everyday words and phrases can be used literally or figuratively. We can *literally* close the door to a room, or we can *figuratively* close the door to further negotiations. Literally speaking, 'Some memories surprise me'; figuratively speaking, 'Some memories jump me like muggers in the dark.' Literally, 'The story was boring'; figuratively, 'The story had the emotional zing of a grocery list.'

Why use language figuratively? We do so because there are times when words, used literally or in a conventional sense, cannot say what we need to say. At such times, we must step beyond the boundaries of the literal ('It's raining heavily') and create our own experiential sense by voicing forms of apparent nonsense ('It's raining cats and dogs').

Figurative usage plays with the sound and meaning of words to create expressive, humorous, experientially precise and multilayered meanings that are unavailable to us in conventional language use. We do this through 'figures of speech.' Think of figurative language as a dance routine, with figures of speech being the various moves within the routine. There are many kinds of figures of speech, all of them described and well illustrated online.[1] Here's a sampling of the more common types: *hyperbole* or exaggeration ('They were starving' rather than 'They were very hungry'); *simile*, comparisons using 'like' or 'as' ('He's as dumb as a doorknob'); *metaphor*, the direct comparison of unlike things ('She's a night owl'); *personification*, the attribution of a human characteristic to something nonhuman ('The leaves danced in the October afternoon'); *onomatopoeia*, words that imitate the sound of the object they describe (oink, meow, giggle, murmur); *oxymoron*, the conjunction of apparently contradictory terms ('Organized chaos,' 'Open secret'); *symbolism* (a blackboard suggests schooling, an owl wisdom); and *puns*, as when Mae West said, 'She's the kind of girl who climbed the ladder wrong by wrong.'

Figures of speech are like miniature word pictures that sometimes seem to explode with meanings and sometimes release meanings in slow, irregular waves. You can decide for yourself which is the case when H.L. Mencken writes 'Happiness is the china shop; love is the bull,' or in this simile: 'Trying to grasp what he was saying was like raking leaves in the wind.' As miniature word pictures, figures of speech often *suggest* meanings by using, comparing, and juxtaposing specific, solid-feeling realia: china shop/bull, leaves/wind/rake, and Mae West's wrong/rung. They even use realia to clarify complex experiences, as in Albert Camus's 'In the depths of winter, I finally learned that within me there lay an invincible summer' (*Lyrical and Critical Essays*).

Figurative usage wrings meanings out of words that literal usage has no inkling of. They suggest meaning through the sounds and rhythms of concrete nouns ('snug as a bug in a rug'); they create evocative comparisons ('He's older than dirt,' or Peter Shaffer's 'If London is a

---

[1] Literal and figurative language are opposite poles on a continuum of natural language use. Over time, words and phrases move easily between the literal and the figurative, as is evident in such words as 'brand' and 'field.' Specific instances of figurative language always originate with individuals, even if their references are cultural (Martin Luther King: 'Let us not seek to satisfy our thirst for freedom by drinking from the cup of bitterness and hatred.') and even though many figures of speech take on cultural lives of their own, as is the case with idioms such as 'Mother Nature' and 'As old as the hills.'

watercolor, New York is an oil painting.'[2]); they capture ambivalence and contradictory experience in a single word, as in 'bittersweet'; and they stir up habitual ways of thinking, as does George Carlin's 'Fighting for peace is like screwing for virginity.' As Carlin's one-liner suggests, there seems to be some deeply anarchic impulse—personal, playful, creative—driving all figurative usage. Figures of speech can be thought of as the expression of the literal, matter-of-fact, nose-to-the-grindstone self—its conventionally available words, its curiosity, and likely its discontent with the constraints of everyday life—bursting at the seams.

Often we can only name something by naming something else. Poets, novelists, and personal writers understand this well, but so have scientists. When Robert Hooke examined a piece of cork through his microscope in 1665, he saw something he called 'cells'—actually the dead walls of cork 'cells'—because they reminded him of the small rooms, or cells, occupied by monks in monasteries. Johannes Kepler developed his concept of planetary motion by comparison with a clock. Christiaan Huygens used water waves to theorize that light is wavelike.[3] To understand and name the things of life, the human mind must often follow something other than a linear, convention-based form of logical reasoning. It must, as it were, move sideways, indeed move every which way. It does this through the *associative* 'logic' of experience-based intuition, guesswork, wordplay, speculation, imagination, the unconscious, and remembering. It creates and finds verbal and pre-verbal juxtapositions, contrasts, and associations. And it repeats, compares, rearranges—plays with—common word meanings, sense-associations and sounds. Talk about bats in the belfry!

---

[2] The Shaffer quotation is from Tom Buckley, 'Why Are There Two U's In Equus?' *New York Times*, April 13, 1975.

[3] These examples are referred to in Cynthia Taylor and Bryan M. Dewsbury, 'On the Problem and Promise of Metaphor Use in Science and Science Communication,' *Journal of Microbiology and Biology Education*, 2018, 19(1). This is a good survey of the historical uses of metaphor in the physical and social sciences.

A mere piece of cloth

There are as many uses of figurative language in personal writing as there are individual writers. Here I have chosen one example, from Vivian Gornick's *Fierce Attachments*, to draw attention to several basic considerations when using figures of speech in your memoir. Gornick is describing growing up amidst the women of a Bronx tenement. She will come around to using a particular figure of speech to suggest the effect of these women in her life.

> I remember only the women. And I remember them all crude like Mrs. Drucker or fierce like my mother. They never spoke as though they knew who they were, understood the bargain they had struck with life, but they often acted as though they knew. Shrewd, volatile, unlettered, they performed on a Dreiserian scale. There would be years of apparent calm, then suddenly an outbreak of panic and wildness: two or three lives scarred (perhaps ruined), and the turmoil would subside. Once again: sullen quiet, erotic torpor, the ordinariness of daily denial. And I—the girl growing in their midst, being made in their image—I absorbed them as I would chloroform on a cloth laid against my face. It has taken me thirty years to understand how much of them I understood.

'I absorbed them as I would chloroform on a cloth laid against my face.' This is the figure, a simile, to which I want to draw attention. First, it works, and only works, because of what precedes and follows it. It emerges naturally from a specific cultural context, and, although the reader doesn't fully know this yet, it introduces the process of self-discovery that preoccupies Gornick in this book. Even as it startles, the figure feels apt. Put more generally, effective figures of speech emerge—and *only* emerge—from the contextualizing flow of our experience as we write and rewrite, especially as we work to capture the essence of an experience inadequately voiced through literal usage.

Second, Gornick's figure makes itself feel needed. If plain language works, stick to it. If your meaning is genuinely amplified by an apt figure of speech, use it.

Third, 'chloroform on a cloth laid against my face' is simple, concise, and clear. Nothing suggests a contrived or forced creative effort. Figures of speech can be complex, and they can release their meaning slowly. A place to begin, however, is with simple, concise, and clear figures. Definitely do not use figurative language that confuses, such as mixed metaphors: 'If we want to get ahead we'll have to iron out the remaining bottlenecks.'

Fourth, Gornick's figure catches us, wakes us from the taken-for-grantedness, the stupor, of the ordinary. We can see and feel it, perhaps even sense it enacted on our self. At first there is the shock of the image, how it so immediately dramatizes or *shows* the completeness of the women's effect on Gornick. Then there are the aftershocks as we continue to wonder over what else is being said, what has been said, what will be said as Gornick's story unfolds– a wondering that is given added power because of the dramatic solidity of the image. All effective figures of speech do something like this. They make the reader's response centres feel an inner *Hmm* or *Huh?* or *Aha!* Inside us something flutters, smiles, feels another's pain, wonders or laughs. Figures of speech pull us towards the story, engage us in the writer's experience, and perhaps whisper questions inside us about the shaping forces in our own life.

Dramatic solidity

I want to pause over how figures of speech so often achieve their effects through what I just called their 'dramatic solidity.'[4] Mary Karr, in *The*

---

[4] Taylor and Dewsbury ('On the Problem'), referring to the work of G. Lakoff and M. Johnson, *Metaphors We Live By*, point out how metaphors 'draw from embodied experiences and look to concrete entities to serve as cognitive representatives.' They see this as an example of what is called 'embodied cognition': 'Conceptual frameworks and theoretical models in science are rooted in the same embodied

Art of Memoir, has one of the best discussions of what I mean. There she describes how, in working on her memoir *The Liars' Club*, she struggled to find a voice that was true to her actually lived experience. What would finally 'unlock the book for me,' she writes, is inwardly hearing the language of 'my barroom aficionado daddy.' 'If a woman,' Karr continues, 'had an ample backside, he [my father] might say "She had a butt like two bulldogs fighting in a bag," which—believe it or not—was a positive attribute . . . . [His] stories hummed through my fibers. It's ironic that the very redneckness I'd spent some time trying to rise above wound up branding my work like a hot iron on a steer's ass . . . . When there was a thunderstorm, Daddy might say "It's raining like a cow pissing on a flat rock" . . . . The crisp image jolts a little. It yanks you out of the quotidian. It operates just beyond the bounds of propriety . . . plus the minute you laugh at it, you become loosely complicit in the speaker's offensive speech. This binds you to the narrator. You've bought in . . . . That single line also evokes an entirely new world in which cows piss on flat rocks and folks stand around to marvel at it.'

Of course 'a butt like two bulldogs fighting in a bag' may not be the sound of your personal voice. That's fine because this voice in this figure already belongs to Karr. Having said this, Karr is certainly affirming the eloquence of tactile figures of speech, whatever form these take for each writer. It's often the solid realness of a figure of speech that makes it 'hum through our fibres.'

Finding your own figures of speech

Karr is making the broader point—confirmed in the passage by Gornick—that each writer needs to find a figurative language that expresses the true, unmistakable voice of their *own* personal

---

understandings of the world as those unconsciously employed in other day-to-day physical and social interactions. Scientific reasoning, then, is situated in what Gerhard Vollmer refers to as the mesocosm, or the "section of the real world we cope with in perceiving and acting, sensually and motorically."'

experience—a voice that 'sounds just like you.' You need to find a language, including forms of figurative language, that 'unlock' what needs writing. The goal of being true to your own experience is paramount. It will gradually pull your language, including your figures of speech, towards a precise freshness that will also, unmistakably, be your own. And it's this very sense of freshness, this singular way of responding to life, that, as Karr says, will yank your reader out of the quotidian, the ordinary and everyday, and begin to really hear your voice.

It follows from this that you must avoid commonplace and other clichéd figures of speech. Never 'drown in a sea of sorrow.' Never say your friend 'has a heart of stone.' You might have a character who speaks in clichés, or you might use 'heart of stone' ironically. Otherwise, clichéd figures of speech don't voice the 'personal' in personal experience, and they detract by their triteness. Avoid them, if not 'like the plague,' at least like a hotel with bedbugs.

Figurative language and imagery

Imagery and figures of speech both evoke rather than state meaning, but they do so in different ways. *Imagery* uses descriptive language, literally understood, to evoke the qualities of a person, place, object, or mood. 'The night was dark and humid, the scent of rotting vegetation hung in the air, and only the sound of mosquitoes broke the quiet of the swamp.' This sentence creates an image but doesn't use figurative language. Every word means exactly what it says. Now consider a similar sentence with *figurative language* added. 'The night was dark and humid, heavy with a scent of rotting vegetation like my great-aunt's heavy and inescapable perfume, and only the whining buzz of mosquitoes broke the silence of the swamp.' Here we have a simile ('like my great-aunt's . . .'), onomatopoeia ('whining buzz'), and even a bit of alliteration in the 'silence of the swamp.' Is the second sentence an improvement on the first? That's a writer's call.

Figures of speech have consequences

'What a different result one gets by changing the metaphor!' That's George Eliot speaking in her novel *The Mill on the Floss*. Eliot is saying that figures of speech have power; they help determine the way we think, feel, and act. Here's an example of what I mean. In a study of metaphorical usage, half of the participants read about a crime-ridden city where 'criminals' were described as 'beasts' preying on innocent citizens (animal metaphor).[5] A separate group read essentially the same description of the city, except that it described 'criminals' as a 'disease' plaguing the town (disease metaphor). Later, when asked how to solve the crime issue, those who read the animal metaphor suggested control strategies: increasing police presence, imposing stricter penalties. By contrast, those who read the disease metaphor suggested diagnostic/treatment strategies: seeking out the primary cause of the crime wave, making the economy more equitable. Changing the metaphor changed the way readers thought about crime.

Do personal writers have things to learn from this experiment—and many others with similar results?[6] At the very least, know that figures of speech have consequences. Yes, they *imply* their meanings, but they still imply *these* meanings and not those. It follows that we need to choose figures of speech that suggest what we intend to suggest—and review them critically before we finalize a piece of writing.

---

[5] Paul H. Thibodeau and Lera Boroditsky, 'Metaphors We Think With: The Role of Metaphor in Reasoning,' PLoS ONE, February 2011.

[6] Metaphors and other figures of speech used in the physical and social sciences often appear to be value-free and merely explanatory. This is rarely the case. Instead, they are often filled with perceptions, beliefs, values, and historical practices that they legitimize by their naive and repeated use. Taylor and Dewsbury ('On the Problem,' cited earlier) review many examples of how metaphors influence and are influenced by thought, values, and feelings across all aspects of culture: the militaristic and ideological figures in biology and ecology ('war on invasive species,' evolutionary 'arms races,' cells being 'hijacked' by viruses); 18th-century references in biology to 'slave-making' ants, scientifically inaccurate but still widely used today; and metaphors that equate the practice of science itself with 'penetrating the unknown,' 'conquering nature,' and 'pioneering new frontiers.'

What role do arrivals and departures play in your life? What are their experiential qualities? And what of the life stories of these remembered times—times, possibly, of loss, sadness, anticipation, excitement, upheaval, or uncertainty? Courtesy Plato Terentev (pexels.com).

CHAPTER 15

THE WRITING PROCESS: FROM ROUGH DRAFT TO 'GOOD ENOUGH' FINAL TEXT

This chapter describes how to develop your rough draft into what I call a 'good enough' final text. We will follow a step-by-step rewriting process, the aim of which is to help you express your life experiences as fully, eloquently, and personably as you can. At the end of the chapter I have included a reader's checklist. This imagines what makes your writing 'work' and not work from the perspective of your reader. Use this as another tool for completing your 'good enough' final text.

The trial-and-error zigzag of the writing process

The writing process, at least in the context of memoir writing, is like hiking to a desired destination through mountainous and sometimes wild terrain. What I just called 'a methodical, step-by-step rewriting process,' and the advice associated with this process, is equivalent to all those things—maps, a GPS, signposts, the sun and stars—that help us keep our bearings along the hike and guide us to our destination. The pathway itself is something else entirely: up and down, rocky, mucky, suddenly perfectly clear, then overrun, forked, and out of range of any map or GPS. This path is the memoir writing process. Indeed, if you write a first draft as if you can see everything ahead—the way is clear and straight—you are probably only reporting your experience as an observer, not exploring it as a participant. Genuine personal writing is the process of discovering what needs saying and how best to say it. Feeling lost or 'turned around,' stumbling, doing some bushwhacking, searching for the way forward: these are all natural parts of the memoir writing process.

To develop a memoir story or personal essay is to follow a zigzagging path of revision, trial and error, research, critical reflection, craft, and creativity. We begin with some notion of a particular life experience, idea, or point or view. We then set out—through a process of caring, curiosity-driven exploration—to find what is most important in our experience, and to express this as engagingly and truthfully as we can. We write a messy first draft, then enter into the sometimes muddled, sometimes unsettling back-and-forth world of reviewing, reworking, exploring, discovering, developing, and refining our material. And we persevere until we are satisfied that we have done the best we can do. It's this that I call the 'good enough' final text: our best writing about this experience or idea at this time.

Every exploratory memoir writer opens themselves to false starts, surprise realizations, errors, blocks, dead ends, and the labour of craft. Good memoir writing requires trust in one's desire to write, and trust in the writing process itself. Listen to how Mary Karr, author of several memoirs, describes personal writing as a process:

> Each page takes you somewhere you need to travel before you can land in the next spot. You zigzag . . . saying the next small thing about which you feel strongly, trying to nestle down into that single instant of clear memory you know without shadow of doubt is both true and important to who you've become . . . . The pushing comes when editor me comes back to comb over—and over and over—the pages, unpacking each moment. Mostly I take general ideas and try to show them carnally or in a dramatic story. I also interrogate a lot of what I believe . . . . All the while I question. Is this really crucial? Are you writing this part to pose as cool or smart? For me, the last 20 percent of a book's

> improvement takes 95 percent of the effort . . . . In the long run, the revision process feels better if you approach it with curiosity. Each editorial mark can't register as a 'mistake'. . . . Remind yourself that revising proves your care for the reader and the nature of your ambition. (*The Art of Memoir*)

Advice like this is worth posting in large letters wherever you happen to write. Nestle into your deep, personal, experiential truth. Listen to your inner creaturely self with curiosity and empathy. Voice your experience through the stuff—objects, voices, gestures, feelings—of its solid carnality. Interrogate what you believe, what you assume, what you take for granted. Bushwhack into hidden, blocked places. Zigzag forward. Focus on what's important. And write from a care for the nature of your ambition.

Begin with your 'rough' first draft

First drafts are called 'rough' or 'messy' for good reason. We begin with a 'clear' but only partially conscious, sometimes barely fluent memory. We write quickly: in complete and incomplete sentences, phrases, single words, crossing out this, adding that, drawing arrows from here to there. All in all, it's a mess—but a necessary one. It's necessary because we are not reporting or writing out the fully known; we are exploring what 'feels' important and needs knowing. We are *discovering* our subject, *figuring out* the story that needs telling, *finding* the best way to voice our experience in an engaging, dramatic, and authentic form.[1]

With our first draft in hand, we can now turn to those tools—the writer's equivalent of maps, a GPS, signposts, the sun and stars, maybe a machete and some bear spray—that will help us journey from our rough draft to a 'good enough' final text.

---

[1] See Chapters 6 and 7 for further discussion of writing the first draft.

Review your first draft

Begin by setting aside your first draft for a few days, then return to it fresh.

Read and listen to it whole—no pausing, no self-correcting. Just listen. Listen to where its energy or feeling centres are, what it seems to be about, how it moves forward, where it goes, when and how it ends. At this stage you are listening for the *possibilities* of your roughly worded material: its personal significance, what you are trying to say, what needs saying.

Ask yourself questions like these: Where is this material's emotional, creaturely heart? Why is this material significant to me? What is this material really *about*? What am I learning about myself? Underline the most important key words, phrases, and images in your rough draft, add any missing key words, bracket off the less important.

In one short sentence with subject, action, and object, write what this story or essay is essentially about. Use this like a fulcrum to develop your material—although remain aware that the actual *aboutness* of your material may shift or appear in some new form over the writing process.

Now, with a provisional sense of *aboutness* in hand, begin revising and further developing your material.

The rewriting process: A few key signposts

Let the writing process explore your life. We are full of competing, often still-to-be-articulated sentences, phrases, and words that vie to express the truth of our experience. Starting or revising this sentence rather than that one, and seeing where things go—all on behalf of what we feel and know—is how writing helps discover what we need to say. That is, personal writing as a process is always helping us discover what needs saying. In this way, memoir writing explores us. Open yourself to its work.

Listen for the known but not yet thought. What needs saying—what I call the essential *aboutness* of your material and the best way to express it—can sometimes emerge through conscious reflection. On the other hand, it is just as likely—perhaps more likely—to appear suddenly, as if unbeckoned, in the form of something deeply sensed or felt but as yet unthought. A word or phrase or an associated memory or sensation suddenly makes you feel sad or elated or lonely or frightened. You 'know' something even if you don't yet have the words to name it. This is the creaturely mind wanting its say on behalf of genuinely personal experiential truths. Listen to these unthought but felt knowns.[2]

This raggle-taggle life. Ensure that *how* you express your experience is faithful to your actually lived experience. Life experiences have no shortage of contradictions, inconsistencies, uncertainties, coincidences, inconclusiveness, and all-round grittiness. Don't gut your personal writing of these qualities. Be wary of tidy, linear narratives, of imposing a self-satisfying psychological 'sense' (driven, for example, by the fantasy of being master of one's fate), and of makeovers aimed at charming your reader. The most genuine-feeling memoirists allow the raggle-taggle qualities of life to be voiced through—and to shape—their writing.

---

[2] The concept of 'the unthought known' is from Christopher Bollas' *The Shadow of the Object: Psychoanalysis of the Unthought Known*. Put simply, Bollas sees evidence of the 'unthought known' in those deep, sudden, powerful, and involuntary felt responses that seem to 'appear from nowhere' inside us as we are listening to a piece of music for example, or reading a novel, turning a street corner, experiencing a taste or aroma. How, Bollas asks, to understand such responses, especially their uncanny quality of seeming to have been lived or experienced, and powerfully so, at another time in our life, as well as their ability, in many instances, to make us feel deeply, satisfyingly complete? Although we cannot cognitively apprehend or name these sensed moments from an earlier time, they are nevertheless 'existentially known' and felt overwhelmingly inside us. I should add that I am bending and broadening Bollas' idea in order to encourage the reader's inner openness to sources of personal experience, insight, and truth beyond the already well-known or readily nameable.

Express your material in your distinct voice. Use language, writing rhythms, figures of speech, images, and intonation to animate and colour your material: to make it 'sound like you.' Keep yourself—your creaturely feelings and thoughts—in your material. Make your material, in itself, demonstrate its importance for your life.

The good doctor's gaze and touch. Bring to the writing process the empathetic as well as the clinical attention of a good doctor. Examine your work with creaturely care, ask the necessary questions, and tell yourself the good news and the bad. We value a good doctor precisely because they have a heart, they're knowledgeable, and they are reliable truth-tellers. When examining your writing, use the good doctor's gaze and touch.

Listen to your writing. One of the best tests of writing is to read it aloud straight and whole. Listen to its inner experiential unfolding and flow. Speak—at least *hear*—the words rather than just scanning the text. Listen for the writing's felt energies. Listen for its forward pull. And listen for hiccups along the way: missing information, implausible-sounding voices, impersonal generalities and clichés, feelings gorged on adjectives and adverbs. Does each part—specific scenes, examples, figures of speech, the beginning and ending—contribute effectively to the whole? Have you varied your sentence forms and lengths? Is your 'through line' —a connecting theme, plot, or characteristic—dramatized and deepened?

Rewrite with more conscious intention. As you review and rework initial drafts, you are developing a clearer sense of what you need to write: your material's essential *aboutness*, how to begin and develop your subject, your narrative through line, what the key 'scenes' and centres of energy need to be, and how to end. Step close to your work, then away, then close again. 'See' or feel the whole, and how its inner workings contribute to this whole, then zoom in on details—adjust word choices, the cadence or rhythm of sentences, figures of speech—then move back out again to get the wider impression. Develop what needs saying with more conscious intention.

Do not overwrite. Overwriting results from being too cautious, too clever, or feeling anxious that 'I haven't said it all.' Our expressive style becomes formal, stilted, impersonal, or florid. It loses the pleasing rhythms needed by the human breath and inner creaturely movements of attention. Read your work for its natural vocal rhythms. Find the necessary, precise words, phrasings, and figures of speech, and let these do their work.

Do not overexplain. Write in a way that enables your material to speak for itself, to enact its meaning and importance. Yes, reflect on what an experience means to you, but don't tell me what an experience is about. Demonstrate or dramatize its aboutness instead. Leave room for your reader to have their own experience. Respect your reader's intelligence. Don't handhold. Know when not to explain.

Do your research. Check factual details. Compare your point of view with others.

Recognize when you have a 'good enough' version. Remember that even very good batters only hit .300 or so, and that's after years of practice. Sometimes we get to first, many times we foul or strike or fly out, and only a few times do we hit a homer. Keep writing, read good writing, and aim for the best you can do.

Revising towards a 'good enough' final text: the practicalities

Here we briefly review the practical craft elements of effective personal writing, everything from narrative development to punctuation. Most of the points noted here are discussed in greater detail in Chapters 10–12 and elsewhere.

- Begin with a strong, contextualizing, immersive opener. Sometimes a single sentence works: 'Mornings were not our best family moments.' Alternatively, use a brief anecdote that immediately brings your reader into your material's experiential world. Don't wait too long to say where you are—and when. Good beginnings are usually written or at least finalized last, once you know what you are introducing.

- Pull the reader forward through a mix of 'close-up' scenes, examples or arguments, and narrative bridges and summaries. Not everything you need to say warrants equal attention. Use your narrative to build curiosity and anticipation. William Zinsser: 'Never forget the storyteller's ancient rules of maintaining tension and momentum—rules you've known in your bones since you were a child listening to bedside stories' (*Writing About Your Life*). Ensure the narrative line unfolds naturally and intelligibly, even given its turns, surprises, digressions, and movements back and forth in time.

- Mix things up. Vary the rhythms of your writing: sentence lengths and forms, long and short paragraphs. Vary the tone as moods and points of view change. Rather than always depending on linear narratives based on conventional time, re-order events and details to create suspense and curiosity.

- Shift perspectives, make them dynamic. Move the point of view between the narrator's (or a character's) inner thoughts, their external behavior, external activities, and the external surround. *I thought. I did. That happened. The place looked/smelled/sounded like.* Let your characters speak and converse directly in their own voices. Where needed, give a voice—including direct speech—to perspectives different than the narrator's own.

- Consider using figurative language to personalize, enliven, suggest, and deepen meaning. Ensure each figure of speech makes a meaningful contribution; nothing gratuitous, or merely smart or pretty. Remember that a single well-chosen noun, verb, or adjective might do the job just as well, or better, than a figure of speech.

- 'Show' (evoke, demonstrate, dramatize) characters, feelings, situations. 'Show' through telling actions, gestures, behaviours, characteristics, and figures of speech. 'Tell' to move between scenes, to create narrative bridges and summaries, and to reflect on an experience.

- Bring characters, actions, and places alive through evocative concrete realia.

- Take into account all the senses, not only sight or hearing. Remember smell, touch, taste.

- Replace the language of anyone's voice ('wonderful,' 'great,' 'nice,' 'beautiful,' or 'ugly') with that of your precise personal voice. Replace clichés ('play my cards right,' 'bed of roses,' 'bad egg') with experientially specific, concrete, evocative, and personalized language.

- Remember humour and its power to lighten misery, reveal stupidity, disclose character, give the finger to abusive or obdurate power, and much else.

- Delete deadwood: unnecessary phrases and words, especially excessive adverbs and adjectives, as well as scenes, details, objects, or people that add nothing of consequence to the story. Follow the advice attributed to the playwright Anton Chekhov: 'Don't put a loaded gun on the stage if no one is thinking of firing it.'

- Use adjectives and adverbs sparingly and precisely. For example, instead of 'I am definitely going to do it today,' write 'I am going to do it today.' Consider precise nouns and verbs instead. Less is often more.

- Aim for a direct, vigorous style. Use the active voice and concrete nouns.

- Review your grammar. Use one of the many helpful websites or grammar correction apps. Reading and listening to your work is often the best corrective. Check, for example, subject–verb agreement, personal pronouns, and double negatives.

- Punctuation. Again there are helpful online advice sites. Use punctuation to make your meaning clear and to support natural and varied reading rhythms.

- Spell out organization or movement names when first used, place the acronym in brackets following this first reference, then use the acronym thereafter.

- Check spelling and typos. Run your work through a spell-checking app. Decide whether to use Canadian, British, or American spelling.

The 'good enough' final text, or putting the octopus to bed

How do we know when we have arrived at the 'good enough' final version of our work? This is a question every writer asks, again and again. How do we know when we are done?

Alas, there is no sure answer. The most we have is good advice from practiced writers. Some of the best advice I've read on this question is by Anne Lamott in her *Bird by Bird: Some Instructions on Writing and Life*. How do you know when you're done? Lamott asks. 'You just do,' she says—which is a response that turns out to be more accurate, even more helpful, than it appears at first glance. Here are Lamott's thoughts on the matter.

> I think my students believe that when a published writer finishes something, she crosses the last t, pushes back from the desk, yawns, stretches, and smiles. I do not know anyone who has ever done this, not even once. What happens

instead is that you've gone over and over something so many times, and you've weeded and pruned and rewritten, and the person who reads your work for you has given you great suggestions that you have mostly taken—and then finally something inside you just says it's time to get on to the next thing. Of course, there will always be more you could do, but you've had to remind yourself that perfection is the voice of the oppressor.

There's an image I've heard people in recovery use—that getting all of one's addictions under control is a little like putting an octopus to bed. I think this perfectly describes the process of solving various problems in your final draft. You get a bunch of the octopus's arms neatly tucked under the covers . . . but two arms are still flailing around. Maybe the dialogue in the first half and the second half don't match, or there is that one character who still seems one-dimensional. But you finally get those arms under the sheets, too, and are about to turn off the lights when another long sucking arm breaks free.

This will probably happen when you are sitting at your desk, kneading your face, feeling burned out and rubberized. Then, even though all the sucking disks on that one tentacle are puckering open and closed, and the slit-shaped pupils of the octopus are looking derisively at you, as if it might suck you to death just because it's bored, and even though you know your manuscript is not perfect and you'd hoped for so much more, but . . . you also know that there is no more steam in the pressure cooker and that it's the very best you can do for now—well? I think this means that you are done.

The reader's checklist

As memoir writers we typically rely on our own perspective to develop a piece of writing. This is as it should be. After all, we are telling our life stories in our voice. At the same time, seeing our writing from a reader's perspective, in terms of their needs as a reader, offers a further qualitative check on our work. Try using this reader's checklist to review your own next-to-final copy.

- Does the first sentence or two get me interested, and keep me engaged, in the story's world, situation, or argument?

- Do I continue to feel engaged, drawn forward, kept curious, moved?

- Do I know where I am in terms of place, time, people, situation? Do I know where I am going? Can I follow the story?

- Does each element—word, detail, dramatic scene, narrative thread—focus on the essential *aboutness* of the story? Does the seemingly extraneous also serve the story's *aboutness*?

- Are the rhythms and overall balance of attention—between, say, dramatic scenes, narrative bridges, and narrative summaries—appropriate to what is being said? Does the writing 'show' where needed (dramatize or demonstrate experiences and character through precise, evocative, telling realia) and 'tell' where needed?

- Does the writing come alive through appropriate, precise, and evocative figures of speech; the use of speech, thought, and dialogue to suggest shadings in character; and attention to the five senses?

- Is there a dramatic, engaging use of time: non-chronological approaches to narrative time; flashbacks, forward hints, recollections?

- Does the whole hold together, even if it includes varied anecdotes and tangents?

- Can I hear the writer's voice in the writing? Does the writer take me beyond the merely reported to a sense of their felt participation in and experience of the material?

- Does the voice sound distinct, personal, necessary, authentic? Where, if anywhere, does it not sound like the writer's own voice?

- Does the writing feel personally genuine and honest? Or does it feel like the writer is skating along surfaces, staying close to what feels familiar and comfortable, sometimes being evasive, reporting rather than exploring their experience?

- Does the ending feel appropriate? Did it work?

- As I read, do I become more aware of why the writer has needed to do this piece of writing, why it is important to them?

- What stands out as one or two key strengths of this piece of writing? If I were to suggest one change, if any, what would this be?

- Does this story or essay stay with me and leave me with something to think about? Has it suggested to me something new about the writer?

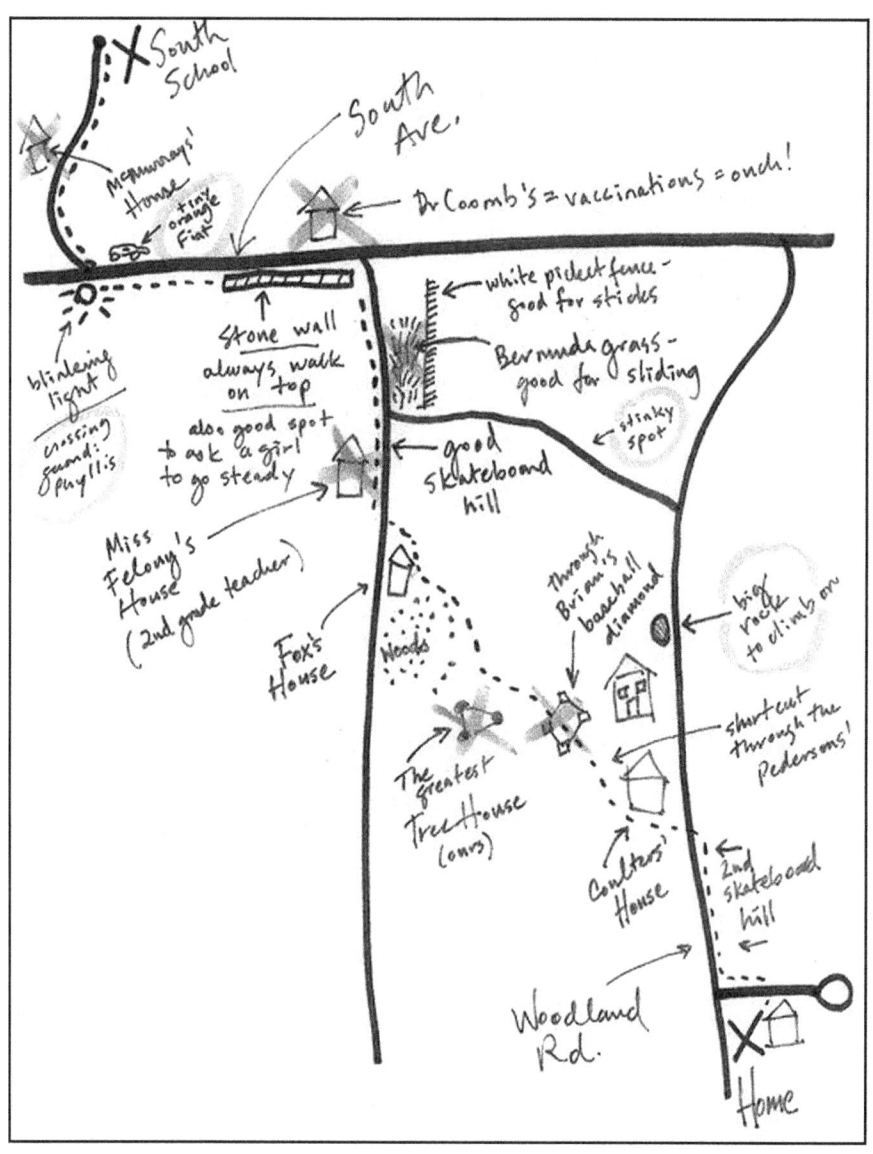

John Fulford, *The Walk To South School, 1964–71*, from Katharine Harmon, *You Are Here: Personal Geographies and Other Maps of the Imagination.* Fulford drew this map for his nieces who, 30 years later, took a similar route to the school he attended. All items crossed out have changed or no longer exist; all items circled were added by the nieces. Try sketching route maps like Fulford's, or floor plans of significant residences in your life. Add experiential details, then begin telling the stories that emerge.

CHAPTER 16

THE MEMOIR WRITER'S BLUES, AND HOW TO BECOME INSPIRED AGAIN

Sooner or later there are times when we find it difficult to write. We have been working on our memoir for a while, then one day we realize we are not making any progress. Perhaps we can't find the next life story. The tank feels empty. Or we have ideas, but then we procrastinate. Or we are having difficulty developing or ending a piece of writing that's already underway. Maybe the inner interest that first inspired our writing feels like it has left town. Or we feel our writing is 'not good enough' or our stories 'not interesting enough' to share.

Welcome to the memoir writer's blues.

We're not talking here about how changing life circumstances—caring for a new grandchild, breaking your wrist, travelling the world—can derail your writing. The writer's blues are something else. They're the inner experience, as a writer, of feeling disheartened, unmotivated, or uninspired. We become overwhelmed with what others are saying or might say about our writing, or whether anyone even cares about what we have to say. Our confidence gets beaten up by a gang of carping inner critics. We get frazzled by a writing challenge that feels so tangled we don't know how or whether to continue. Or we become immobilized by a particularly difficult life experience. Whatever the reasons, 'the thrill is gone,' as B.B. King used to sing, or as the blues master Albert Collins once wrote, 'When I left I had corn flakes for breakfast, now there's a bone from a T-bone steak.'

How to get writing again? How to write through what's blocking or frustrating us? How to send those worrying, scolding inner voices packing? How to again feel that desire and curiosity that brought us to the memoir writing table in the first place? Here are a few practical steps to get us back on our way.

Take your writing challenge to members of your memoir group. Ask for advice. Read your work, present your problem, then have a frank discussion. Participants will be naturally receptive. At least some members will recognize what you are talking about and have their own insights and suggestions. The very act of describing your problem to others can help clarify matters to yourself. Here's something else you might try. Focus on your writing challenge, write 'What I really want to say is . . . '—then complete the sentence and see where it takes you.

Don't force yourself to write. 'Your unconscious can't work when you are breathing down its neck,' writes Mary Karr in *The Art of Memoir*. Take a break for a few days. Enjoy other activities, enjoy your friends and family. A writing routine is fine, but a routine taken over by a mood of 'I should write' can murder your writing spirit. Remember, too, that 'writing' needn't always take a more-or-less completed form. 'Writing' can also be research, notes, phrases, and story 'mapping.'

Use your personal writer's journal. Everything here is for yourself only. No nagging—from yourself or others. Here, all is perfect in its imperfection. Make brief notes on a situation, feeling, person, idea, or photo. Write words and phrases (names, objects, sensations) that hold memories. Write out favourite passages from writers. Include story or idea 'maps.' Make notes on what your grandchild's birth or smile feels like, or on that ornery person who grabbed mandarins right out of your fingers at the fruit counter. The physical act of hand writing in your journal—its intimacy, the change from keyboarding—can itself draw water from what seemed like a dry well.

'I feel overwhelmed, I'm not sure where it's all going, I'll never get done.' Remember that image from the beginning of this book: writing your memoir is like crossing a river step by step, stone to stone. A preoccupation with the river itself, or reaching the far shore, can overwhelm you. Enjoy the water, enjoy the feeling of each stone. Feel for that first stone, write one memorable life experience in rough form. Tomorrow, feel for another stone, or get a better feeling for the stone you are already standing on. You are gradually making your way forward across the river. Indeed, in finding your way you are *creating* your way—you are telling us about your becoming, about who you are, step by step.

'My family, partner, or friends don't want me to write this'—a particular experience or your memoir itself. Discouragement comes in many voices: *'Let bygones be bygones,' 'Don't you dare,' 'That's not what happened,' 'Why would you even want to write about that?'* Personal writing is already demanding without having these nagging, oftentimes censorious voices whispering over your shoulder. Yes, ask for and decide whether or not to acknowledge the viewpoints and memories of others, but never become the voice of their values, timidity, and fears. Others can tell their own stories. This is your story, your best, thoughtful, caring effort at being true to your experience. Determine for yourself what needs remembering and saying, and say it with your own voice. If your inner scolds persist, acknowledge their power by writing 'It is difficult for me to write about . . .'—then continue this sentence in your own voice. See Chapter 21 on the challenges of 'being true.'

'I have nothing original—or important—to say.' I have heard this said many times by participants in personal writing workshops, but I have never seen it confirmed in practice. By the fact that you live inside your own skin—your creaturely self—you are an 'original,' with your own important felt experiences, memories, and forms of self- and life-understanding. Your friends and family are interested in your personal 'take on life,' including all those 'small,' personal, and fundamentally human moments that constitute your life: that first lover's kiss, the death of a dear friend, riding through golden September corn on the tailgate of your uncle's 1950s Dodge pickup. Bring these moments alive in your own voice. Your reader will relish your human beingness as told through these 'small,' true moments of life. They will grasp—appreciate, get the idea of, enjoy—the inner personal importance of what you have needed to remember.

'This is just not written the way it needs to be.' Perhaps so, in which case try to identify what is not working (use the suggestions in Chapter 12 or take the problem to your writing group), then try a new approach. If your dissatisfaction is more general and chronic, remember what I said earlier: that even good batters hit only .300 or so. Maybe you are being too hard on yourself. As we have seen, each piece of writing has a 'good enough,' not perfect, final version. Allow yourself to feel satisfaction with what's perfectly good enough.

Writing flows but also drips. Memoir writing takes many forms. A sentence, a paragraph. An essaying 'map.' A figure of speech. Hasty, scribbled notes about some suddenly felt memory. Rubbishy first drafts. The final 'good enough' story. Be happy with writing's drips, shout for joy when writing flows.

Don't wait for 'ideal' writing conditions. Sure, 'everything will be perfect tomorrow' and your writing will flow like the mighty Fraser River. Or maybe it won't. Perhaps tomorrow will be a little like today—not yet 'perfect.' Write what can be written today. And remember E.B. White's admonition that 'a writer who waits for ideal conditions under which to work will die without putting a word on paper.'[1]

Writing doesn't always happen when you sit down to write. Go for walks, lull the logical mind, wonder sideways. Talk with others about a memory you have been thinking about. Make quiet times only

---

[1] From an interview in *The Paris Review*, Fall 1969.

for yourself and your thoughts. Welcome the wanderings of memory as you fall asleep or wake up. Keep some note-taking device nearby. Welcome the surprises that memory enjoys springing on us.

Stir up your memory, feed your storytelling self. Paste up memoir-related photos where you write. Thumb through family albums and public archives. Visit an art gallery. Experience other stories and creative voices through films, theatre, paintings, and musical concerts. Read writers that inspire you.

Write a memoir story in the form of a letter to an acquaintance. The acquaintance could be a family member or friend, either living or dead. The act of personal letter writing materializes your reader, bringing them into the room as it were, where the two of you can have a conversation. The setting of writing, and our inner sense of what we are doing, thus becomes more relaxed. Try it out. You may find that you write with a greater ease and confidence, and with more immediacy and warmth.

Take a non-writing approach to writing. Make a sketch of a childhood neighbourhood or favourite place or room, then circle places of felt energy and begin making notes on what's happening in these circles. Revisit the memoir writing topics listed in Chapter 5, choose one page, select one topic that catches your attention, and begin 'mapping' (Chapter 7) your own experience of this topic.

Claim your time and your space. Dedicate a private, quiet hour or so every couple of days to 'writing' your memoir. No interruptions. 'Writing' can include writing a rough draft, journalling, 'mapping,' research, or revising.

It is what it is. Accept that there are times when writing simply feels too difficult, maybe impossible, to do. Personal writing is full of stops and starts, trial and error, doldrums and fair winds, laborious challenges and breakthroughs. Don't give yourself a hard time about the slow times. Shrug them off, turn to other enjoyments, and let your inner life simmer away. It's preparing something tasty for later.

Remember why you wanted to write your memoir in the first place. Return to notes where you first described why you wanted to create a personal life story. What did you write then? Use this to re-write your purpose in your personal writing journal. Put what you write on a sticky note over your desk. *'I want to write my memoir because . . . .'* Because why? So that my grandchildren or parents or friends have a more complete, truer sense of who I am—or was? To chronicle my life in my own voice? To relive and relish my life experiences? To redeem past mistakes? For greater self-understanding? In order to better understand others? As an act of resistance to the oblivion of mortality? *'I want to write my memoir because . . . .'* Now complete this sentence in your own words.

Visit the Rag Bag man. Here are some wise concluding thoughts from Anne Lamott:

> I've always told my writing students that I think writer's block is a misnomer. I don't think we get blocked, but rather that we get empty. We need to fill back up. I believe there is a creative partner inside of me whom I call the Rag Bag man, who has a burlap sack of my memories, insights, visions, observations, from which I will eventually construct the quilt of my stories. My job is to search out these bits of cloth and thread, of velvet and unbleached muslin and corduroy, red cords and dental floss and grosgrain ribbons. So instead of sitting at my desk in full clench and despair, I go about accumulating snippets and chunks of cool stuff: I do informal interviews with brilliant friends on childhood, soul, the meaning of life, etc; I take my most articulate friends to marshes and museums, and I write down every brilliant observation either of us has; I look through old photo albums; I read more poetry. In other words, I fill back up.[2]

---

[2] From an interview in *Lit Hub Weekly*, March 1–5, 2021.

Many of us have had some experience of being in an intimate relationship with another person. What stories and reflections arise from your own relationships? Photos, clockwise from upper left: Julian Stein (pexels.com), Ketut Subiyanto (pexels.com). Dainis Graveris (unspash.com), Anastasia Shuraeva (pexels.com), Rodnae Productions (pexels.com), and Matej (pexels.com).

PART III

FINALIZING AND SHARING YOUR MEMOIR

CHAPTER 17

BRINGING IT ALL TOGETHER: ORGANIZING, PREPARING, AND SHARING YOUR MEMOIR

This chapter helps you prepare your memoir materials for print and discusses today's printing and publishing options.

Arranging your memoir materials

Early in this book I cautioned against becoming preoccupied with the final arrangement of your memoir materials. I encouraged you instead to just start writing. Sure, begin imagining the overall form, direction, and final 'look' of your memoir. Even jump ahead to this chapter to consider your options. But, I advised, hold these ideas lightly—and watch how your emerging material begins to suggest its own organizational form.

It's easy to understand that our reader learns about us through *what* we write. But *how* we express each story or essay, and *how* we give an overall shape to our memoir, also imply things about how we understand our life and who we are. For example, by adhering closely to conventional chronological time throughout our memoir, we imply that our life has followed a path of more or less orderly development, one experience building on a previous experience. At the very least we are retrospectively imposing a logical order over our life, despite the fact that actual life is always life-in-progress, with its yet-to-be-determined array of choices, surprises, external forces, and still-to-be-knowns sitting out there in the future.

To put this another way, the *form* of a memoir is part of the evidence of how the writer understands their life. One person wrote about their life in 108 short chapters, the number of beads on a Buddhist prayer string. Another based their life stories on rooms in a house; yet another on a number of favourite places: the woods, a cemetery, a mountain top, places of joy and places of misery. The narrator of Patti Miller's *The Last One Who Remembers* compared herself to a bowerbird, a collector of bits and pieces, and structured her memoir accordingly.

In considering the overall form of your memoir, ask questions such as the following:

- If the *form* of a memoir is part of the evidence of how I understand my life, what should the form of my memoir be?

- Given what I know about the dramatic development of individual life stories and essays, do I want to give a dramatic, engaging, forward-pulling form to my material—and what might this look like?

- What arrangement will best represent my understanding of the relation between the parts and the whole of my life story?

- Where and how do the pieces connect? Do they suggest their own natural arrangement?

- Do I want to arrange my materials in a way that represents the actual process of exploring and understanding my life experiences?

- Are there pieces that must appear first, second, and so on, and other pieces that must come last—perhaps a meditative personal essay in which you reflect on and assess what has come before?

Whatever overall form you are considering, don't become overly concerned that your material might not 'hold together.' Each memoir has built-in organizing signposts: the writer's name, title, introduction, table of contents, and, if you include one, a personal timeline. With these in hand, your reader will know where they are, and you as the writer will have enough elbow room to arrange your material in a way that brings alive the overall story you want to tell.

A closer look at some possible arrangements

What follows are a few options for organizing your material.

Chronology. This is the go-to approach of many memoir writers. The overall narrative follows conventional time: birth until the present, or the beginning of a particular experience or phase of your life through to its conclusion. Chronology has a built-in beginning and end, and it's easy to organize and follow. It can be based, for example, on stages of your life, places you have lived, or a specific sequence of events.

Be mindful that chronology, strictly adhered to, can feel predictable, lifeless, tedious, and, as suggested above, false to actually lived life. On the other hand, you can give a greater true-to-life feeling to the chronological approach by rearranging the temporal order of events and mimicking the work of memory. Eva Hoffman does exactly this in the first section of her memoir *Lost in Translation*. The section, called 'Paradise,' chronicles her childhood in Poland, prior to the family's emigration to Canada. The narrative begins in 1959 with the 'highly agitated' family aboard a ship that is leaving the Polish port of Gdynia and headed for North America. Within moments, however, Hoffman shifts to a childhood experience ten years earlier, then from here the narrative gradually moves forward through her childhood until she arrives again at the 1959 departure and the end of both her childhood and the 'Paradise' section. The form of the narrative frames the section, describes how Eva came to be on that ship, and sets the stage for what will turn out to be her traumatic removal from 'paradise.'

Hoffman even spurns conventional chronology in the page-to-page narrative of the 'Paradise' section. In rendering ten or so years of her childhood, she does move forward through the years, but she does so along a zigzagging, back-and-forth path. It's the path of the inner dynamics of Hoffman's remembering. That is, the narrative *form* of the section follows the activity of recollection. It represents the activity not of retrospectively imposing an unlived logic over her life but of allowing memory to recollect the complex unfolding of life. The narrative is an act of remembering—the narrative of memoir—and is all the more authentic-feeling for being so.

Collage—or mosaic or patchwork. Collage is the intentional arrangement—literally a gluing together—of diverse materials, often fragments, into a single work. In memoir writing these materials can include life stories, personal essays, journal entries, letters, quotations, photographs, and other writings and documents. Although collage is used in many contexts and for a variety of reasons, a number of autobiographical writers adopt it in order to express their experience of the *discontinuousness*—volatility, arbitrariness, and unintelligibility— of modern life. Indeed, collage is an especially useful form for memoirists from tumultuous life worlds, such as the world of racism, social violence, displacement, and cultural amnesia recalled by Jordan Abel in his memoir *Nishga*. For writers like Abel, conventional chronology and linear narratives negate what they need to say. They need a form, like collage, that represents the never completed work of investigating, deciphering, and piecing together an overturned and fragmented life. Collage has the added benefit of creating experiential spaces—inside and between each of its parts—for your reader to build their own impressions of who you are and where you have come from. Reader and writer become collaborators in the continuing work of making sense of the material at hand.

Linked thematic clusters. Arrange your material by theme or subject matter, such as family, mother or father, relationships, friendships, childhood, school days, passions, travels, inner life, working life, old age, key turning points, and being a father or mother. This approach gives you freedom to name and organize themes as you wish.

An overarching, shaping question or topic. For example: How did I become who I am? Or: Who am I? Or: How can I better understand that phase of my life? Or: How and why did a specific experience or person or time in my life deeply influence my life forever? Name the overarching issue(s) in your introduction, then organize your material in ways that take the reader through a gradually unfolding journey that itself is your answer to the question—or at least contains the makings of a provisional answer.

An organizing device. Stories or essays are linked through a shared organizing device. This 'device' could be a set of concrete things of experiential value ('My life in 12 essential objects'); a series of character studies based on people who have significantly influenced your life; rooms in a house, or places in which you have travelled; or the metaphor of life as a journey or pilgrimage, with stories about encounters with people and places framed as an ongoing quest for learning, meaning, or happiness.

A specific life experience. The year I backpacked around the world. Living with a challenging condition. Our family's move between countries or across a continent. My years in a seminary or prison. Aunt Mamie and me. Building a boat, trying my hand at homesteading, learning to paint or play the piano.

Begin to imagine possible titles for your memoir

Your memoir's title might have already come to you, although don't be concerned if it hasn't. Reflect on your memoir's key experiences, reflections, and understandings—then daydream possible titles. Titles—typically up to a few words long—can *describe* your memoir in literal terms, as in Thomas DeBaggio's *Losing My Mind: An Intimate Look at Life with Alzheimer's*, or more figuratively, as with Maya Angelou's *I Know Why the Caged Bird Sings*. Titles can also be based on key words or phrases that you use or that have been used against you, such as Gary Shteyngart's *Little Failure*, or they can allude to a core aspect of your experience (*Uprooted*) or self-understanding (*My Assorted Lives*). If you are lost for ideas, look at the titles in the Selected Readings list. Keep notes on possible titles, then get on with other things.

Review and rationalize informational details

Ensure that your dates, name spellings, and other matters of fact are accurate and consistent. If you say 'B' happened before 'C' but after 'A' then maintain this same temporal order of events throughout. If you have two or more characters with the same name, help your reader keep them straight: Uncle Joe, Grandpa Joe, my friend Joe.

Include a personal timeline

See Chapter 2 on creating a personal timeline. Harmonize your timeline and your written material. In brief chronological order, include key dates, characters by name and relation to you, and key activities and events. Also include social-cultural events where these are relevant to your material. Place your timeline at the end of your memoir, list it in your table of contents, and refer to it in your introduction.

Create a consistent overall 'look'

Choose a standard, easy-to-read **typeface (font) and size** and use this consistently throughout your main or 'body' text. You might want to use a second but visually complementary typeface for story titles and your main title. Serif fonts are often used for body text, sans serif fonts for titles. Use the same font and type size for the same categories of text. Some standard body text fonts include Garamond, Palatino, Jenson, Minion, and Adobe Caslon. Twelve-point type (size) is usually standard for body text. Chapter title and subtitle fonts include Open Sans, Helvetica, Montserrat, and Verdana.

Bold, underlining, italics. Use these sparingly and only as aids to your reader. Within the body of your text, set direct speech and quotations in quotation marks. Use italics for book titles. Possibly use italics to suggest inner thought or voice or to give emphasis. In the latter case, it is usually better to use language that communicates emphasis, without recourse to italics. Use bolded text for various forms of titling. Avoid underlining. Overall, keep the appearance of your pages simple and clean.

Spaciousness and ease of reading. The pleasure of reading is influenced by choices of typeface and text size and by the reader's sense of spaciousness on the page. Typical margins are set at a minimum of 2.5 cm on all sides. Either indent the first line of each paragraph or, if you do not indent, add a bit of vertical spacing at the end of each paragraph. Whatever approach you choose, use it consistently.

Number pages. Choose from among the numbering styles in Word or your publishing service. Run numbers continuously from first to last page.

Begin each story or equivalent with a **title** in bolded, larger type.

Photos and other graphic material. Online publishing services will have their own advice and aids for setting images in your text. Digital writing programs like Word easily set .jpg image files into text. Include **captions**: who or what is depicted, date of image, image source, and copyright if applicable.

Contextual notes. Most of your entries should be intelligible in themselves. Where this is not the case—letters, juvenilia—include brief, contextualizing introductions.

Dedication, introduction, acknowledgements

Dedication. If you wish to especially recognize, honour, or express appreciation to a particular person or persons, name them here. The dedication usually sits between the title page and introduction. A dedication is optional. It is also different than recognizing people in your acknowledgements (see below).

Preface or introduction. This—the last piece you write—orients your reader to what they have in hand and who wrote it. Given that this is your memoir, write your introduction in the tone of a personal letter to your reader. Remember that this reader may know you firsthand, but they might also be opening up your memoir 100 years from now.

There are a variety of approaches to writing an introduction. One option is to play it straight: tell your reader what this document is, why you wrote it, that there's a personal timeline at the end, and anything else you want to add. A second, more engaging and personable option is to immediately immerse your reader in your own thinking about how you came to write your memoir. Use a personal experience to *show* what got you started writing about your life, what prompted this memoir, and why it's important to you. Let your reader immediately experience your personal, storytelling voice.

Possibly describe elements of your writing process: your research, the context of your writing (e.g., your participation in a memoir writing group), and memoir writing's pleasures and challenges. Finally, orientate your reader to how your memoir is organized: what elements they will find where.

Remember as well to briefly include essential facts about yourself: where you are in your extended family, your birth year, and other basic identifiers. You can do this in your introduction or in a separate **'Note about the author.'**

Your name and the date. Add these to the end of your introduction.

Acknowledgements. This is the place to thank those who have given you support on your writing and life journey.

Sharing your memoir: the changing world of publishing

The options for sharing your memoir with others have changed significantly in recent years. When my mother produced her life stories in the 1970s, she arranged to have the manuscripts photocopied in limited numbers, each with a hand-written letter from her, and bound in a simple 'report' cover on which was pasted a typed title. One of her granddaughters created a set of delightful illustrations in pastels. Each copy is still cherished.

Although you can still take this approach today, by using print services or home printers, you do have an array of other options. These include professionally printing limited copies of your memoir in book format, sharing your memoir through a personal online blog or website or media such as Google Docs, or using one of the digital self-publishing or e-publishing services.

> **Keep your work safe**
>
> Whatever option you choose for sharing your memoir, make sure you create a personal digital copy, plus a second back-up copy. Print at least one copy, archive the electronic file and print copies in a secure place, let others know what you have done and, if you have a will, include a note on what you have done.

Print options

Print options—as distinct from the publishing options discussed later—include your local print shop and online print companies. This may be your best choice if you need only a few published copies. Online companies—such as Blurb, MyCanvas, Lulu—produce individual, full-colour, bound copies in book format. You choose a template or 'look,' then you upload and arrange your materials online, create a cover, sign off on your book when you are ready, and order the number of print copies you need. Only you can order copies. The company will store your book online, which means you can edit the file as needed and print more copies later. No special 'techie' skills are needed. Note that while all companies handle combinations of text and graphics, some online book printing companies, such as Shutterfly, create mostly photo books. Ensure that the company you choose makes it easy to format mostly text content.

Blogs and websites

Creating a personal blog or website has never been easier, although you still need some experience and confidence with computers. Popular blog hosting companies—such as Blogger, WordPress, Squarespace, Wix, and Medium—do the behind-the-scenes programming and provide preset design templates. Blogs are easier to set up than websites and are arguably more suitable for the presentation of memoir material. If you are considering this option, remember the transient nature of the web and that it doesn't come with print copies.

When researching blog or website hosting companies, check the following: ease of set-up, whether there are free online set-up tutorials, choices of 'look,' ease of posting new material and updating features, whether or not the site displays ads on your published pages, what free apps are available to build into your site (e.g., apps connecting it to social media), types of domain name (some have their corporate name combined with your site's name, some offer a distinct name), cost of hosting, and how long the company is likely to be in business.

Digital self-publishing or e-publishing

The digital self-publishing or electronic publishing option makes your writing available on-demand to anyone anywhere in both digital and printed book formats, in black/white or colour, and, in most instances, at no cost to you. In essence, you upload your manuscript to an e-publisher website and convert it into a book format which anyone can purchase in a digital or printed (print on demand) version. Increasing numbers of today's one-time memoir writers are turning to this option. Popular e-publishers include Kindle Direct Publishing (KDP, an Amazon company), Smashwords, Draft2Digital, and IngramSpark. Each has its own online distribution system.

Digital self-publishing is relatively easy to do on your own. Companies like Smashwords provide free how-to videos, a style guide and an extensive FAQ section. Draft2Digital also has a good reputation for making e-publishing easy for new users. If you need help, companies such as Tellwell provide assistance for a fee, including editing, layout, cover design, and marketing. In choosing an e-publisher, pay particular attention to whether you will find their manuscript preparation and posting system manageable; the quality, types, and cost of support they provide; and the formats and distribution systems they offer. Check online as well to see what others are saying about the helpfulness of a particular e-publisher.[1]

Basic self-publishing puts the onus on you to provide final text organized as you want. KDP and Smashwords accept Word .doc files which they help convert into publishable e-files. You will also be expected to design your own cover. You can usually add page navigation to digital versions of your book, as well as an identifying ISBN (international book identification number), an author blurb, and other features.

Once uploaded, formatted, and made available to distributors online, your memoir can be purchased in an e-book format or as a print on demand book that is mailed to the purchaser. If they know your name and your memoir title, any person with access to your e-publisher or distributer can access your book. Each time a person purchases your book in either form, at a price set by you, the publisher and the distributor take a percentage of the listed price. The main companies have wide e-book distribution systems through Apple Books, Kobo, Kindle, and Nook. You should be able to set the limits of distribution, for example only to North America, and you can, if you wish, arrange for the online promotion of your memoir.

---

[1] There are a number of websites that independently review current e-publishing options, such as https://selfpublishing.com/self-publishing-companies/.

E-publishing has many advantages. There is no cost to you if you upload and prepare your book on your own. The preparation process is also relatively simple, with support available. As well, e-publishing turns your memoir into a solid, long-lasting book, with you controlling the 'look' and copyright. Your work is readily accessible to any interested person, and at a modest cost you can give presentation copies to particular individuals.

Are there reasons not to choose the e-publishing option? Possibly. You must be prepared to move through the steps of uploading and finalizing your book, although online assistance is available and you might even have a tech-savvy grandchild or friend who can help. Will your e-publisher be around five years from now, and does this matter to you? It probably shouldn't, if you have kept a digital copy (and back-up) of your manuscript. Finally, remember that once your memoir is posted as an e-book, it may be accessible to any interested person who knows the whereabouts of or stumbles on the title. You might not have foreseen or want this public access. At the same time, few people other than family and friends will know that your memoir is available online.

What publishing option should I choose?

Consider your goals in writing your memoir and sharing it with others. Who is it written for? How many copies do you want? Might it be of interest to people beyond the circle of readers you originally had in mind? Is cost a factor? How important is the physical presentation and appearance of your memoir? Is a certain format more likely to be read, enjoyed, and preserved by your readers?

Remembering childhood. Frederico García Lorca: 'My oldest childhood memories have the flavour of earth.' Jay Griffiths: The piece of land called Cow Common 'was the scruffy-normal from which all else diverged . . . no manners, no wealth, no restriction and no clocks . . . the Unoccupied Territories.' E.E. Cummings: Children are happy sliding, slipping and getting wet, 'when the world is mud-lucious and puddle-wonderful.' Griffiths: 'You no more have to teach a child to make dens [or treehouses or forts] than give a mouse training in burrowing. Dylan Thomas: In childhood 'my body was my adventure.' Griffiths: 'All children are natural shapeshifters'—today a mom or an architect, tomorrow a pirate or a goat. All passages from Griffiths, *A Country Called Childhood*. Photos, clockwise from upper left: localecologist.org (March 6, 2009), Daryl Wilkerson Jr. (pexels.com), the author, and an unknown source.

PART IV

FURTHER REFLECTIONS ON MEMOIR WRITING

Remembering, as Campbell McGrath imagines it, is like climbing up into his mother's unfinished attic, a space hot with ghosts, where a light bulb shatters against his mind and the shadows deepen. Somewhere in this dimness sits a dust-covered shoebox, the past sealed in duct tape, resistant, but gradually yielding when he returns to the bright kitchen light, its cargo of photographs spilling out like playing cards—like a game of chance?—into whose layers he must reach, further in, deeper down, amongst the world of crimped, yellow-margined, fingered images and pencilled notes, each a tender act of resistance against forgetfulness—a cargo which he, the rememberer, now rescues and begins to interpret.

McGrath's poem delivers up a memory of a book read in my own childhood—the story of a boy who climbs at nightfall into his family's attic. It's a place 'old and grey where hundreds of things are tucked away,' in this instance a tattered straw hat, an oil lamp, a kettle, a once-colourful patchwork quilt, a collection of masks, and a can of paint that suddenly, frighteningly, comes alive, tumbling from a rafter and splashing bright red across the floorboards. A warm memory this is, not least of all because it and I are held snug against my mother's body where every adventure—its wonder, its disquiet—always, finally arrives at a place of safety, of love.

McGrath writes evocatively about memory as a retrieval of and fascination with his family's past. It is this particular sense of memory and 'the past'—understood as a family's past, as ancestry—that is so popular today. Witness the ubiquity of genealogical charts, DNA kits, ancestry tourism, and the search for 'roots,' heritage, and 'homeland'—along with related forms of memoir writing. This is 'the past' as beguiling in itself.[1] It is also a use of memory that can quickly slide into agreeable

---

[1] The 'ancestry' boom is not entirely as it appears. While it is thought to be objective and encourage cross-cultural understanding, the last genealogical revival in the 1970s–1980s became a catalyst for white Christian North Americans with mostly northern European lineages to affirm 'blood,' nation, and (often imaginary) ethnic origins; to distance themselves from those unlike 'Us'; and to identify with 'struggling immigrant' as distinct from 'conqueror' life stories. Left

but enervated forms of reverie and nostalgia: a sentimentalizing and idealizing of 'the past,' its use as a hideout from the present.[2]

McGrath's remembering looks back. But surely the point of remembering is to also help us live today and tomorrow. Remembering in this other sense means *using* memory to reflectively understand who we are in terms of our complex becoming, to remember what we have forsaken, what we might do and who we might be. To do this more complete work, remembering needs imagination, especially our ability to form images, ideas, wishes, and more complete 'pictures' —and their words—from remnants of experience.[3] The memoirist in particular needs imagination—especially, as I will suggest in this chapter, an imagination attuned to our creaturely, empathetic centres. Imagination in this sense does not only help us recollect both our enacted and our felt but unrealized pasts; it helps us make sense, today, of our life experiences, and it uses the past to recall abandoned hopes and generate new ones.

---

critically unexamined, ancestry research is easily used to reinforce pre-existing racial and ethnic self-ideas. Although appealing to a wish for clarity, if not certainty, about one's 'origins,' the truth is that ancestry research often relies on inferences from data based on unreliable and culturally skewed records. It also biases an understanding of ancestry very narrowly on the side of 'bloodlines,' despite the frequency of cross-cultural and mixed-raced relationships, and the role of social-culture experience in people's lives. On 'heritage tourism' and fabricated ethnicity in the case of the Scottish diaspora, see Paul Basu, *Highland Homecomings*.

[2] I say 'enervated' because nostalgia can also prompt subversive thoughts in response to the present. The word has roots in the Greek *nostos* (return home), *algia* (longing), and *algos* (pain, grief, distress). Its origins are associated with homecoming, to escape to or reach or return to a place of safety, as well as to recover or heal. 'Nostalgia' was only coined as 'homesickness' in the seventeenth and eighteenth centuries. At that time it was used to refer to a psycho-emotional condition—a yearning to return home, to safety, to the familiar—experienced by sometimes forcibly displaced people, such as domestic servants and soldiers fighting abroad. Nostalgia has long been common among soldiers in combat where it has been seen, by superiors, as another form of slacking and dodging. Nostalgia in this sense is an active longing to feel safe, to be home, to heal.

[3] No less so does imagination depend on acts of remembering.

Personal remembering

There are many ways to think about memory and remembering, both in life and in the specific context of memoir writing. I find it helpful to begin by differentiating between what I call *workaday memory* and *autobiographical* or *personal memory*. Workaday memory is attuned to our day-to-day functioning within our social-cultural surround. Workaday memory helps me remember that a red traffic light means STOP, that on Tuesday at 9:00 a.m. I have a work project deadline, and that the furnace filter needs changing and where I can find a new one. The basic functions of our everyday social surround have echoes in our workaday memory. Especially 'useful' experiences and their memories are repeated and reinforced by the routines of our day-to-day lives; they often feel close to consciousness (often it's as if we are not remembering them at all); they more or less jibe with 'what works' socially; and, because they often 'work,' they can feel rational and efficient. All this is the case even in cultures that do *not* work at all well from a human perspective, and where to function more efficiently can involve betrayals of creaturely life. In other words, rational-feeling workaday memory can participate in the irrational. The main point I want to make about workaday memory, however, is that we tend to see it as that part of our memory that is reliably accessible, functional, efficient, rational—like searching for objects in usually well-lit, well-organized, reliably signposted rooms.

The memory room up into which McGrath climbs is something else—more like a changeable world of shadows, light beams, floating glitters of dust, and dark corners. This is what I call our autobiographical or personal memory. Found here are traces of personal life as lived in the emotions, nervature, and musculature of the single-bodied self. Here are memories that are stored, shaped, and retrieved in ways determined by one's needs, interests, fears, and longings. Workaday memories may be found here as well, although with new shapes and colourings. What distinguishes autobiographical memory and remembering are their rootedness in the life of the creaturely self—that nervature and musculature I just referred to.[4] This is where the clues to the truths of our actually lived life are stored, waiting to be found and interpreted—and waiting to be made eloquent in our memoir writing voice.

Workaday memory works to help us function efficiently in the day-to-day. Let up on this work, however, and we are quickly reminded of how our memory is wider, deeper, and more complex; how its jostling 86 or so billion neurons are alive, electric, fluid, always on the move. A light bulb shatters. McGrath's 'shoebox' resists opening, but then suddenly things 'spill' out. I am in a 'serious' workplace meeting when suddenly the aroma of a colleague's homemade muffins makes me hear fiddle tunes in a farm kitchen visited decades before. Forgotten things suddenly break into consciousness 'out of nowhere.' Sensations in the present evoke an experience about which we swear we have 'no knowledge.' Sleep can help us remember; shame or trauma or social proscription can make us forget. The body–mind switches swiftly between a smell, a taste, a voice, a texture, a weight, a volume—and does so with an indifference to customary time. In McGrath's attic, something viscerally familiar suddenly brushes against my cheek; sitting over there is something 'known' but indecipherable; in a corner, mostly hidden, is something else I have forsaken, covered up in the reasons I have invented to 'account for' and 'make sense' of what has happened.

Somewhere inside myself, McGrath's imagining of remembering set up a ladder to the hot unfinished attic of my personal memory, then invited me to climb, in an instant, to where my childhood 'reading' memory was waiting. No ordinary, everyday signposting took me to this memory. Nor does it have much of an echo—any use-value—in workaday life. Its return to awareness can only be explained by some out-of-the-ordinary form of reasoning. Indeed, we need other ways of thinking about words like 'reason' and 'sense' if we are to understand the value of personal remembering and how it works.

---

[4] On my use of the terms 'creaturely,' 'the creaturely self,' and 'the live creature,' see Chapter 19.

Although our memory contains considerable cultural material, and although it uses our everyday adult experience to organize aspects of itself, all our memory is personal memory, although 'personal' in a specific sense. Perceptions and experience are taken in, stored, and remembered not as a camera records and produces the objects before its lens, but in terms of an individual's needs, interests, emotions, social situation, and bodily-sensuous engagement with the world. That is, personal memory is life *passed through* the single-bodied, creaturely self. It's here that the experiential wellsprings of memoir writing are to be found. *This is life as I have experienced it, as I remember it, as I understand it, and as expressed in my own voice,* says the memoirist through their every word. They have taken up memoir's built-in invitation not simply to voice their personal take on life but to do so as experienced and remembered within the skin of their creaturely self. This means that a memoir is not only the outcome of the writer's choices and descriptions of personal life events and relationships. It is also the result of how each person explores and resists memoir's inherent invitation to listen to the creaturely self and its memory.

Creaturely memory has its own reasons

This is how Meir Shalev describes the give-and-take between memory, creaturely remembering, and the process of memoir writing:

> Human memory awakens and extinguishes at will. It dulls and sharpens actions, enlarges and shrinks those who perform them. It humbles and exalts as it desires. When summoned, it slips away, and when it returns, it will do so at the time and place that suits it. It recognizes no chief, no overseer, no classifier, no ruler. Stories mix and mingle, facts sprout new shoots. The situations and words and scents — oh, the scents! — encrusted there are stored in the most disorganized and wonderful manner, not chronologically, not according to size or importance or even the alphabet.[5]

---

[5] Shalev, *My Russian Grandmother and Her American Vacuum Cleaner,* translated from the Hebrew by Evan Fallenberg.

The scents—oh, the scents! The memoirist Patti Miller describes how the smell of nutmeg 'connects' her not to other spices, 'as the logical side of the brain would have it,' but to her 'father and the Golden Key café in a small country town where, for the first time, [she] tasted a malted milk with nutmeg sprinkled on top' (*Writing True Stories*). Miller is describing how personal, creaturely remembering 'reasons' sideways, through processes such as sense association and synesthesia, where one sense experience or word stored in one part of the mind connects with and activates another associated sense experience or word in another part of the mind. The poet John Keats once wrote that 'touch has a memory.' In my own version of this thought, I'd say that we remember through what touches us, through how we grasp the world through the touchings of our senses.

Marcel Proust offers a much-cited example of what I mean in a passage from *À la recherche du temps perdu* (*In Search of Lost Time*). Weary at the day's end, Proust lifts to his lips a spoonful of tea with crumbs of a *madeleine* cake. Suddenly, he writes (as translated from the French): a 'shudder ran through my whole body' and an 'exquisite pleasure . . . invaded my senses.' Reflecting later on the origins of this 'exquisite pleasure,' Proust writes, 'when from a long-distant past nothing subsists, after the people are dead, after the things are broken and scattered, still, alone, more fragile, but with more vitality . . . the smell and taste of things remain poised a long time, like souls, ready to remind us, waiting and hoping for their moment, amid the ruins of all the rest; and bear unfalteringly, in the tiny and almost impalpable drop of their essence, the vast structure of recollection.'

Ghost tastes, ghost smells, ghost touches, but as solid as shudders running through the body. There they sit 'poised' as trace sensations in creaturely memory, waiting for their moment to 'invade' the rememberer.

I have quoted how Meir Shalev describes the relation between memory, the activity of remembering, the creative mind, and the emergence of memoir stories. Here is how Patti Miller describes it in *Writing True Stories*:

Underneath the efficient mind there is another darker, dimmer mind that cannot even tie a shoelace—but it does know how a story works. Not that it could tell you how, it cannot explain anything logically, it cannot argue a point, it cannot define the case. It does try to make itself heard and seen in daily life but because we have neither the time nor the quietness to see the connections, it comes across as confused and incoherent.

This dark mind seems to be made of infinite multi-coloured patterns of physical and emotional memory, insights, sensations, even dreams, flamboyantly filed in its intricate 'Indra's net' structure[6] where everything is connected to everything else—not by logic, but by poetic association. It's at the point when the rational organizing mind gives up that a writer—or anyone who demands the time and quietness—enters the dark mind. There one writes memoir, paints pictures, finds theorems, designs a new object, rediscovers childhood, realizes one has been on the wrong track, sees how change can be made . . . something new has found form.

Let's say you are writing in response to some memory—your father's characteristic mannerisms, your first funeral—and you do so mostly with your workaday, bill-paying mind. You will get the job done, but you will give the impression of observing and then reporting on your experience as if from outside yourself. You haven't done what

---

[6] Francis H. Cook describes 'Indra's net' this way: 'Far away in the heavenly abode of the great god Indra, there is a wonderful net which has been hung by some cunning artificer in such a manner that it stretches out infinitely in all directions. In accordance with the extravagant tastes of deities, the artificer has hung a single glittering jewel in each "eye" of the net, and since the net itself is infinite in dimension, the jewels are infinite in number. There hang the jewels, glittering "like" stars in the first magnitude, a wonderful sight to behold. If we now arbitrarily select one of these jewels for inspection and look closely at it, we will discover that in its polished surface there are reflected *all* the other jewels in the net, infinite in number. Not only that, but each of the jewels reflected in this one jewel is also reflecting all the other jewels, so that there is an infinite reflecting process occurring.' Francis H. Cook (1977), *Hua-Yen Buddhism: The Jewel Net of Indra*.

memoir writing as such invites you to do: to step into the skin of your memory—your physical and emotional memory, its insights, sensations, dreams—then given these memories, the fuller range of your actually lived experience, their voice.

It is in the creaturely mind and body where memory has stored the vestiges of personally lived interests, passions, fears, pleasures, annoyances, convictions, and furies—and linked them all in Indra's net. A personal example of this comes to mind: how, one day, the smell of an overheated fireplace in northern Ontario—the danger smell of scorching stone, metal, wood—suddenly set me inside my child self in front of another fireplace many years earlier . . . the smoldering fireplace of my childhood home in the 1950s into which my father had just told me to throw my 'good-for-nothing' comic book collection (*Superman* and *Wonder Woman*, of course, as well as copies of *Frontline Combat*, *Weird Suspense Stories*, and *Mad* magazine), the acrid smell of over-heated brick, my father's hurt admonishments ('Is this who I have raised you to be?'), my own cheeks burning, head hung down, speechless . . . then I am somewhere else, a few years on, kneeling in boring work, making up adventure stories in which, again and again and again, I, the full-voiced hero, stand in triumph over vanquished enemies that become more overwhelming with each telling . . . then to overheard ghost stories in a southern Ontario farmhouse, and back much further to some primordial time when all stories, no matter their disquiet, ended well . . . and now forward to here and now, remembering all this, and reflecting on my love of storytelling and writing, and my attraction to matters of voice and voicing and freedom of expression.[7]

---

[7] For people of my generation, born in the mid-1940s, it is important to recall how, during the early 1950s, North American parents were easily persuaded to see comic books and publications such as *Mad* magazine as a powerful threat to their children's moral well-being, including, perhaps most importantly, their children's acceptance of the productivist ethic of post-war culture. See David Hajdu, *The Ten-Cent Plague: The Great Comic-Book Scare and How it Changed America*. My parents, like many others, would have heard about the comic book 'plague' through politicians, their church, parent-teacher associations, and the many newspapers and magazines that published articles on how comic book

Creaturely memory does not only have an 'extravagant taste' for remembering. It also takes pleasure in using its out-of-the-ordinary reasoning to *re-member*—assemble and reveal the sense of—our inner, actually lived life. No wonder it finds favour among memoir writers.

Bodily experience and remembering our childhood

> Paradise is bolted, with the cherub behind us; we must journey around the world and determine if perhaps somewhere there is an opening to be discovered again.
>
> —Heinrich von Kleist, *On the Marionette Theatre* (1810), trans. Thomas G. Neumiller

As part of our animal—creaturely—inheritance, humans are hardwired to build memories from stored and associated bodily, sensory, emotional, and perceptual experience. As the memoirist Patricia Hampl writes, 'The beauty of memory rests in its talent for rendering detail, for paying homage to the senses, its capacity to love the particles of life, the richness and idiosyncrasy of our existence' (*I Could Tell You Stories*). All this we share as a species. At the same time, the content and workings of the human memory are highly individualized: unique inside the skin of each person. Each memory comprises trace sensations of how the

---

reading was a primary contributor to childhood deceit, mental disturbance, sexual depravity, and violent delinquency. The leading proponent of comic books as 'pollution,' Dr. Frederic Wertham, published his *Seduction of the Innocent* in 1954, followed by widely circulated interviews and articles. This was the same year that Allen Ginsberg was working on 'Howl,' and white, urban youth were quickly abandoning the music of the Crew-Cuts and Doris Day and embracing Bill Haley's 'Rock Around the Clock' (1955), Elvis Presley, Chuck Berry, and Fats Domino. Meanwhile, children were enlisted to act out comic book trials and burnings—public versions of the shame-soaked ceremony that my father arranged in our family livingroom—and legislators brought in laws to shut down the comic book trade. During my own childhood I read comics alongside novels such as H. Rider Haggard's *She* and *King Solomon's Mines*, and Robert Louis Stevenson's *Kidnapped*. As with these novels, so with the comics: it was almost certainly the dark, crazy mysteries, adventures and eroticism of their story lines and illustrations that so attracted me.

individual has physically *grasped* the world in specific material settings at specific times in their life.

By way of an example, there is a well-known story of the writer and filmmaker Jean Cocteau wanting to experience again a favorite place from his childhood. He returned to what he thought must be the site and ran his hand against a nearby wall. But the memory, the trace sensation of the experience, wasn't there. Something was missing. Had he returned to the wrong place? Only when he bent down into the position of the child he once was, and again ran his hand along the wall, did the once-experienced solid place touch him. That is, it touched and brought alive the 'particles of life' of the original, significant experience, including the associated smells, voices, expressions that were lovingly stored in Cocteau's memory. As Ernest G. Schachtel writes of such experiences: 'The forgotten experience is revived by the recurrence of a sensation that has left a record, a trace behind; or it is revived by the understanding and reliving of the bodily attitudes, muscular and vegetative, which the forgotten experience produced.'[8]

Personal memory's 'loving' storing away of the body's sensuous engagement with the immediately perceived surround has important implications for how, and whether, we remember our childhood experiences. To explain what I mean, we need to make a detour into evolutionary biology.

Humans as a species live through an exceptionally long stage of dependency, from infancy through childhood and youth. During this period, infants and young children engage the world primarily through the proximity senses: touch, smell, taste. Articulate speech doesn't yet exist or is only developing. The experiential world of infants and children is fully embodied, immediate, kinesthetic, immersive, and alert, whether

---

[8] Schachtel, *Metamorphosis: On the Development of Affect, Perception, Attention, and Memory*. Referring to Cocteau's and many similar experiences, Stephen J. Smith writes that personal memories are 'inscribed in the body, the lived body'; they are 'really the residues of our physical being.' Smith, 'Physically Remembering Childhood,' in *Phenomenology + Pedagogy*, Volume 10, 1992, available online.

this involves basic needs (hunger), emotional responses, or physical and fantasy play. Healthy children are naturally live creatures. They grasp the world—literally, sensuously, and as primary understandings—in a 'haptic' way: touching everything not only with their fingers but with their entire physical-perceptual being.[9] Children live amidst an intense, sensuous *WHY?* of curiosity, testing, and figuring out. Fantasy and actuality intermingle freely. They take great pleasure in creatively re-shaping materials; they are 'uninhibited' (an adult term) regarding their bodies; and they live amidst quick changes to their existential emotional states, such as fear, anxiety, loneliness, and the need for attachment.

As humans become 'adults,' this creaturely, haptic way of being in the world is overlaid by a more distanced, culturally defined 'rational' way of being. The distancing senses, sight and hearing, become dominant as 'adult' speech and reasoning develop. While this transformation is shared in essence by all humans, it takes specific forms from culture to culture. In his essay 'On Memory and Childhood Amnesia,' Schachtel examines the process of becoming 'adult'—and the fates of childhood and memory—in the context of modern Western culture. What he finds is a unique metamorphosis in modern humans' sense and perceptual life, in our engagement of the natural and cultural surround, in the structures of our thinking, and in the nature of our language.[10] Personal or autobiographical memory is overlaid with an impersonal, conventionalizing cultural memory. As a result, Schachtel says, the 'schemata' of the modern adult's functional, workaday memory—that is, how it organizes itself in terms of cultural milestones (first job, buying

---

[9] 'Haptic' (from the Greek *haptein*) refers to physical grasping, touching, holding, latching onto. Haptic perception refers to the way the whole creaturely self actively, sensuously interacts with and 'grasps' its environment: physically experiences its shape and volume and other material qualities, and uses this to understand where it is. In sensuously 'grasping' the things of the world we grasp their meaning. See the discussion of haptic perception in Chapter 7 of E.V. Walter's *Placeways: A Theory of the Human Environment*. Laura Crucianelli has a fine essay on 'touch hunger,' expressive touch, therapeutic touch, touch and mutualism with others, and how touch gives a sense of embodiedness and bodily ownness. Crucianelli, 'The Need To Touch,' in the online magazine *Aeon*, October 2020.

[10] Schachtel, *Metamorphosis*.

a house), everyday functioning, and cultural conventions—simply cannot 'receive and reproduce experiences of the quality and intensity of typical early childhood.'

A curtain falls between the personally charged, haptic world of children and the more distanced, conventionalizing, and calculated world of adults. Adults come to experience childhood as something like a foreign land, where the 'locals'—often viewed with a mix of condescension, sentimentality, and nostalgia—are seen as 'playful,' not 'serious,' and in need of 'discipline' and 'development.'[11] Meanwhile, adults develop what Schachtel calls, again in the context of cultural modernity, a 'normalized childhood amnesia' (in contrast to amnesia's pathological forms). We adults do not only struggle to recall, *in a personal way*, the events in our early life. More specifically, we have difficulty remembering, and finding the words for, their original, personally experienced *felt qualities* and the creaturely, haptic way-of-being-in-the-world that they represent.[12]

Remember Cocteau's experience: how his adult memory felt somehow mistaken—until, that is, he re-created the original situation by

---

[11] Heard in this are the echoes of the 'civilizing' ideology—emerging in Europe over the seventeenth to nineteenth century—that propelled the promotion of early mass schooling, industrialization, nationalism, and Europe's colonizing or 'civilizing' mission. Both the colonizers and school promoters saw their 'foreign' subjects as 'infantile,' threateningly sensual, and in need of 'development' and 'discipline'—in particular, work and time discipline, and the 'stilling' of the body. Large clocks became an essential feature of the classroom and many colonized settlements. For their part, the colonizer-adults believed (and said repeatedly) that they were acting 'for the good' of the child or the 'uncivilized.' This is part of the historical context that leads Schachtel to write: 'The world of modern Western civilization has no use for this [the child's haptic, creaturely] type of experience. In fact, it cannot permit itself to have any use for it; it cannot permit the memory of it, because such memory, if universal, would explode the restrictive social order of this civilization.' See my discussion of 'schooled' culture and writing in Chapter 1.

[12] 'We adults' should not be taken to mean all adults. Probably each of us knows a few people who have retained something of a creaturely, haptic sensibility in adulthood. One of the appeals of certain modern-era artists, such as elements of Paul Klee's work, is in how they remind us of our haptic past and dreams.

re-entering his childhood body and grasping the world, a specific wall at a specific time, with that earlier body. In order to remember his childhood, Cocteau had to break through, almost by happenstance, the curtain created by his adult acculturation. He had to *reincarnate* the earlier body–self–world connection.[13]

Opening ourselves to creaturely memory

How then can we open ourselves to autobiographical, creaturely memories, especially from our early childhood? Here are a few suggestions. See as well the advice and story prompts in Chapter 5 and the discussion of 'mapping' in Chapter 7.

Begin by removing yourself from outward, workaday commitments. Quieten your thoughts. Let them slip along the natural streambeds of your felt experience. 'Let your soul dangle' (*Die Seele baumeln lassen*), as the German saying goes.

Go to your sense of smell or touch, our most memory-laden and evocative senses. Fully take in the smell of a flower, a forest, a spice, an outhouse, your father's shirt, a perfume. Let your musing body-mind take you where it wants. Pick up a significant keepsake or tool and turn it in your hands. Like McGrath's photographs, feel the 'crimps' of the many handlings of this object.

Sketch a diagram of the floor plan of your childhood home, your bedroom, a favorite outdoor play area, family kitchen, a workplace, a secret place. Or sketch the view looking down a hallway towards other doors or rooms, or up a flight of stairs. Now physically move through one of these sketched places, stopping and turning where your feelings invite you. What do you smell or hear or find? Who else is there, or are you alone? What is happening there?

---

[13] On the experiential worlds and needs of children, see Jay Griffiths, *A Country Called Childhood: Children and the Exuberant World*. On how children create their own experiential spaces in the city, see Colin Ward, *The Child and The City*.

Choose a personally important memory for which you have only a few details. Using the details you have, your sympathetic creative imagination, and some of the phrasings listed later in this chapter from Jane Taylor McDonnell's book (the list beginning: 'I only know that . . .), create a story or personal essay associated with this memory.

Keep some note-taking device close by. Be ready for what memory suddenly offers up to awareness.

Here are a few more suggestions specific to remembering childhood experiences:

Handle objects from childhood. A doll, stuffed toy, game, cup or spoon, piece of music. Hold them, play with them, smell them, put them to your cheek and mouth.

Play as a child with children. Let go of your adult awareness and enter physically, sensuously into a child's muscular–spatial–tactile world. Get in synch with a child on their terms: down and dirty, pre-verbally, in fantasy. Immersive physical play with children can connect us directly to body sensations from our own childhood.

Return as a child to the sites of childhood experience. Do as Cocteau did—or my sister, who once returned late in life to a country road she had walked each day as a child, to and from school. She remembered a small stream running under this road, a stream where she had often stopped to play. On her return she found what she thought must be the stream, but it didn't feel right—that is, not until she crouched down low along the stream edge, ran her fingers through the buttercups and grass, then bent lower and breathed in the mosses along the water's edge. Suddenly she knew she was back inside the place, the world, of her childhood.

Return to sites that reproduce the favoured places of your childhood. Under a stairwell, under a table nestled between its legs, in a closet or attic, in a tree house.

Read books from your early childhood, or books evocative of early childhood experience. On the latter, stories and illustrations like those found in Maurice Sendak's *Where the Wild Things Are* and *In the Night Kitchen* give us a license to enter into—surrender to—states of fantasy play and reverie that can lead into the wild lands of our own earliest experiences.[14]

Read memoirs, novels, or short stories that give you the feeling of capturing the realness of childhood life. Wait for keys—a word, an image, a place, a feeling—that open doors to your own felt memories, then begin some free note-keeping on where your feelings take you.

Listening for the hooves, or getting at the truth of the past by 'making it up'

How do we write about important memories that seem to resist expression? For example, we might be missing needed details, or many similar memories have combined into inchoate feelings. Possibly we *sense* a momentous event in our early childhood, before we had the words to describe it. Or we simply must write about a family secret—our mother was taken away somewhere, that hidden letter we discovered—but where and why and what was this event really about?

When the memoirist Vivian Gornick was asked how to write about situations that resist sufficiently complete or distinct remembering, she replied 'Well, just make it up. Then see if it is true.' What did Gornick

---

[14] In recent decades, few children's book author-illustrators have evoked the world of early childhood (before about seven years old) as vividly as Sendak. Loneliness, anxiety, fear, anger, defiance (sticking out of tongues), revenge, cannibalistic and megalomaniac fantasies, exuberant dancing and playing, screaming and howling, the deep need for loving attachment, the resolving of life's times of awfulness through fantasy and reconciliation—it's all there in Sendak's stories. During the 1950s and 1960s Sendak transformed children's literature away from the nice, pretty, and docile children of the adult imagination to what he called the 'authentic liveliness' of the children he experienced firsthand, and the one he knew in himself through his personal memories. See the interview with Sendak by Nat Hentoff, 'Among the Wild Things,' *The New Yorker*, January 22, 1966.

mean? Note that she doesn't advise just making up the past. She says make it up and 'then see if it is true.' Her test of the 'made up' is whether or not it is 'true.' She suggests, as I understand her, that the aim of 'making up' an insufficiently remembered experience is, or needs to be, to make its experiential truth as eloquent as possible. The following examples, drawn in part from Jane Taylor McDonnell's *Living to Tell the Tale*, show what this can mean in practice.[15]

In *A Childhood: The Biography of a Place*, Harry Crews wants to depict his first awareness of his Self, his first 'awakening,' at four years old. In the absence of complete memories, he chooses to write as an older adult on behalf of the child. He combines the few details he does know with imagined sensate and probable details, and he then follows the boy's perceptions and emerging self-awareness as they move amongst these details: sleeping at the curved roots of a giant oak tree, waking, seeing a white dog, then seeing a house, then a red gown with little pearl-coloured buttons he was wearing, then his 'knowing' that 'my grandma made this gown' and that 'the dog belongs to me and keeps me safe.' Crews acknowledges what he doesn't remember, and evokes what is humanly probable, even likely. He uses two perspectives: the older writer's and the boy's imagined movement of attention. And he makes the situation feel real through sensate detail.

How can we bring alive a momentous but much-repeated experience that has become one soupy, generic memory? Jane Taylor McDonnell

---

[15] In an interesting parallel, historians are usually thought of as limiting themselves to available, factual evidence. But what if, despite meticulous research among the most obscure archives, the historian decides that these archives preserve only the voices of power? What about the lives and voices of people whom the record leaves mostly unheard? Answering this question, imagining a voicing of the unheard, guides the work of historian Saidiya Hartman and her research into the lives of slaves in the U.S. (*Scenes Of Subjection* and *Lose Your Mother*) and Black women in late nineteenth-century New York City and Philadelphia (*Wayward Lives, Beautiful Experiments*). Hartman attends closely to archival material but, as she says, her method of 'critical fabulation' 'troubles the line between history and imagination.' See Alexis Okeowo, 'How Saidiya Hartman Retells the History of Black Life,' in *The New Yorker*, October 19, 2020.

faced this question while writing about raising and gradually coming to understand her autistic son Paul. As a young child, Paul became transfixed by the rapidly flickering lights of the city's movie marquee. He insisted that he and his mother return to these lights night after night. There were many similar experiences—flicking light switches on and off—repeated many times. Paul loved flashing lights. When McDonnell came to write about these experiences later in life, they had merged into one inchoate memory. What to do? She began by deciding to set aside her long-held resistance to 'making up' life stories. She then proceeded to create *one* scene 'experienced many times and not remembered as a single time, but told now as a single event so that it stands for all that is forgotten.' Standing one evening under the theatre marquee, holding two-year-old Paul's hand, McDonnell uses her later understanding of her son to make his inner life more visible at this moment. She also uses this invented scene to capture her motherly acceptance of his life-world, even though she doesn't yet understand this world. It's with this one pivotal but 'made up' scene that McDonnell begins *News From the Border*, a memoir that tells the story of Paul's life and the mother's deepening understanding of her son.

In cases where you experience gaps and silences in memory, or its material evidence, McDonnell recommends acts of thoughtful wondering and speculation—and involving your reader in your efforts to fill out an incomplete past. 'It is your reflections on what you cannot know and what you imagine to be true, your frustration at not knowing more, and your willingness to actively engage the unknown which, finally, will give your narrative candor and power,' McDonnell writes in *Living to Tell the Tale*. She cites the example of Maxine Hong Kingston's *The Woman Warrior*. Early in this memoir the mother tells her daughter, the author, a cautionary story about the mother's young pregnant aunt, a mysterious 'no name' woman who drowned herself in a well. To even tell this story is to break a family taboo. This sets Kingston wondering and speculating—and we as readers wonder with her. How did the aunt become pregnant? Love? Rape? Vanity? Who was the father? The aunt is a mystery, her fate a warning, and Kingston finds she must tease out the meaning of both as a way of telling her own life story.

Important mysteries and unknowns invite us to wonder and speculate. One approach is to draw on the little you know and, using your sympathetic imagination, complete sentences such as the following and see where they lead:

- I only know that . . .
- Perhaps this is what happened . . .
- He must have thought this . . .
- To the best of my knowledge . . .
- I have not been told all of this story because . . .
- The weather at that time of year would have been . . .
- When I return to the place where he was . . .[16]

Consider inventing a diary to express a character's inner life: 'I have wondered if she kept a diary and what she might have written about at that time in her life.' Create an imagined set of letters or conversations between two people. Whatever your approach, let your reader see the limits of your reliable memory and knowledge, and see as well where you are making things up as a way of picturing missing but possible parts of a story that needs telling.

In her memoir *Object Lessons: The Life of the Woman and the Poet in Our Time*, Eavan Boland needed to remember her grandmother who died during childbirth at the National Maternity Hospital in Dublin in 1909. Boland has heard only a few facts about her grandmother's death, but finds herself returning again and again to the last hours of the woman's life outside the hospital. 'The building is still there' she writes. 'If you approach from the south . . . look down a tunnel of grace made by the houses of Fitzwilliam and Merrion squares, your view will end abruptly with the hospital, red brick and out of character, blocking the vista.' The grandmother arrived in October—and so Boland uses her knowledge of a Dublin October day, the chilled air, 'the trick of light' at this time of year, 'how the sunlight cuts the houses in half.' But then, Boland continues, the woman 'may not have come that way. She might have traveled down the unglamorous back streets . . . . It is not a long

---

[16] I have adapted these from McDonnell's *Living to Tell the Tale*.

drive. But whatever she saw that morning, it is lost. Whatever that journey yielded—the child with a hoop who never existed, the woman with the red hat I am now inventing—they were her last glimpses of the outside world.'

So far we are following a woman, seemingly alone and about to give birth, entering a maternity hospital. The situation is made all the more real-feeling by those small, almost incidental touches: the woman 'may not have come that way' but by another back street, it's 'not' a long drive. I have said that this is Boland imagining her grandmother, although Boland herself has not told us this yet. Having brought us with her thus far, Boland now, self-reflectively, draws our attention to her creative, empathetic imagining of this situation:

> This is the way we make the past. This is the way I will make it here. Listening for hooves. Glimpsing the red hat which was never there in the first place. Giving eyesight and evidence to a woman we never knew and cannot now recover. And for all our violations, the past waits for us. The road from the train to the hospital opens out over and over again, vacant and glittering, offering shadows and hats and hoops. Again and again I visit it and reinvent it. But the woman who actually traveled it had no such license. Hers was a real journey. She did not come back. On October 10 she died in the National Maternity Hospital. She was thirty-one years of age. She was my grandmother.

As McDonnell says of this passage, Boland resists 'the impulse to "know" what cannot be known [and] instead invites the reader on her imaginative journey' (McDonnell, *Living to Tell the Tale*).

What lessons might we take from these examples? Above all, don't be stymied by the unknowns and half-knowns that sit amidst personally significant memories and other experiences. Use the little you know. Empathetically imagine the possible. Give eyesight and evidence to the absent and the dead. Set in the scene the red hat that the mother might have worn but may not have. Try this street, but possibly another. Listen for the hooves. Invite your reader to be comfortable yet curious inside the always imperfect work of your remembering. Write from a sensitivity to the violations in our rememberings. And finally and always, let your remembering be guided by your creaturely sympathies.

⸺

In describing how 'the act of imagination is bound up with memory,' Toni Morrison develops this suggestive image:

> You know, they straightened out the Mississippi River in places, to make room for houses and livable acreage. Occasionally the river floods these places. 'Floods' is the word they use, but in fact it is not flooding; it is remembering. Remembering where it used to be. All water has a perfect memory and is forever trying to get back to where it was. Writers are like that: remembering where we were, that valley we ran through, what the banks were like, the light that was there and the route back to our original place. It is emotional memory—what the nerves and the skin remember as well as how it appeared. And a rush of imagination is our 'flooding' . . . . [L]ike water, I remember where I was before I was 'straightened out.'[17]

Good memoir writers are never satisfied with merely writing about their 'straightened out' self. Instead, they *remember*—in the sense of listen for, feel around for, wonder about—where and who they were before or beyond this straightened self. As Morrison says, they especially listen for what 'the emotional memory—what the nerves and the skin remember': the inner, natural flow and turns of the floodwaters or energies within us. And they work to bring to life these energies, these actually lived, creaturely qualities—Morrison's 'valley we ran through, what the banks were like, the light that was there'; Boland's hooves and red hat—through a new flooding, 'a rush of imagination,' that aims to 'get back' to what they felt, and something of where and who they were. They do so because the past is never just 'the past' but rather a source of creaturely intelligence that we can use today.

---

[17] Morrison, 'The Site of Memory,' in William Zinsser (ed.), *Inventing The Truth*.

Tony Luciani, *Talking With Her Self*. With permission © Tony Luciani. See the caption to the photograph set between Chapters 1 and 2, and other photographs from this project—*MAMMA, In the Meantime*—at tonyluciani.ca

CHAPTER 19

LISTENING TO THE VOICE OF THE LIVE CREATURE WITHIN

The mind contains more than intellect. It contains a history of what we learn through our feet. It grasps the world that meets the eye, the city we know with our legs, the places we know in our hearts, in our guts, in our memories, in our imaginations. It includes the world we feel in our bones.

—E.V. Walter, *Placeways*

All deliberation, all conscious intent, grows out of things once performed organically through the interplay of natural energies.

—John Dewey, *Art as Experience*

[A] story must be judged according to whether it *makes sense*. And 'making sense' . . . is *to enliven the senses*. A story that makes sense is one that stirs the senses from their slumber, one that opens the eyes and the ears to their real surroundings . . . sending chills of recognition along the surface of the skin. To *make sense* is to release the body from the constraints imposed by outworn ways of speaking, and hence to renew . . . one's felt awareness of the world.

—David Abram, *The Spell of the Sensuous*

If you can articulate the feelings in your body, present or past, you can generally reach your own complex truth.

—Tristine Rainer, *Your Life as Story*

As memoirists we need to return to our senses. Open ourselves to them. Let ourselves feel the *actually lived* qualities and energies of our felt experience. And in reflecting on these qualities and energies, discover how we are living and could live.

'The live creature,' a concept that I refer to often in this book, helps me think about the life of the sensing, single-bodied 'I' that is so critical to successful—exploratory, authentic-feeling—memoir writing. I take the concept from John Dewey's *Art as Experience*, where he uses it to anchor his understanding of human experience, expressiveness, and aesthetics. I have brazenly lifted Dewey's idea out of its original context and adapted it to my own purposes, although I believe I have remained true to key elements of his thinking.[1]

Dewey's sense of 'the live creature' asks us to attend to the felt qualities and energies of human experience. In the context of memoir writing, this means attending, in what Dewey would call a 'caring,' 'loving' way, to our single-bodied, felt, and actually lived *creaturely* life, as distinct from our cultural life. In this chapter I will consider certain key words

---

[1] *Art as Experience*, published in 1934, was first presented as a series of lectures in 1931. The first chapter or lecture is called 'The Live Creature.' I should note that Dewey does not discuss memoir or personal writing. My own sense of 'the live creature' is influenced by the work of writers in addition to Dewey, some of whom are referred to in this chapter and elsewhere in this book. One writer I don't mention is Maurice Merleau-Ponty and his work to understand the embodied (sensuous, sentient) experiencing self in its interactions with its expressive surroundings. Aspects of Merleau-Ponty's work have close affinities with Dewey's thinking about 'the live creature'—see, for example, Chapter 2 of David Abram's *The Spell of the Sensuous: Perception and Language in a More-than-Human World*. Abram describes his book as an 'animistic' and 'sensuous' account of Western culture's understanding of 'reason' and how this 'reason' underpins the culture's antagonistic relation with nature. Abram calls attention to the 'carnal' field' or 'biosphere' of earthly life within which we smell and taste and listen. This, he adds, is not the biosphere as 'it is conceived by an abstract and objectifying science,' but rather 'the biosphere as it is experienced and *lived from within* by the intelligent body—by the attentive human animal who is entirely a part of the world that he, or she, experiences.' I am setting aside what in my view are Abram's reductivist claims for the role of 'alphabetization,' claims that he later qualifies, somewhat, in a 2017 Afterword.

and ideas that I think are critical to successful memoir writing. Among these are *experience*, felt experiential *energies*, a *caring* attentiveness to (and engagement with) our surround, and the *qualities* of *actually lived* embodied experience. I will also ask us to reflect, perhaps in unfamiliar ways, on the meaning of the 'I' of memoir writing: both the 'I' of our single-bodied self and the 'I' of our cultural self.

It's my view that the most true-to-life memoirs are written from a 'caring' attentiveness to the shared but also disparate needs, experiences, claims, and truth criteria of both our cultural self and our single-bodied, feeling self. I will also put forward the view that attention to the life of the single-bodied creaturely self gives us a critical means of exploring the actually lived qualities of our experience at some distance from the cultural status quo and on behalf of the single-bodied 'I.' In short, a creaturely attentiveness strengthens our ability to acknowledge, name, and voice life very literally *for ourselves.*

The interplay of natural energies

For Dewey the human being is, naturally and importantly, a 'live creature.' By this he means an embodied organism understood in terms of its 'natural needs,' its 'basic vital functions,' and the 'biological commonplaces' humans share with 'birds and beasts.' Dewey asks us to consider the 'human' as something not separate from our natural, animal being, but rooted in and inseparable from it. Indeed, he says we are 'more fully alive' when we are actively engaged through our 'natural vital functions.'[2] Dewey certainly values the human ability to reflect on and make reasoned, intelligent judgments in response to our

---

2   Dewey is critical of the traditional Western cultural view that rigidly separates mind and body, and the human and natural, and extols the 'human' mental faculties while denigrating and claiming power over the body and the natural world—French thinker René Descartes's claim that the aim of knowledge is to be 'masters and possessors of nature' is representative of the still-prevailing view (see as well Footnote 14 later in this chapter). Dewey is also critical of the view that aesthetics is a unique sphere of experience and activity quite separate from everyday life.

experiences. At the same time, he argues that these processes, at their most intelligent, are grounded in the qualities and energies in our sense-based creaturely experience. His 'reason' resembles what E.V. Walter calls 'a grounded intelligence' or 'a kind of sensuous reasoning.'[3]

'The senses,' Dewey writes, 'are the organs through which the live creature participates directly in the ongoings of the world around him. In this participation the varied wonder and splendor of this world are made actual for him in the qualities he experiences.' We 'grasp' the world haptically by means of an engaged, interactive, sensuous 'touching' between ourselves and our surround.[4] This sensuous engagement in turn 'makes possible the drawing of a ground-plan of human experience upon which is erected the superstructure of man's marvelous and distinguishing experience.' In other words—and whatever else our cultural self tells us—our *creaturely grasping* of life is a foundational dimension of our *perceptual-intellectual grasping* or making sense of the world and ourselves.

One way to consider Dewey's meaning is to listen to the language he uses—active, sensuous, appetitive, qualitative, charged with energies—to describe what he calls 'the animal grace' of the live creature:

The interplay of natural energies. The self taut with energy. Inner commotion. Stir.

---

[3] Walter, *Placeways: A Theory of the Human Environment*. In *The Spell of the Sensuous*, David Abram writes: 'Whenever I quiet the persistent chatter of words within my head, I find this silent or wordless dance already going on—this improvised duet between my animal body and the fluid, breathing landscape that it inhabits.'

[4] By 'senses' I include the familiar ones (sight, hearing, touch, taste, smell), as well as others, such as our sense of another's expressive face, the experience of social touch, our sense of time, distinct sexual feelings, and our sense of movement, weight, and volume. I use the term 'perception' in its conventional sense of referring to how the mind organizes, identifies, and interprets sense experiences, although I don't follow the modern habit of associating 'perception' primarily with sight. The Latin roots of 'perception' suggests 'apprehension' not only through sight but through a sensuous 'gathering or receiving.' Sense, perception, and understanding for Dewey are always in a state of interaction, but the foundations of experience are to be found in the sensate, embodied live creature.

Places that are charged with energy.

Waves of feeling that extend serially throughout the entire organism.

Zest. Fascination. Heightened vitality.

Engaged. Interested. Events that hold the attentive eye and ear . . . arousing [the person's] interest and affording him enjoyment as he looks and listens.

Pleasurable activity. Finding satisfaction. Delightful perception.

Imaginatively participating.

Caring. Objects made with delightful care. Loving attention.

Hunger for beauty—towards the pleasing, shapely, graceful, satisfying, fulfilling.

Everything that intensifies the immediate sense of living.

Active through one's whole being.

'The live creature' is the human wanting to be—and enjoying being—'fully alive,' 'fully there,' sensuously and imaginatively engaged. Dewey gives the example of a person poking the burning wood in their fireplace. When asked why they are doing this, they say to make the fire burn better. It's a reasonable response, writes Dewey, but not the whole story. Notice, he says, how that same person's eyes concentrate on the darting flames, crumbling logs, sparks. Notice the 'zest' in their face, their fascination with the 'colourful drama enacted' before them, a drama in which they 'imaginatively participate.' What we are seeing is a dimension of experience that transforms—infuses, enhances, draws pleasure from, brings fully alive—the functional and ordinary (poking the fire). What we are witnessing, that is, is the life of the live creature: some 'inner commotion,' as Dewey puts it, 'waves of feeling,' an emotionally 'charged' moment, the satisfying of a hunger for delight and beauty, an expression—a creaturely experience—of natural animal-human pleasure and wonder.' 'Energy is Eternal Delight,' the poet William Blake once wrote, and Dewey often seems to be saying.

At one point Dewey asks us to compare ourselves to a live animal, say a fox or thrush. Notice, he says, how an animal is 'fully present, all there, in all of its actions: in its wary glances, its sharp sniffings, its abrupt cocking of ears . . . .' Dewey agrees that such creaturely or animal grace is 'so hard for [modern humans] to rival.' Nevertheless, he sees traces of the live creature everywhere: in how the 'intense grace of the ball-player infects the onlooking crowd,' the 'delight' and 'intent interest' of the woman tending her garden plants, and 'the intelligent mechanic engaged in his job, interested in doing well and finding satisfaction in his handiwork, caring for his materials and tools with genuine affection.' I'd add to this what Tess Taylor calls a parent's 'deeply animal . . . profound care' for their children,[5] and our fulfilling embraces as sexual lovers. I think as well of phenomena like the *canang sari*, the scent and flower-rich morning and evening offerings the Balinese make in their doorways: small, ephemeral ritual gestures, a frangipani blossom tucked behind the ear, 'its scent then going through your words,' according to one Balinese, the making of beauty in ways that 'your mind is surprised and happy,' says another.[6] In each instance, to use Dewey's language, we humans as live creatures 'steep ourselves' in or 'plunge into' our experience with 'loving,' 'delightful care.'[7] We become 'more fully alive,' or can sense the possibility of being so.

---

[5] Speaking with the voice of the live creature, the poet Taylor says in an interview: 'To become a mother of small beings is to realize immediately that you are deeply animal, connected to all the mothers through time, back into the dark chain of the past. It is to also realize, profoundly, that everyone alive was born, was mothered, or parented, was brought up (even if in flawed or radically imperfect ways) through acts of profound care. It also, I think, makes us aware of our common vulnerability, on the planet, as beings that need care.' From 'Writing Place in a Time of Crisis,' *Book Marks* online, April 21, 2020.

[6] Jay Griffiths's 'Daily Grace,' in *Aeon*, January 31, 2019. Griffiths brings the same creaturely observational skills and sensibility to *Wild: An Elemental Journey*.

[7] Dewey has what is today called a holistic, mind–body sense of the human, although one that is importantly grounded in the natural life of the body, its energies and sensorium. Considerable recent research supports Dewey's general view. For example, see Sarah Garfinkel, 'How the Body and mind Talk to One Another to Understand the World,' *Aeon*, February 15, 2019; Frans de Waal, *The Age of Empathy: Nature's Lessons for a Kinder Society*, 2009; Noga Arikha, 'The Interoceptive Turn,' *Aeon*, June 17, 2019; Stephen T. Asma, *The Evolution*

'Intakings and outgivings': The live creature interacts with its surroundings

Our creatureliness has a life inside us. But it also has a second life, interwoven with the first, made up of our interactions with other people and the social and natural surround. Dewey sometimes describes these interactions, in their most elementary, natural form, as energy that moves expressively *outward* from the individual into engagement with the world, then back through the live creature and out again. He associates this movement with a 'caring,' 'loving,' creative state that he compares to heliotropism in plant life: the organism's turning toward and thriving on the surrounding light. He seems to see in nature a cycle of outgoing attentiveness and engaged activity followed by a 'taking in,' 'like breathing is a rhythm of intakings and outgivings' or, cast in human terms, an 'active and alert commerce with the world.'

If nature is based on rhythmic cycles of 'intakings and outgivings,' our distinct human interactions with others, nature, and culture give these rhythms a specific shape. 'Human energy gathers, is released, dammed up, frustrated and victorious,' Dewey writes. 'There are rhythmic beats of want and fulfillment, pulses of doing and being withheld from doing.' These, in Dewey's view, are the wellsprings of human curiosity and expressive action. In the face of frustration, want, lack, the unknown, the ephemeral, and the formless, the live creature hungers for insight, for solutions, to create 'sense' and beauty. This, Dewey says, is why humans learn, how we change, and why we create—including, I'd say, why some of us might feel a hunger to write our life story.

The live creature lives between worlds of want and completion, lack and fulfillment, threatening and hospitable surroundings and relationships. We can feel 'fully alive' and we can feel fearful, anxious, dulled, and depressed—divided from others, the world, and within ourselves.

---

of Imagination; Melanie Challenger, *How To Be Animal: A New History of What It Means to Be Human;* and Laura Crucianelli, 'The Need to Touch,' *Aeon*, October 26, 2020. On the other hand, modern laboratory science is only revealing hints of what writers, painters, musicians, and other artists have long been disclosing through a 'caring' attention to their actually lived, creaturely experience.

Circumstances can encourage an 'active and alert' engagement with the world, and they can prompt a need to contract or flee. The 'interplay of natural energies'—zest, care, hunger for beauty, interest, delight—can be blocked and mutate into their contraries: nervousness, anger, guardedness, discontent, indifference, depression, and sensory withdrawal. Among these many possibilities, attention to the lived, creaturely qualities of experience helps us acknowledge and articulate the truth of the actually lived. We become more vigilant towards our 'pulses of doing and being withheld from doing'—a creaturely phenomenon so clearly expressed by Maya Angelou in her poem 'Caged Bird':

> A free bird leaps
> on the back of the wind
> and floats downstream
> till the current ends
> and dips his wing
> in the orange sun rays
> and dares to claim the sky.
>
> But a bird that stalks
> down his narrow cage
> can seldom see through
> his bars of rage
> his wings are clipped and
> his feet are tied
> so he opens his throat to sing.
>
> The caged bird sings
> with a fearful trill
> of things unknown
> but longed for still . . .
>
> . . . a caged bird stands on the grave of dreams
> his shadow shouts on a nightmare scream . . . .[8]

---

[8] Angelou's immediate reference is the experience of Black people in the United States, but the image also widens the poem's reach. Angelou's birds remind me of Paul Klee's painting *Twittering Machine* in which tiny birds, the embodiment of delicate sensate life, are caught by and being turned into extensions of some

The live creature speaks the truth of the sensate body, present and past: its doings, its feeling withheld from doing, and its longings. It is the voice not of cultural convention, expectation, and propriety, but of the more 'complex truth' of the actually lived life of every successful memoir's 'I.'

Creaturely attentiveness and authenticity in personal writing

The best memoir writing is the result of what I think of as a creaturely attentiveness or creaturely vigilance. It is this, or something like it, that I believe people who write about memoir writing are referring to when they stress the importance of attending to the sensate details and emotional charge in remembered experiences, to the energies of the directly-heard voice, to how our sympathies flow and recoil, and, as Mary Karr writes in *The Art of the Memoir*, to rendering experience with a 'carnal' or 'physical clarity, enabling your reader to get zipped into your skin.'

Karr also writes that '[i]n memoir the heart is the brain. It's the Geiger counter you run over memory's landscape looking for the precious metals to light up.' In a similar spirit, when Dewey describes the process of creaturely remembering, he writes about how 'Moments and places . . . are charged with accumulations of long-gathering energy. A return to a scene of childhood that was left long years before floods the spot with a release of pent-up memories and hopes' (*Art as Experience*).[9] Authentic personal writing always feels 'charged,' natural,

---

    mechanical, pain-inflicting apparatus, their upturned, panicky heads twittering, crying out in desperation.
[9] In his study of how humans sensuously–perceptually interact with and 'grasp' the felt energies of places, E.V. Walter describes how the ancients of the Mediterranean world talked of an 'organic mode of active observation—a perceptual system . . . that encouraged an open reception to every kind of emotional, cognitive, symbolic, imaginative, and sensory experience—a holistic practice of thoughtful awareness that engaged all the senses and feelings,' the sources of what Walter calls 'a grounded intelligence' and 'a kind of sensuous

and necessary—something that has emerged from under the skin of this writer and only this writer; something that feels like *it must be told*. Authenticity says: *This is my honest, best attempt to explore my creaturely life, and to accurately express what I have found in my own voice.*

When I feel authenticity in a memoir, it is precisely the writer's effort to remember in this way that I am feeling. Every effective memoir story, even one about another person, is a story *passed through* the memoirist's single-bodied creaturely self and made meaningful in this passage. The truest stories have been tested on the body, in the creaturely self, then listened for by the writer's 'I.' If I am reading your memoir, it's these stories I want to hear, it's this 'I' that I want to connect with.

A seeming paradox: this very attentiveness to writing from inside our skin can in turn create within the reader—even across vast distances, cultures, and centuries—an echo of creaturely recognition. The writer's 'heart' material 'lights up' the 'precious metals' in the reader, the first step in a kind of invitation to the reader to connect with the writer, even inwardly re-enact (at least feel) their experience, and use this to reflect anew on their own life.

The live creature speaks

The voices of the live creature are heard in many different forms and contexts in personal writing and other modes of personal expression.

For example . . .

I hear the live creature in the full-blossomed adolescent erotic swagger remembered in Jaquira Díaz's 'Beach City' (see excerpt in Chapter 13);

---

reasoning'—as distinct from the cool, visually centered, detached reasoning of modern science and technology (*Placeways*). The pre-modern sensibility is evident in *The Temptation of Eve* (carved by Gislebertus in the 1130s, for the lintel of the Cathedral of Saint Lazare), in contrast to the eye-centered, measured, controlling, and alienated from nature modern sensibility in Albrecht Dürer's *Artist Drawing a Nude with Perspective Device*, from his 1525 *The Painter's Manual*.

in Jay Griffiths's essay on *canang sari* mentioned earlier; in how Griffiths, in *Wild: An Elemental Journey*, renders her own sensuous experience, and that of Indigenous peoples, in the immediate natural world; in personal essays such as Virginia Woolf's 'The Death of the Moth,' Robert Louis Stevenson's 'An Apology for Idlers,' Junichiro Tanizaki's 'In Praise of Shadows' (see excerpt in Chapter 11); in Eavan Boland's poem 'The Carousel in the Park,' quoted and discussed in the introduction to this book; and through every word of Sharon Olds's memoir-like poetry, whether her subject is one's parents, childhood and youth, social events, making love, the end of love, giving birth, or dying and death.

The poet Ted Hughes imagines the live creature as a 'thought-fox' that enables him to write. In this instance it is a bold, creative, disquieting energy in the form of a fox approaching out of the night; a creature alive and delicate and curious-seeming, but also injured (a 'lame shadow'), its nose sniffing its wary way forward, its eyes' greenness brilliant, concentrated; 'a body that is bold to come,' 'coming about its own business' (in Hughes' poem 'The Thought-Fox').

The live creature appears as weight, clatter, warmth in the memory story 'Two Brass Bands' in Walter Benjamin's *Berlin Childhood Around 1900*: 'The lake lives on for me in the awkward cadence of feet weighed down by skates, when, after a run over the ice, they would feel anew the wooden planks beneath them and enter, clattering, the hut in which a cast-iron stove was glowing. Nearby was the bench where we gauged the load on our feet once again before deciding to unbuckle. When one leg then rested aslant on the other knee, and the skate slipped off, it was as though our heels had sprouted wings, and, with steps that nodded in greeting to the frozen ground, we strode into the open.'[10]

Throughout *The Old Ways,* Robert Macfarlane describes moving fully alive in—and being changed by—the natural world, as in this passage from a trek in the Guadarrama area, Spain: 'I spent that night in a dense part of the forest, surrounded by an untuned orchestra of crickets. At sunset the day's light came amber and slantwise through the pines, and

---

[10] Translated from the German by Howard Eiland.

I saw millions of particles of pollen ticking down through it, gilding by the light, a steady shower of tree dust that settled on my skin and set the air seething . . . . [Landscape] is not something to be viewed and appraised from a distance, as if it were a panel in a frieze or a canvas in a frame. It is not the passive object of our gaze, but rather a volatile participant—a fellow subject which arches and bristles at us, bristles into us . . . . [L]andscape scapes, it is dynamic and commotion causing, it sculpts and shapes us . . . .'

Late in Eva Hoffman's memoir *Life in Translation*, the live creature becomes the voice of critical self-reflection: of complaint, of questioning. Middle-aged, separated, living in New York City, navigating a busy international writing career, Hoffman writes that she has learned, 'along with my generation of American women, how to travel further; how to gain some detachment and nurture a sense of self-worth . . . . Ambition, achievement, and self-confidence are the pieties I've picked up from the environment, and if I don't always work hard, I compensate by a sort of anxiety, an inner simulation of running hard . . . . I'm in a hurry all the time . . . [But as] my father would say, 'For what is the purpose?' . . . . [While] I'm moving on, and moving away, I have a fantasy of being more like the lilies of the valley, a fantasy of quietness . . . . But we have so little time of that kind. We've become underdeveloped on the receptive side . . . . We're efficient even in telling our stories . . . though we don't always have the extra leisure for the surprise of empathy, which takes place in slow time and is hard to catch between cocktails and taxicabs.'

In the opening, 'personal' chapter of *The Spell of the Sensuous*, David Abram describes what happened to his live creatureliness on his return to North America after studying magic and medicine with shamans in rural Nepal and Bali. During his studies he has learned to sense the energy-filled, meaning-filled presence of his non-human natural surround: the 'meaningful speech' of birdsong; the life inside a ray of sunlight pouring through a chink in a roof; the way the sun's heat expresses itself in the precise rhythms of the crickets; how Balian offerings of fruit at household thresholds complete the 'gift' relationship with the nearby ants. 'I learned to slow my pace and feel,' Abram says. 'I entered a wordless dance always already going on, an improvised duet between my animal body and the fluid, breathing landscape that it inhabits.' When Abram returns to North America, some of his behaviour (like chattering with squirrels) startles his neighbours. But then he gradually begins to lose his sense of 'the animals' own awareness. He starts 'observing' the natural surround 'from outside,' as he had done before travelling. 'As the expressive and sentient landscape slowly faded behind,' Abram writes, 'I began to feel—particularly in my chest and abdomen—as though I were being cut off from the vital sources of nourishment. I was indeed reacclimating to my own culture . . . [the air] was not, here, a sensuous medium . . . [and I was left with merely] a host of body memories.'

In her 'lunch lady' story, Sonya Huber brings a creaturely honesty to her marvelling over her mid-life folds of skin: 'I raise my arm to write on the chalkboard, and the skin draped over bone and muscle swings in contrapuntal melody. I am ashamed to be caught in the act of living in skin. I hope my students are not hypnotized by the distracting motion. I hope no one sees this hammock of flesh and lumps me onto a mind's-eye heap of sad discarded women. I look up the name for loose upper-arm muscle and see "bingo arms" or "lunch lady arms." . . . As a child I didn't know this upper arm of an older female had a name. I saw a unified whole, an older woman whose flesh was a cool miracle of softness and solidity swathed in mysterious folds. You came to her with problems and she both solved them and smiled at you through layers of fondness and days, sorting like a savant all the miracles in the heart's mansion-chambers. Her hands and muscles and mind could do anything that was needed.'[11]

Dying and death, when rendered authentically, always resound with the voice of the live creature—as when the Colombian mother Fabiola Lalinde describes how at night she dreams 'with' her missing [politically 'disappeared'] son, seeing him 'return home with the smile he always

---

[11] 'The Lunch Lady and Her Three-Headed Dogs,' *Brevity*, January 14, 2017.

has' (Michael Taussig, *The Nervous System*), and in passages throughout Simone de Beauvoir's *A Very Easy Death*, her memoir on the death of her mother. '[In front of Cardin's I saw] beautiful downy dressing-gowns, softly coloured . . . . Scents, furs, lingerie, jewels: the sumptuous arrogance of a world in which death had no place: but it was there, lurking behind this façade, in the grey secrecy of nursing-homes, hospitals, sick rooms. And for me that was now the only truth . . . .' 'By her eyes she [my mother] clung to the world, as by her nails she clung to the sheet, so that she might not be engulfed. "Live! Live!"' At the funeral '[t]he priest spoke again . . . [a]nd emotion seized both of us by the throat when he said, "Françoise de Beauvoir."'

It may well be, as Dewey says, that we humans find genuine creaturely or 'animal grace' 'so hard to rival.' But writers like the ones referred to here are surely proof that the live creature lives within us—'seizing us,' 'finding' the child riding the alive carousel, challenging the 'pieties,' liquefying us, sitting in 'the heart's mansion-chambers,' dreaming loved ones back to life, clinging to the death-bed sheets. Memoir writing is our opportunity to listen for the voices of our creaturely life—to use them as guides to our actually lived life, and to see where they lead.

The memoirist listens to the voice of the live creature

Here I want us to experience the voice of the live creature through a more complete piece of memoir writing, in this case the opening scene of the first chapter, called 'Growing Up Black,' of Maya Angelou's memoir *I Know Why the Caged Bird Sings*. The scene focuses on the girl-child, Marguerite. I've chosen this scene because it invites us to experience a moment of life-changing struggle in Marguerite's life between her cultural and creaturely selves. Standing in front of her church congregation on Easter Sunday, Marguerite has forgotten the lines of the verse she is supposed to read. She suddenly feels caught inside a self that she has dreamed of being but which at this moment feels profoundly false. It is her creaturely body that prompts a questioning and, in the end, a rejection of this wishful but alien idea of herself.

Marguerite begins by trying to recite her poem in front of the congregation.

> 'What you looking at me for?
> I didn't come to stay . . .'

I hadn't so much forgot as I couldn't bring myself to remember. Other things were more important.

> 'What you looking at me for?
> I didn't come to stay . . .'

Whether I could remember the rest of the poem or not was immaterial. The truth of the statement was like a wadded-up handkerchief, sopping wet in my fists, and the sooner they accepted it the quicker I could let my hands open and the air would cool my palms.

> 'What you looking at me for . . . ?'

The children's section of the Colored Methodist Episcopal Church was wiggling and giggling over my well-known forgetfulness.

The dress I wore was lavender taffeta, and each time I breathed it rustled, and now that I was sucking in air to breathe out shame it sounded like crepe paper on the back of hearses.

As I'd watched Momma put ruffles on the hem and cute little tucks around the waist, I knew that once I put it on I'd look like a movie star. (It was silk and that made up for the awful color.) I was going to look like one of the sweet little white girls who were everybody's dream of what was right with the world. Hanging softly over the black Singer sewing machine, it looked like magic, and when people saw me wearing it they were going to run up to me and say, 'Marguerite [sometimes it was 'dear Marguerite'], forgive us, please, we didn't know who you were', and I would answer generously, 'No, you couldn't have known. Of course I forgive you.'

Just thinking about it made me go around with angel's dust sprinkled over my face for days. But Easter's early morning sun had shown the dress to be a plain ugly cut-down from a white woman's once-was-purple throwaway. It was old-lady-long too, but it didn't hide my skinny legs, which had been greased with Blue Seal Vaseline and powdered with the Arkansas red clay. The age-faded color made my skin look dirty like mud, and everyone in church was looking at my skinny legs.

Wouldn't they be surprised when one day I woke out of my black ugly dream, and my real hair, which was long and blond, would take the place of the kinky mass that Momma wouldn't let me straighten? My light-blue eyes were going to hypnotize them, after all the things they said about 'my daddy must of been a Chinaman' (I thought they meant made out of china, like a cup) because my eyes were so small and squinty. Then they would understand why I had never picked up a Southern accent, or spoke the common slang, and why I had to be forced to eat pigs' tails and snouts. Because I was really white and because a cruel fairy stepmother, who was understandably jealous of my beauty, had turned me into a too-big Negro girl, with nappy black hair, broad feet and a space between her teeth that would hold a number-two pencil.

'What you looking . . .' The minister's wife leaned toward me, her long yellow face full of sorry. She whispered, 'I just come to tell you, it's Easter Day.' I repeated, jamming the words together, 'IjustcometotellyouitsEasterDay,' as low as possible. The giggles hung in the air like melting clouds that were waiting to rain on me. I held up two fingers, close to my chest, which meant that I had to go to the toilet, and tip-toed toward the rear of the church. Dimly, somewhere over my head, I heard ladies saying, 'Lord bless the child,' and 'Praise God.' My head was up and my eyes were open, but I didn't see anything. Halfway down the aisle, the church exploded with 'Were you there when they crucified my Lord?' and I tripped over a foot stuck out from the children's pew. I stumbled and started to say something, or maybe to scream, but a green persimmon, or it could have been a lemon, caught me between the legs and squeezed. I tasted the sour on my tongue and felt it in the back of my mouth. Then before I reached the door, the sting was burning down my legs and into my Sunday socks. I tried to hold, to squeeze it back, to keep it from speeding, but when I reached the church porch I knew I'd have to let it go, or it would probably run right back up to my head and my poor head would burst like a dropped watermelon, and all the brains and spit and tongue and eyes would roll all over the place. So I ran down into the yard and let it go. I ran, peeing and crying, not toward the toilet out back but to our house. I'd get a whipping for it, to be sure, and the nasty children would have something new to tease me about. I laughed anyway, partially for the sweet release; still, the greater joy came not only from being liberated from the silly church but from the knowledge that I wouldn't die from a busted head.

If growing up is painful for the Southern Black girl, being aware of her displacement is the rust on the razor that threatens the throat.

It is an unnecessary insult.

This is writing that is only possible by a memoirist who is listening to her creaturely memories and current creaturely self. It is what authentic, true-to-personal-experience memoir writing sounds like.

Angelou succeeds here because of her 'loving,' creaturely attention to the child's physical being and self-consciousness, to the carnal realities of her situation. She looks for the truth of the girl's experience as if by moving her fingers not only through the 'angel's dust' of the girl's understandable longings, but also over the raw scraped skin of her actual life—the life of the child's physical body, her emotional life, and the associated materiality of things, such as how her anxious breath rustles her taffeta dress. By attending to the girl's embodied experience, Angelou brings alive, without sentiment or editorializing, a creaturely understanding of Marguerite's longings, clothed as they are in everything alien, everything that denies who she is.

Angelou invites us to experience something of how the girl's *natural* longings, especially for her own voice, are being distorted and betrayed at each step. She does this not by declaring this to be the case, but rather through the actual *felt* experience and thought responses of the child. We witness Marguerite's creaturely self half unable, half refusing to speak. It is as if the musculature of the girl's throat and her creaturely mind have suddenly decided, despite her anticipation of the performance, that enough is enough.

This scene's context is growing up Black in the American South, a life that is described as being 'painful' in itself and having an effect like 'the razor that threatens the throat' of the Black girl. Marguerite seems to have mostly thought and spoken in a voice not her own. Today the girl's throat-mind will scream, or refuse to speak at all. Is it surprising that she tastes a sourness on her tongue and at the back of her mouth? The body appears to be protesting the agony of the moment, but also the cultural self-ideal it has lived and voiced but can voice no longer.

Living—voicing—a false self is painful, all the more so when it is the oppressor's, as it is here. Hardly less painful is the live creature's refusal to conform, and the girl's sense of isolation that results from her new awareness. In the same breath, though, is Marguerite's experience of 'sweet release'—from peeing, of course, but also in the act of running from, being 'liberated' from, a false self. Angelou builds the scene through multiple, discordant points of view: the girl's immediate feelings and alienated wishes, the girl as more self-observant, the girl as feeling herself being watched, what her audience experiences, the narrator's objective description of the girl's material situation, and Angelou's own later, critical reflections on the girl in this situation. Each view takes its cue from the responses of the 'charged,' 'natural energies' of the girl's creaturely self. It's precisely because of Angelou's 'loving' attentiveness to the live creature in Marguerite's experience that we as readers come to participate in—feel as something of our own—the girl's struggle to understand who she really is.

This, as I said earlier, is writing that is only possible by a memoirist who is listening to her creaturely memories and current creaturely self. This is what authentic, true-to-personal-experience memoir writing sounds like.

Writing memoir as a live creature in the modern world

> [E]xperiences have never been refuted more thoroughly than strategic ones were by trench warfare, economic ones by inflation, physical ones by mechanical warfare, ethical ones by the ruling powers. A generation that had gone to school in horse-drawn streetcars found itself under open sky in a landscape in which only the clouds were unchanged and below them, in a force field crossed by devastating currents and explosions, stood the tiny, fragile human body.
>
> —Walter Benjamin, 'The Storyteller' (1936) [12]

Dewey's thinking invites us, as the explorers and tellers of our lives, to consider our interactions with the world from the perspective of the needs of the live creature—that creaturely self that Benjamin reminds us is 'the tiny, fragile human body.'

If our creaturely self was given its voice—as Angelou gives Marguerite her voice—what memoir stories would it tell of our own interactions with the world? How would it characterize the current built world and its experiential qualities? What are the qualities of our 'commerce'— our creaturely, experiential interactions—with the world? Are they characteristically 'alert and active,' or something else—and if 'active,' with what consequences for creaturely, natural life inside and around us?

When Eva Hoffman reflects on herself at mid-life in her memoir *Lost in Translation*, she notices how 'ambition, achievement'—'the pieties' of her gender and generation—create 'anxiety,' a 'moving on, and moving away,' a reduction of 'empathy,' a self that is 'underdeveloped on the receptive side.' That is, she 'grasps' the world with the attention of a live creature—a grasping or understanding that leads to a questioning of, even a momentary protest against, the prevailing 'pieties.'

---

[12] Benjamin is referring, in the mid-1930s, to the First World War, the increasing persecution of the Jews (and, I'd add, Roma and LGBTQ people) across Europe, a permanent state of economic crisis, and the re-arming of national states.

Hoffman's reflections—and Angelou's writing of that Easter Sunday scene—point to one of the live creature's most important gifts to memoir writing. By giving us a place to write that is just beyond the reach of cultural 'pieties' and everyday necessities, it creates an opportunity to reflect on *how* and thus who we actually are. It gives us the means to explore our experiences and tell our life story in their more complete, actually lived form. It gives the voice of our creaturely 'I' its rightful place in shaping our life story.

In the final chapter of *Art as Experience*, Dewey considers his primary theme in the context of the experiential qualities of modernity's institutions and everyday life. Rather than a surround that 'enhances the experience of living,' he sees the 'ugliness' of many workplaces and housing developments; 'the destruction of natural beauty'; the alienation of labour; the alignment of science and inventiveness with mechanization and profit-making; an attention to the qualities of life replaced by a calculus of quantification and profit; and a situation where 'art is [merely] the beauty parlor of civilization.' In sum, Dewey describes an 'esthetically repellent' built world that fosters not a fulfilling 'active and alert commerce with the world' but a 'narrowing' and 'dulling' of the sensorium, a 'hunger of the organism for satisfaction through the eye,' and 'less fulfillment and more repulsion than at any previous time.'[13]

I include this summary of Dewey's evaluation of modernity's built world—what I see as a live creaturely evaluation—not so much to here seek agreement or disagreement with his point of view. Rather, I include his responses, as well as Hoffman's, Angelou's, and Marguerite's, as demonstrations of what the creaturely 'I' attends to, what it notices for itself when attention is loosened from culture's own necessity-saturated

---

[13] Dewey developed his thinking for *Art as Experience* during the first 30 years of the twentieth century: that is, during the era of high imperialism, colonialism, and the First World War. He witnessed mass industrialization, the human precarity created by capitalism, the advance of corporate 'oligarchical control,' the emergence of the modern megalopolis, the forces of anti-Semitism and racism, and a resurgence of authoritarian regimes. Do not memoir writers today write amidst the continuation, and more likely the intensification and expansion (the climate emergency), of these same forces?

realisms (paying the mortgage, getting 'schooled'), its 'pieties,' the comforts of the familiar, and the rewards of 'staying in line.'

Dewey is not anti-science, -technology, or -business as such. What he asks, however, is that we attend to their effects on the creaturely sensorium, and thus on our perceptions, understanding, and actions. Dewey's 'live creature' offers us a second, and critical, perspective through which to consider (in memory and in the present) the qualities of our personal interactions *with* the world—what we experience and what we do—across our working lives, our forms of social engagement, and our relations with others and the natural world.[14]

Writing with 'loving' attention to our creaturely experience helps us fill out the 'complex truth' of our actually lived life: the life of our hearts, our guts, our memories, and our imaginations. It is to take very seriously—to respect, to really care about—the single-bodied 'I' of our life story.

---

[14] Trauma, withdrawal, dissociation, affective numbing—the responses of the live creature to the monotonous, ugly, or menacing surround—contain important truths about the actually lived effects of various elements of modernity that the 'adjusted,' 'practical' mind hides from view. Considerable evidence suggests that the sensorium of the modern live creature is 'taking in' (and warding off) the world under duress. Consider the trauma resulting from war, poverty, and environmental degradation (Griffiths, *Wild*: 'the razed Amazon [is] a mirror of terrible truth for the soul of modernity'), work-related 'burnout' (the World Health Organization calls this a 'state of vital exhaustion'), abusive behaviors, suicide, depression (a form of shutting out the disturbing surround), increasing prescription drug use, and the lengthening list of 'industrial culture' or 'modern civilization' diseases. In this context, the psychoanalyst Christopher Bollas has written about what he calls the increasing prevalence of an 'absent subjectivity' among people who struggle to be 'normal'—individuals with a need to 'lose themselves in busyness' and institutions, and an attention to things, details and 'facts,' not people. They are 'unusually steady and sound,' but they 'launder' their responses to others, 'vaporize conflict,' speak in pat phrases, and lack playfulness and imagination ('Normotic Illness' in Bollas, *The Shadow of the Object*).

Memories of looking out through a window . . . while sitting with your grandmother, or in your bedroom, during a school class, on a train or plane, in a new house, or in an unfamiliar country. Courtesy Kieran Mannix (unsplash.com).

CHAPTER 20

MEMOIR WRITING AS EXPLORATION

Memoir writing, says William Zinsser, is the 'best search mechanism that writers are given.'[1] It offers us a unique opportunity to explore our life experiences, perhaps for the first time. Memoir writing as exploration is an invitation to review, reflect on, wonder about, decipher, be surprised by, and learn from our life. It takes our writing beyond mere description while re-shaping what we began to describe. It is an occasion to ask which life experiences have been most important and why. It is a chance to better understand how and where and who and why we are. Rather than beginning with 'My memoir is about . . .,' the memoirist-as-explorer uses writing to go in search of what their actually lived life is about. They are explored through the process of writing.

Memoir writing as exploration includes two closely related activities: first, exploring our life for *personally* significant experiences, and, second, inquiring into what I call the actual 'aboutness,' the significance, of these experiences, and their influence on and meaning for our life.

Examples of memoir writing as exploration abound. Mary Karr writes in *The Art of Memoir* that she once thought that one of her stories, in an early draft, was about her mother's struggles with Alzheimer's. Later she realized that it was more likely about how 'we siblings re-discovered

---

[1] *Inventing the Truth: The Art and Craft of Memoir.*

each other through our mother's illness.' In writing his memoir *The Duke of Deception: Memories of My Father*, Geoffrey Wolff describes how he had lived with an image of his father as 'extraordinarily seedy or criminal,' only to realize later that 'the things I'd dined out on weren't emotionally accurate.' Gary Shteyngart's family held that he was an ugly ingrate as a child and youth, but in writing his memoir *Little Failure* he realized that he was actually a dutiful son and probably handsome as well.

Where are the truths of our life experiences? What people, relationships, activities, places, objects, and other sources of our personal experience really matter—and why? What really is of consequence among the familiar stories I tell about my life, those charged memories that have not yet become stories, those crucial stories I have resisted telling, or those other stories hidden until now in the folds of my life? Listening especially to my creaturely self, what stands out in the journey and the mysteries of my becoming? Who am I, this ongoing work in progress I call my 'self'?

The examined life

We humans have always reflected on our experience. We have wondered about how things work, where and why we are, who we are in relation to other people and nature, and how to live a good life. Memoir and memoir-like oral stories and writings across time and cultures demonstrate a human hunger to examine and better understand our life—and thereby live more fulfilling lives.

In the European cultural tradition, the concept of the examined life is traced back, in part, to the Greek teacher and philosopher Socrates. Traditional Greek education during Socrates's lifetime was being narrowed to what today is called 'skills training.' Learning was being reduced to a means of gaining wealth and power in society as it existed. Socrates opposed this approach. He argued that the primary goal of learning was not personal social-material ambition but rather to live a virtuous life. For this he was convicted of 'corrupting' Athenian youth and given a choice of exile or death. He chose death. In defending his refusal to go into exile, which meant for him the loss of the ability to teach and learn with others, Socrates declared, in a now-famous statement, that 'I can never keep silent, because the unexamined life is not worth living for human beings.'

Socrates was defending with his life a primary maxim of ancient Greek culture: *Know thyself*. He was also living out the meaning of the ancient Greek word *philosophy*: philo (love) and Sophia (wisdom), or love of wisdom. He believed that, as human beings, we have a unique opportunity to explore and learn from our experience, to reflect on our values and beliefs, and to seek out, live in accordance with, and defend those views that make for a well-lived, meaningful life—a life lived in the spirit of truth-seeking and integrity. When Socrates looked at his society, he saw people living like puppets of the status quo rather than from their *personal*, *creaturely* understandings and considered values. Today we call this being 'other-directed' or alienated. Socrates argued that competitive self-interest and mutual exploitation was becoming the norm. This, he said, invites increased social-administrative regulation, which in turn creates people intent on, as we now say, gaming the system. Far better—indeed, more truly human, he said—to encourage the development of inner virtue and responsibility towards others.

Socrates is a challenging model for the memoir writer. He links self-understanding with an understanding of one's interactions with the social surround. He associates thoughtfulness with questioning the status quo—a questioning based on ethical considerations. And he understands the examined life as a continuing process based on open dialogues with others and the self.

Socrates's is not the only voice from the ancient Mediterranean-Indo-Persian world of relevance to the modern memoirist. After all, the wise ones from that region gave us Mnemosyne, goddess of memory and mother of the Muses, including poetry, history, and comedy. They also gave us two other concepts that I believe add to our thinking about memoir writing as exploration. One is the ancient Greek word *theoria*, meaning in one of its senses to 'see the sights for yourself' in order to gain a broader understanding of the world. E.V. Walter says that *theoria* originally implied a specific approach to experience: 'a complex but organic mode of active observation—a perceptual system that included asking questions, listening to stories and local myths, and feeling as well as hearing and seeing. It encourages an open reception to every kind of emotional, cognitive, symbolic, imaginative, and sensory experience—a holistic practice of thoughtful awareness that engaged all the senses and feelings.'

Walter associates the term *theoria* with a second word: *therapeia*. Again the focus is on a way of engaging the subject of one's experience. *Therapeia*, he says, means 'close attendance' to or 'caring' for something, in the sense that farmers cultivate their fields and parents attend with care to their children. According to Walter, the ancients called philosophy '*therapeia* of the self.'

Applied to the concept of 'the examined life,' *theoria* and *therapeia* suggest the active, sensuous, receptive, caring, creaturely experiencing of and inquiry into the world *for oneself*—or as Walter writes, a 'holistic practice of thoughtful awareness that engage[s] all the senses and feelings.' It is something like this, I believe, that memoir writing as exploration invites us to undertake.[2]

Interestingly, Walter adds that many early '*theorists*' were travelers. Among them was Socrates's contemporary Herodotus, who used what he experienced and heard firsthand to inquire into and learn about the world. Herodotus eventually gathered his chronicles under the title *Inquiries*, a word translated today as *Histories*. Herodotus explored the near world of his time. The modern memoirist explores their self in the world. As active, caring observers, as 'theorists' and 'therapists' in

---

[2] Walter, *Placeways: A Theory of the Human Environment*. Although Walter is not using *theoria* in the context of memoir writing, his subject (the human experience of place) is not far off. His reference to a 'caring' attentiveness is reminiscent of John Dewey's sense of the live creature's 'caring' or 'loving' attention (see Chapter 19).

the senses just described, both undertake inquiries based on an open receptiveness to the experienced present and past—and both chronicle their findings in 'histories,' partly cultural, and deeply personal.

Unearthing our actually lived experience

As explorers of their life in the world, the most interesting memoirists actively, receptively observe with all their senses. They listen and question with a caring, creaturely curiosity. They haptically, thoughtfully grasp—sense and make sense of—the evidence held in their single-bodied, creaturely self. What I call 'the evidence' Mary Karr calls our 'actual lived experience.' As she writes in *The Art of Memoir*:

> [U]nless you're looking at actual lived experience, the more profound meanings [of your life] will remain forever shrouded. You'll never unearth the more complex truths, the ones that counter the convenient first take on the past. A memoirist forging false tales to support his more comfortable notions—or to pump himself up for the audience—never learns who he is. He's missing the personal liberation that comes from the examined life.

We will return to a number of things Karr says in this passage. For the moment, however, I want to ask what it means to 'unearth the more complex truths.' Here is one example, taken from Vivian Gornick's *The Situation and the Story*. Gornick has attended a memorial service where one eulogist in particular has deeply moved her. The eulogist had been trained by the deceased person, a doctor, who she recalled as a conscientious, effective mentor. Why, Gornick wonders, had the speaker's words been so affecting? Gornick concludes that in preparing for her presentation, the eulogist seems to have really opened herself to the *actual lived* material of her relationship with the doctor, including how painfully vexing and dismissive the doctor could be. Gornick calls the two women 'talented belligerents.' The eulogist then seems to have asked—honestly, for herself—who the doctor was in her life, and who she was to the doctor. What does it mean to have known her? What do I want *my* remembrance to really evoke about this person and our relationship? What is it that I really need and want to say for myself?

All the other eulogists saw the service as an occasion to offer the customary praise. Gornick's eulogist considers what she will say by exploring what mattered most in the raw material of her personal experience: her admiration for the doctor as well as the doctor's 'profoundly cutting,' hurtful behaviour. Then she 'composes' and communicates to others the results of this inner exploratory effort. She has searched for what she, the person in her own skin—her creaturely self—feels and thus needs to say. She has been true to the 'more complex truths' of her 'actual lived experience.' The result? As Gornick says, 'The better the speaker imagined herself, the more vividly she brought the dead doctor to life.'

Some impediments to exploring our life experiences

There are a variety of forces that can confound the exploration of our life experiences. Among these is a concern about what others actually say or might say or think—a subject I discuss in Chapters 8 and 21. Among other impediments I would highlight the following:

Familiarity. Frequently told life stories—told by oneself, family, or friends—can develop an aura that makes their significance self-evident and resistant to questioning. These are often the stories with which first-time memoirists begin. They are readily accessible to consciousness, they can be told with relative ease, and they feel comforting. At the same time, they come to act like a fixed photographic image that replaces the original experience. This image becomes the source of the story and can even come to set limits on 'sensible' questions about itself. By contrast, memoir writing as exploration de-familiarizes the familiar. The writer questions the 'sensible'—and the lore and wished-for truths that have become bound up with oft-told tales. They try with 'attentive care' to feel something of the original experience: to restore its sensations or recreate their physical presence in the situation. What actually *did* happen? What *did* I feel? What *was* all that about?

Rationalizing the past. There is a form of 'making sense' of our life that can impose a false rationality over our life story. This may be especially true for those of us writing later in life. We write as if this life event or stage followed naturally from the previous stage and led naturally to the next stage. But whose actually lived life is like this? Isn't life an unfolding of immediate experiences, something about to be ventured into, a thing that is sometimes planned but mostly unknown? Writing-as-exploration remembers those personal crossroads and thresholds where we have stood, uncertain, eager, wondering. It recalls the surprises a few steps beyond the crossroad, those interests pursued and longings forsaken, the role of both determination and good luck, of both plans and happenstance. It notices how things can gather and then collapse and then come together in a new way, leaving you confounded or alarmed or elated. The mind works hard with memory to make sense and create order, retrospectively. Actual life—life in progress—is something else. The most compelling memoirists return to their life in its unfolding—and look for sense in this.

The anxious ego is another force against writing-as-exploration. Here is Karr's memoirist who forges 'false tales to support his more comfortable notions—or to pump himself up for the audience.' It's rare for memoirists to tell 'false tales' deliberately. What I am referring to are memoir stories selected and shaped by mostly unconscious inner needs. The writing flows not from a genuinely exploratory approach but from fixed ideas the writer has of himself. He needs to see himself and be seen in a certain way: often, at least in modern Western society, as a grinder, as inwardly 'together,' 'resilient,' always progressing, not infrequently overcoming challenging odds. He's the memoirist as hero, or hero-like. Writing-as-exploration hammers away at the wall of fixed ideas and monuments to the heroic self. Questions from friends or from fellow writers in the memoir workshop setting might serve the same purpose.

Family secrets and lies can misdirect or block our inquiries into our life. In a particularly dramatic example of this, Mary McCarthy writes in *Memories of a Catholic Childhood* about a photograph of her and her siblings, 'all looking very happy,' well-nourished, clean, enjoying a pony ride. The photograph and others like it were sent to distant relatives by the children's family guardians as proof that the children were being well cared for. In fact they were malnourished, regularly beaten, denied toys sent by the relatives, and had their mouths taped nightly 'to prevent mouth breathing.' The photograph's misrepresentations were part of a pattern in which the guardians surrounded the orphans with lies about their dead parents and background, and insisted that any personal memories the children had were also lies. For McCarthy and her brother Kevin, these lies led, she writes, to a lifetime of 'burning interest in the past.' They became explorers in search of their actually lived childhoods, 'like two amateur archaeologists, falling on any new scrap of evidence, trying to fit it in, questioning our relations, belaboring our own memories.'

Trauma. A kind of amnesia—at least an inability to voice what we know—can come to surround traumatic experiences, such as childhood and domestic abuse, war and civic terror campaigns, or a broken relationship. Emotional pain is difficult to re-enter, as are the often-associated feelings of humiliation, self-loathing, self-pity, resentment, and murderous rage. Even aspects of 'ordinary,' everyday life can induce forms of stupor that makes precise, qualitative recollection (and exploration) difficult. How to explore such experiences? The writer's journal is one safe place to examine—find the words and syntax for—a distressing experience. Your memoir writing group can be another safe space, with the added benefit of empathetic listeners. Some writers write out pain by switching to the third person pronoun (she/he)—as Thomas Bernhard sometimes does in *Gathering Evidence: A Memoir* when describing the anguish of living in a Nazi-era boarding school. Alternatively, professional counselling may be your best choice, especially combined with journal writing and a writing group. Finally, take courage from those who have been able to name the actually lived, felt truths of their lives. And offer courage to others by being loving, creaturely listeners. With courage in the room, who knows what might happen?

Exploring what is important in our experience

How does one experience come to be seen as important and another not so much? What do we mean when we suggest that such-and-such an experience is important? How have we made that choice? Family members, friends, and the external and internal voices of culture are often ready to choose for us, although on their own behalf, using their own perspective, values, and norms. Writing-as-exploration seeks to answer such questions for our self.

Here we look at three varied examples of what I mean.

In 'Ruth's Song (Because She Could Not Sing It),' Gloria Steinem's reflections on her mother's mental illness, Steinem asks why the family saw the mother's illness as 'natural,' whereas Uncle Ed's breakdown was seen as a 'mystery of importance.' 'Happy or unhappy, families are all mysterious,' Steinem writes. 'We have only to imagine how differently we would be described—and will be, after our deaths—by each of the family members who believe they know us. The only question is, Why are some mysteries more important than others?' Why was the family fascinated with the 'mystery,' the claimed unexpectedness of the man's breakdown, whereas the woman's was to be expected? An important piece of the answer, Steinem argues, is in how the 'natures' of men and women are understood culturally. Because of this, and in order to not betray her mother's life experience, Steinem can only write about her mother by thinking *against* the family's internalized cultural assumptions and understandings.

In her essay 'He and I,' Natalia Ginzburg juxtaposes Western cultural commonplaces about marriage—compatibility, for example—with her take on her actually lived marriage. She quickly draws us into a curiosity-driven, candid, sometimes irritated, and often humorous cataloguing of the actualities of her and her husband's aggravations, differences, trade-offs, appreciations, gratitude, her own misgivings, her own complicity in the annoyances—and the mystery of why *him*, why *her*, and why the two of them who have stayed together all these years. Each detail implicitly questions the veracity of the learned and familiar cultural platitudes associated with married life; indeed, the essay is a good example of de-familiarizing the familiar. We are being invited to become newly sensitive not only to the complexity of our own marriage but to the extraordinariness of marriage itself, especially those aspects that leave us so helplessly convinced and unconvinced, so implicated and so incredulous. As Vivian Gornick says, Ginzburg not only digs and digs through the truisms towards the lived truth; she allows herself to be surprised, stunned even, by what marriage *actually* means.[3]

In *Writing About Your Life*, William Zinsser includes several examples of how cultural assumptions about 'significant' personal experiences can block the recognition and exploration of the actually lived. One story in particular concerns his involvement in the Second World War. This 'involvement,' he writes, was the 'turning point' in his life, 'broadening what I knew and how I thought about the world.' At first glance, we might think Zinsser is going to write about military service and battlefields. It's this that will be personally life-changing. But no, that's not what happens. Instead, he summarizes the 'turning point' as follows: 'the only stories I ever wrote about the war are the two I've briefly retold here: one about a train ride across North Africa, the other about a summer in Florence. Neither is about the war itself. They are stories about how the war changed *me*.'

The lesson Zinsser draws from this? 'Your biggest stories will often have less to do with their subject than with their significance: not what you did in a certain situation, but how that situation affected you.' Zinsser is moving 'significance' away from what we have been acculturated to think of as its rightful home (the commonly recognized social-cultural event, a war, and our involvement in it) to the event as actually lived

---

[3] Gornick, *The Situation and the Story*.

under our skin. He is not saying that the direct experience of the Second World War cannot be a 'turning point' in a life, cannot be lived from within as 'significant' experience. His point is that the exploration and naming of what is 'significant' experience in memoir writing is not to be arbitrated by the collectively defined event. Instead it needs to be named in relation to how the broader 'situation' associated with this event is lived out inside the human body, one person at a time.

Writing as a discovering of what is important

As these examples suggest, the personal meaning and meaningfulness of a memory or experience—what I call its actual lived *aboutness*—can be but is often not self-evident. Rather it is something we have to go in search of. 'I write entirely to find out what I'm thinking, what I'm looking at, what I see and what it means,' says the essayist Joan Didion. James Baldwin takes this a challenging step further: 'When you're writing, you're trying to find out something which you don't know. The whole language of writing for me is finding out what you don't want to know, what you don't want to find out.'[4]

I write to discover what I know. I repeat this while being aware that another adage of personal writing, in fact one I use many times, says: *Write what you know.* How can both be true? Well, they just are. 'Write what you know' is an excellent place to begin writing. It gets us going. If we interpret it to mean 'Write what you know in your creaturely self,' it's good advice to follow at any time.

On the other hand, 'Write to discover what you know or what needs more complete knowing' introduces a new dimension to writing: the act of writing from a place of critical, self-reflective curiosity. This is the basis of the exploratory approach. The memoirist-as-explorer does not 'know it all.' Indeed, one principal reason they write memoir is to

---

[4] Didion, 'Why I Write,' *New York Times*, December 5, 1976. The Baldwin quotation is from an interview in *The Writer's Chapbook: A Compendium of Fact, Opinion, Wit, and Advice from the 20th Century's Preeminent Writers.*

become newly aware of their life here and now, to be open to being surprised, to come to an understanding, for today, of where they have been and who they are.

Anne Lamott includes an excellent example of this in *Bird by Bird: Some Instructions on Writing and Life*. She compares writing-as-exploration to watching a Polaroid image develop. 'You can't—and, in fact, you're not supposed to—know exactly what the picture is going to look like until it has finished developing.' By way of example, Lamott describes how she once assigned a writing topic on eating school lunches, and then how she wrote on the topic along with her students. She chose the subject because, as she says, 'It only *looked like* a bunch of kids eating lunch. It was really about opening our insides in front of everyone. Just like writing is. It was a precursor of the showers in seventh- and eighth-grade gym, where everyone could see your everything or your lack of everything . . . . The contents of your lunch and whether or not you and your family were Okay.'

As Lamott continues her own piece of writing, she remembers how school lunchtimes are fraught with so many invisible codes ('regulation' white bread versus the mortifying other kinds) and an intense self-consciousness. Then suddenly, emerging out of the Polaroid's murk, she is standing 'alongside the kid against the fence,' his scuffed shoes, the guy who walked not on sidewalks but through weedy lots, dogs yipping at him . . . and 'If you so much as glanced at him, a visible empathetic arc would stretch between you, like a rainbow . . . .' As she realizes later, 'the boy against the fence appeared out of nowhere—I had no idea when I started writing that he was in my memory. To me, he is the most important thing that came out of that exercise.'

School lunches and all those life-sucking codes? Sure, they may be important enough. But for Lamott they are not as important as the power of the sudden memory of that rainbow arc connecting her and the scuffed-shoed kid against the fence—a *body-lived arc* that will surely become conscious if she dares look his way. It's writing and the remembering, feeling, creatively self working together that make this discovery, that lift the past at its most significant—the sudden tremorings of that fascinating, consequential, connecting erotic rainbow—out of the murk of memory.

As Lamott says, you can't have any way of fully knowing what a particular piece of writing will look like when you first begin. If you do, you're writing within the four walls of the already obvious. You're writing to be reassured, not to learn. Writing to learn is to be open to the life that emerges from the Polaroid's grey murk. It's to patiently, feelingly allow the writing process to reveal what it, the 'subject,' is actually, personally about. The best memoir writing takes us to that *something compelling* that has lodged itself somewhere hardly conscious in the nervature of our memory. But what and why? To get closer to an answer, to allow it to disclose itself, the memoirist explores their experience. They write. They open themselves to their deep creaturely self. They wonder, question, reflect, keep writing, do some research, then re-write to build on what they and their writing are discovering: that charged element in an experience that the live creature knows is 'significant' and has never forgotten.

Exploring the context on the way towards understanding

Exploring our life experiences includes exploring their *contexts*. Indeed, human understanding depends on knowing the context—the who, what, where, when, how, why—of a situation, experience, or person. We understand things in context. When my logging-truck-driver friend thinks of a forest, he 'sees' food on the table and a roof over his family's head. When my ecology teacher friend thinks of a forest, she sees trees communicating with each other and feels the earth's, and our own, healthy breathing. Our understanding—of a forest, a 'Canadian,' what someone says, and how we hear it—depends on our sense of the context. Contexts are always constructs: a particular naming, selection, and arrangement of 'the facts' forged from a mix of material circumstance, values, interests, and perceptions that are themselves determined by personal experience and cultural factors.

Indeed, cultures themselves create a multitude of contexts (e.g., for understanding work, love, fear, the body, gender, measures, time, death) which, although also constructed over time, can come to appear inevitable and 'natural'—that is, not constructed at all.

'Context' in personal writing can include details about a character's appearance or behaviour, circumstantial and background information, facts that establish the temporal or physical setting, and the writer's biases, values, and beliefs. Contextual details are always orienting our thinking as writers as well as our responses as readers. Context creates understanding through implied comparison and relationships. It suggests this person, not that one; here, not there; then, not now; *this* emotion among possible emotions; *these* reasons rather than those; *this* smell compared to that, *this* touch, *this* tone of voice, *this* characteristic quirk.

Context is essential for self-understanding and thus for memoir writing. By way of example, I have found that my own work of self-understanding must attend, at least in part, to those experiences that hinge the 'personal' and 'family' to the specific social-historical and geographical surround of my childhood and youth. My self is a bodily self entwined with a historical-cultural being. My parents' economic success during the 'boom years' of the 1950s enabled the beginning of my life of often-assumed, unaware privilege. I grew up middle class and white on Canada's west coast, far from the cultural centres of political power and Anglo-Canadian nationalism, even while I experienced both very immediately through my father. I, like so many others of my generation, was invaded by the mass media of radio and, soon after, by television and its mass, image-centered ceremonies (e.g., Kennedy's assassination and funeral), as well as by market-driven mass music, by 'youth culture,' and by the relentlessly hectoring world of advertising. Into every living room, tucked between dinner and bedtime, came images of 'weapons testing,' Cold War menacing, and historical images of the bombings of Japan—the germination, deep within, of what Czesław Miłosz calls a 'terror . . . and a foreboding of what was to come.'[5] Being born into this specific time and place was a matter of happenstance. But its particulars—its materials-become-experience-become-self—are touchstones of who I am.

The critical exploration of the contexts of our experience can name the *actually* disturbing and abnormal in 'the normal.' On the other hand, unexamined contextual 'facts' can narrow and create blind spots in one's self-understanding. For example, in recounting the place where I grew up near Vancouver in the 1950s, I'd likely begin by describing the familiar built environment of the time: the orderly, gridded streets with European settler names, like Johnston, Stevenson, Scott, and McLellan; the recently assigned Arcadian place names like Ocean Park and Crescent Beach; playing television and comic-book cowboy-and-Indian adventures deep in the dark woods. Life there and then was 'as it should be' and good.

All this is factually true. But stopping here leads to a historically myopic, naïve sense of the near world in which I grew up. It is to not explore my childhood world as the inquiring, historically sensitive Herodotus would have: listening to stories, asking more questions, exploring local myths, experiencing 'for themselves,' moving back and forth in time, being receptive to every kind of emotional, cognitive, symbolic, imaginative, and sensory experience. I can only claim to begin to understand where I grew up if I also take into account how, a mere fifty years earlier, those same settlers had clear-cut the nearby ancient forests in a single decade. Or the fact that beneath those surveyor's streets and the nearby shorelines—beneath our children's feet—once wound the footpaths of the Semiahmoo, Kwantlen, and other Coast Salish peoples, people (at least the few then still alive) who in the late nineteenth century were hemmed in on a stamp-size parcel of land on the margins of the town of White Rock where 'they' ('those Indians') were mostly invisible to 'us.' Or how the adults of my childhood seemed to see everything in these so recently manufactured surroundings, and the violence at their centre, as

---

[5] From Miłosz's memoir *Native Realm: A Search for Self-Definition*.

unremarkable—my father did have a keen interest in Canadian history, but only of the settler, nation-building kind.

The memoirist-as-explorer questions the context, especially its taken-for-granted 'facts.' Exploring my boyhood pleasures as an adult means revisiting the circumstances of those pleasures in themselves, but also exploring how the child's soft soul was imprinted with the culture's amnesia, turning predation into racially laced and appealing play, adventures, and romance.

Some last words

Use writing to go in search of your life—to discover what you know, the actual personal significance or aboutness of an experience, what your body remembers but you don't yet understand, what you don't want to know and yet feel a need to know.

Begin writing about an experience in your private journal. Use this private place to discover what really needs saying—and say it. You can decide later what you want to develop and share.

Run your heart's Geiger counter over your live creaturely memory. See what lights up. Listen for the tremorings.

Approach your memoir writing as if you are a stranger returning to the world of your life from afar. Question the context: the personally 'obvious' and collective commonplaces. Ask about things that your 'at home,' 'local' self stopped asking years ago. Yes, you know something about humans and how the world turns. But as a stranger arriving from afar *here and now* in the land of your life, set out to make sense for yourself what others (and your 'at home' self) take for granted.

Don't rush to conclusions about what is important and why. Mull, weigh, guess, sense, think, wonder. Set aside your know-it-all self long enough for the Polaroids of your actual experience to develop.

Have courage to question your normal human vanities and their defenses, the self's blind spots. Explore your self's dislikes and yet-unmet longings, your passions, those moments when you stood at your own crossroads and thresholds.

In the end, show yourself trying to more fully understand your becoming and who you are. This is what will bring you alive—feel authentic—in my experience. This is what interests me as your reader.

A number of things have been said in this book about 'modern times' and 'modernity,' especially what I call its experiential quality of 'overwhelmlitude' (see chapters 11 and 19). But modernity is many things, and our lives are not entirely shaped by its forces. How have you experienced 'modern times' in your own life? What life stories best express these experiences? Courtesy René Böhmer (unsplash.com).

CHAPTER 21

ON BEING TRUE, OR WRITING TOWARDS THE REAL RELATIONSHIP WITH WHAT IS

> Truth for anyone is a complex thing. For a writer, what you leave out says as much as those things you include. What lies beyond the margin of the text? The photographer frames the shot; writers frame their world.
> —Jeanette Winterson, *Why Be Happy When You Could be Normal?*

> Tell the truth, or someone will tell it for you.
> —Stephanie Klein, *Straight Up and Dirty*

> Truth seems to want expression.
> —Anne Lamott, *Bird by Bird*

> It is a joy to be hidden, but a disaster not to be found.
> —D.W. Winnicott, *Playing and Reality*

In her *Memories of a Catholic Girlhood*, Mary McCarthy writes, 'This story is so true to our convent life that I find it almost impossible to sort out the guessed at and the half-remembered from the undeniably real . . . . I am not absolutely certain of the chronology; the whole drama of my loss of faith took place during a very short space of time.... The conversations, as I have warned the reader, are mostly fictional, but their tone and tenor are right. That was the way the priest talked, and those, in general, were the arguments they brought to bear on me.'

In clarifying what she means by 'this story is so true,' McCarthy is speaking to a set of tacit but binding understandings between the memoir writer and their reader, what Mary Karr calls the 'truth contract' between writer and reader.[1] Under this implicit contract, the memoirist is understood to be exploring and writing about their actually lived experience. They are making a serious, self-reflective effort to be true to what they remember, feel, and understand, here and now. Their writing is a working *towards* the real relationship with what is. In effect, the memoirist is saying: *Here is my best take on my experience. Here are the facts as I know them. Here is what feels important. Here are the edges of what I know and don't know. Here is how I understand things at this time.*

Given this starting point, we can set out several key elements of the work of 'being true': the writer's representation of their real relationship with the actually lived. First, experiential truth is *constructed*: something created out of McCarthy's undeniably real, the uncertain, the guessed at, the half-remembered, and the 'fictional' but 'right.' Second, experiential truths are the result of individual self-reflective work that takes place amidst the complexities of remembering, and the play of various perspectives, interests, values, and understandings in the here and now. Third, it follows that all representations of our experience are contingent and provisional. There are no fixed, final truths in

---

[1] Karr, *The Art of Memoir*. The word 'truth' has varied meanings, most of which are touched on in this chapter: (a) a class of real things and events, as in 'facts,' (b) capitalized Truth, referring to a transcendent, fundamental or spiritual reality, (c) a judgment, proposition, or idea that is said to be true or accepted as true, (d) fidelity to an original, a usage associated with 'authenticity,' (e) an accepted social standard or cultural norm or ideal, and (f) sincerity (sometimes authenticity) in action, character, and utterance.

experiential matters, and there is definitely no unconditional Truth. We will likely 'see things' differently in a few years, just as we 'saw' our life experiences differently 10 or 60 years ago. Finally, although our search for experiential truth uses facts and the 'undeniably real,' it is something *beyond* facts and their mere reporting. Truth is what we make of the evidence. It is that something new that is worked up using the evidence. This 'working up' is the activity of critical self-understanding.

As Winterson says, truth in personal writing is a complex thing. It's mutable as well. Nevertheless, memoirists like McCarthy and many others still lay claim to the possibility of expressing the actually lived truth of their experience.[2] Not only this, many of the most interesting memoirists let their reader experience something of this truth-seeking work for themselves. They expose what Karr calls the 'edges'—Winterson's framings—of their memories and understandings. They let us see how these 'edges' are determined by their interests, values, longings, biases, and prejudices. In other words, we experience them feeling and thinking in search of personal truth on the page.

---

[2] Some personal writers disagree. Willie Donaldson argues that personal writing is the avoidance of the truth. 'The version of ourselves we present to the world bears no resemblance to the truth. If we knew the truth about each other we could take no one seriously. There isn't one of us who could afford to be caught. That's all life is. Trying not to be found out.' Quoted in William Giraldi's *American Audacity: In Defense of Literary Daring*. For his part, André Aciman writes that 'all memoirists lie. We alter the truth on paper so as to alter it in fact; we lie about our past and invent surrogate memories the better to make sense of our lives and live the life we know was truly ours. We write about our life, not to see it as it was, but to see it as we wish others might see it, so we may borrow their gaze and begin to see our life through their eyes, not ours.' Aciman, 'A Literary Pilgrim Progresses to the Past,' *New York Review of Books*, August 2000. On writing to see our life 'as we wish others might see it,' see the discussion of 'self-idea' in the next section of this chapter.

Some obstacles to 'being true'

The memoirist is expected to adhere to basic, widely shared facts (dates, places, names). They are not supposed to invent details, or if they do, they are supposed to tell us what they are doing and why. These are basic understandings between memoirist and reader, part of the 'truth contract.' Beyond this, however, we enter memoir's unique 'truth' world of uncertainties, approximations, and mutability, what Karr calls memoir's world of 'perhaps' and 'maybe.'

The work of 'being true' is delimited from the start by what we remember, how we remember, and how we interpret and represent what we remember. Each memoirist includes some experiences and excludes many others. We highlight this element and avoid another, we compress and elaborate, we speculate and fabricate. We rationalize the irrational. *They meant well. It must have had a purpose.* Perfectly natural-seeming experiences—how familiarity makes things unremarkable—can also operate against truth-seeking. And, on top of everything else, there's intimidation and threats of libel.

Well before we get to threats of libel, human relationships can confound and constrain the work of being true in many other ways, not infrequently making it, as Patti Miller says, 'messy, confronting and fraught with danger' (*Writing Life Stories*). Each person we know and each grouping with which we are associated has its own understandings of and attachments to what is true. As a result, we 'edit' what we say and write, some of us more, some of us less. We do this for many reasons, including the comfort of 'fitting in' or a fear of 'standing out' or feeling apart and alone.[3] We leave unexpressed a lived truth in order not to antagonize or inflict pain on others, cast ourselves in a less than admirable light, or embarrass ourselves or others. Do we or don't we write about our father's affairs, and risk breaking our mother's heart or

---

[3] One noteworthy novelistic study of the self's fear of 'standing out' is Christa Wolf's *A Model Childhood* (also translated as *Patterns of Childhood*, the German title is *Kindheitsmuster*), in which Wolf reconstructs and reflects on her childhood and youth in Nazi Germany.

deeply upsetting our brother or sister? Perhaps we don't want to invade another person's privacy or breach our own. We might feel unease about where an expressed truth might lead. What will your children feel, for instance, if you write that you never wanted to have children, least of all the three that followed the first?

Social conventions—those around us as well as those that have insinuated themselves inside us—can also lead us to not write what we know, including truths that define who we are. If people had known in the 1960s and 1970s that the marvellous children's book writer-illustrator Maurice Sendak was gay, would they have introduced his books to their children? Do you write about the several years you worked as a prostitute during university in order to pay your way to becoming a doctor? What parts of our self get ignored or denied by internalized cultural ideals such as 'success' and 'resilience,' 'manliness' and 'womanliness'? In addition, we live amidst external and internal pressures to 'be nice,' to 'let bygones be bygones,' to 'not stir the pot.' Women especially may be acculturated to feel they should 'think of others first,' 'keep the peace,' and ensure everyone 'gets along.' Miller comments that '[f]or many women writing a memoir, this can be the least conscious, but strongest, pressure against truth-telling' (*Writing True Stories*).

One more obstacle to being true, at least a complicating factor, warrants special attention. I am referring to our ideas about who we are, what I call our *self-ideas*. Self-ideas are the expression of a need to see ourselves in a certain light and to give our life coherence and intelligibility. As such, they are major influences on memoir writing. Indeed, to the extent that self-ideas guide our writing, the memoir we set out to write—and actually do write—typically becomes a case for their defense. By contrast, the exploratory approach to memoir writing discussed in the previous chapter challenges our self-ideas. In this case 'truth' becomes a truth-seeking, a writing towards the memoir that *wants to be written*—especially the memoir that our creaturely self and its actually lived life wants written. This is difficult work, not least because the writer finds himself disputing what offers succor. We will look at an example of this in a moment, but, first, a few more thoughts about self-ideas.

Self-ideas are formed from a charged, shifting mix of experiences, memories, interests, needs, and yearnings that are largely semi-conscious or unconscious, especially in the absence of critical self-reflection. They are integral elements of our reflexive, unthinking sense of self, at least that part of the self that 'makes sense' of our inner blind spots and illusions. Yes, self-ideas can be involuntarily challenged—and sometimes modified, even overturned—by new experiences, such as the arrival of adolescence, the experience of displacement and dispossession (e.g., becoming a refugee), a 'brush with death,' the attraction of new ideas, becoming infatuated, an injury or chronic condition, or approaching death.[4] The best memoirists zoom in on these especially revealing, transitional, new experiences in their lives. But self-ideas also lead the resistance to the 'new' by promising to re-establish—even adapt and deepen—a familiar, reliable, often wishful and reassuring coherence to life, in spite of our actually lived experience. It is in this role, as instruments of a kind of inner *enchantment*, that self-ideas become a powerful adversary of the work of 'being true.'

Many novice memoir writers use writing to make a case for their self-ideas. At least this is how they begin. Not that they do so consciously, which is precisely the point: their writing simply does not come from a demanding, self-reflective sense of wonder about themselves. Instead, they use their blind spots and illusions to jack up the story they need to tell about themselves. By contrast, self-reflective memoirists, whether intentionally or in spite of themselves, use writing to explore something of the creaturely needs, interests, values, and desires—the driving energies—of who they are. They let us see the edges of their self-ideas and how they developed. In doing so, some inner, inquisitive impulse seeks to better understand who they are and what drives them. 'Being true' in this case—searching for and naming the real relationship with what is—is, or aims to be, a process of *disenchantment*.

---

[4] No one has more revealingly depicted how approaching death can challenge self-ideas than Leo Tolstoy in *The Death of Ivan Ilyich*.

Seeking what's true by writing against what life has taught us

Our life experiences give rise to truths—about our past, about being human, about life itself—that come to take on an aura of inevitability and certainty. Memoir writing as exploration is a process of unearthing and examining the experiential foundations and truth of such truths. I refer to this as thinking and writing against what life has taught us to be true.

Loren Eiseley's memoir *All the Strange Hours: The Excavation of a Life* is a good example of what I mean. Eiseley (1907–1977) was a well-known anthropologist, paleontologist, and poet. He once described himself as a 'bone hunter and naturalist'[5]; in his memoir, written in the last years of his life, he calls himself a 'student of broken things.' Eiseley's professional writing is in the 'schooled' manner—informed, detached, inquisitive—although it can also be uniquely ruminative, evocative, even mystical-feeling. His poems are preoccupied with loneliness, separation, and death. He suffered from insomnia and likely from depression.

I hear at least two contrasting voices in *All the Strange Hours*. The first—experienced, measured, intentional, and conscious—avows a stoical resignation to what Eiseley calls the 'machinery of life': life as determined by a 'throw of dice' in childhood and youth, a 'gambler's war we all lose eventually,' life ruled by the despondent Fates and 'promising nothing.' This feels like one of Eiseley's deep, late-in-life truths. His second voice is the remembering, storyteller voice of his emotional life: sometimes hot with anger, sometimes guilty, sometimes tender, and often lonely, tormented, perplexed, and consumed by longings for emotional attachment. We hear both voices right from the first pages, when Eiseley remembers standing over his mother's grave. 'We, she and I, were close to being one now, lying like the skeletons of last year's leaves in a fence corner. And it was all nothing. Nothing, do you understand? All the pain, all the anguish. Nothing. We were,

---

[5] In the foreword to his first book of poetry, *The Innocent Assassins*.

both of us, merely the debris life always leaves in its passing . . . not more than that.'

All the pain, all the anguish, now the mere debris life always leaves. Nothing.

Nothing? Really? Eiseley may call this anguish 'nothing,' 'mere debris,' but something in him is not convinced. The pain lives on in what he calls his 'scarred brain,' his aloneness, and his longing for emotional warmth. Indeed, his memoir, as the excavation of a *made* anguish, is testimony to the fact that it is not 'nothing,' nor is it part of some existential 'machinery.' This is what makes Eiseley's memoir so affecting: his use of personal writing to try to unearth and examine the big Truth about the 'machinery of life' that so much of his early life experience has left buried in his soul.

Eiseley's parents were loveless in marriage, and emotionally erratic and often distant towards the young Eiseley. He recalls growing up amidst 'a thousand home repressions.' His mother, he says, was 'savage and stone deaf,' 'paranoid, neurotic and unstable,' her voice a 'harsh discordant jangling.' She could lavish affection, but in a 'tigerish silent way.' When, in late adolescence, he visits his father on his deathbed, the man only responds when he thinks, mistakenly, that he is looking at his son from his first, happier marriage. There was, as Eiseley still remembers late in his life, 'an instance of recognition . . . from which I was excluded.'

Everything indicates that Eiseley quickly came to mistrust and fear human relationships. As a child, he writes, 'I was . . . already old enough to know one should flee from the universe but I did not know where to run.' He seeks emotional nourishment in birds, animals, and fossils, and empathizes, deeply so, with an escaped convict who is hounded to death by a posse.

At 19 Eiseley tramps with the jobless across Depression-era America. Once, when a brakeman tries to push him off a moving train, 'A thin hot wire . . . began to flicker in my brain . . . "Kill him, kill him," blazed the red wire.' He has experienced this 'hot wire,' this 'savagery,' before—in his mother and in stories of the 'mad' members of his mother's family—and he comes to fear in himself 'the murderer who had not murdered but who carried a red wire glowing in his brain.' Over time he becomes a life-long 'running man'—running from his parents, from his memories, from his emotions, and finally from every living human being. It is this Eiseley who makes a career out of 'seeking refuge in the depersonalized bones of past eras on the watersheds of the world.'

Amidst all this *running from*, the act of personal remembering was for Eiseley an anguished endeavour. At one point he writes, 'Men should discover their past. I admit to this. It has been my profession. Nevertheless, I now believe there are occasions when . . . to tamper with the past, even one's own, is to bring [on] that slipping, sliding horror which revolves around all that is done, unalterable, and yet which abides unseen in the living mind . . . [and makes] us lonely beyond belief.' Elsewhere he compares the effort of remembering his emotional life to staring through brick or stone 'as if it were not quite there.' In page after page he pushes back against—writes against— everything that has taught him to mistrust and discount his feelings and keep himself apart from creaturely attachments. For Eiseley, lived, emotional truth wants expression.[6]

In a memory that can be read as a story about the need and the struggle to remember the creaturely truth of his experience, Eiseley recalls falling through a pond's ice-covered surface as a child. 'After such an event,' he writes, 'there was no one's arms in which to fall at home. If one did, there would be only hysterical admonitions, and I would be lucky to be allowed out. Slowly my inner life was continuing to adjust to this fact. I had to rely on silence. It was like creeping away from death out of an ice hole an inch at a time. You did it alone.' Indeed it

---

[6] There is one noticeable exception to this. Although Eiseley was married to one woman for most of his adult life, you would hardly know this from his memoir. Mabel Langdon Eiseley only receives incidental mention. The couple had no children.

is this experience, he says, that 'impelled me to become a writer.' In writing 'I feel as though I were still inching out of that smashed ice bubble.' Personal remembering and writing are Eiseley's way of refusing the world's disregard and his own learned belief in the immutability of circumstance—like crawling out of a frozen pond one word at a time. Through writing as truth-seeking, the boy in the man is no longer silent, nor his emotional needs ignored and denied.

Eiseley's memory stories often take tormented, hallucinatory-feeling, and incomplete forms. But there are other stories, each surprising in light of his claims of 'stoical indifference,' in which he embraces memories of warm emotional attachment. On a dig in Texas, for example, he is moved by the 'tenderness' (the word is his) of an unearthed child's skeleton wrapped in shreds of a rabbit-skin blanket and laid in a cradle frame created from sticks. Elsewhere he recounts with affection his many encounters with mongrel strays. The beseeching eyes of more than one dog 'haunted me,' he writes, despite his attempts to resist their appeals. Kindred spirits, he calls them. 'I think we dreamed the same dreams.'

On one wintery night, Eiseley hears a stray cat's 'eloquent' cries of distress. The cat appears and runs toward him, then rolls on its back 'in a gesture of trust.' 'It was more than I could bear.' The cat, Eiseley remarks, 'was not merely saying he was lost and complaining about it. With a perfectly amazing eloquence he was going up and down the scale of animal grievance . . . . [It] was informing me of the nature of the world, of his deliberate abandonment, of his innocence of wrong . . . . A strong compulsion took me. I loved this animal from the cold night.' Up and down the scale of animal grievance. It is hard to imagine a better description of Eiseley's own protest against his childhood, and his struggle to be true to his more complete, creaturely affections.

In an uncannily similar scene from fifty years earlier, Eiseley describes an encounter with a baby squirrel that appears to be separated from its mother ('his mother must have been careless'). The 'little waif,' he writes, was 'blissfully lying on its back [in the sun] . . . without a trace of fear,' seeming to invite Eiseley to tickle its belly. Eiseley obliges, and enjoys the squirrel's pleasurable 'wriggle.' In doing so, he offers the following commentary:

> I think, you know, it is the innocence. A violent dog-eat-dog world, a murderous world, but one in which the very young are truly innocent. I am always amazed at this aspect of creation, the small Eden that does not last, but recurs with the young of every generation. I can remember when I was just as innocent as that baby ground squirrel and expected good from everyone, as a puppy might. We lose our innocence inevitably, but isn't there some kind of message in this innocence, some hint of a world beyond this fallen one[,] some place where everything was otherwise?

Many memoirists write from a hardly conscious conviction that 'we lose our innocence inevitably.' In doing so, they make important dimensions of their experience, especially their creaturely need for pleasure and trust, seem irrelevant to 'real' life. Eiseley does not choose this approach. Instead, he uses writing in a struggle to be more completely true to the full range of his life experience: not only what happened, but also what was denied, and what remains as expectation and as longing. This is what I hear in his question 'but isn't there . . . ?,' in his being amazed by creaturely trust and the expectation of good, and in his wish that 'everything was [and could be?] otherwise.'[7] In reflecting on his life over the twentieth century, Eiseley is saying that the memoirist's truths need to include, but cannot be limited to, those taught by the given 'murderous world.'

Eiseley is aware of writing about 'harsh events and of those memories I wish that some might be effaced, scratched over with great black erasure marks.' But, he adds, 'this is not the way the essayist [the memoirist] writes.' Instead, they acknowledge the 'bricks and stone' of their actually lived experience even while they work to 'stare through [them] . . . as if they were not quite there.' By writing against the

---

[7] Having said this, it is also worth noting Eiseley expresses an unqualified revulsion for the university student activists and dissenters of the 1960s–1970s.

truths life has imposed on us, we can discover ourselves to be far more complex creaturely beings than we might otherwise believe.

Writing towards the real relationship with what is

What does it mean, what could it mean, to write towards the truth of our actually lived experience? What does this mean as a form of attention, a process of thinking, and as a writing practice? What follows are a number of suggested prescripts and other considerations—a framework—for reflecting on these questions for yourself.

Write in your own voice, whatever that is, and whether or not the result meets anyone else's expressive standards. Be true to your personality, sense of privacy, and creaturely experience. Follow the advice of Anne Rice: 'Don't bend; don't water it down; don't try to make it logical; don't edit your own soul according to the fashion.'[8]

Write as if posthumously. In *Prepared for the Worst*, Christopher Hitchens recalls hearing the South African writer Nadine Gordimer say that '[a] serious person should try to write posthumously.' Hitchens goes on to explain: 'By that I took her to mean that one should compose as if the usual constraints—of fashion, commerce, self-censorship, public and, perhaps especially, intellectual opinion—did not operate.' The idea of writing 'as if posthumously' is a reminder of how we can forsake our voice to appease the actual or imagined gaze of others. By writing posthumously, our fealties, fears, guilt, and silences become life experiences to explore rather than forces that impede inquiry.

Be your creaturely self. Don't pretend to stand above your experiences, don't mock them, don't be coolly ironic. Like the rest of us, you are a needful, emotion-propelled, at best half-unknown, unfinished live creature. Use your writing to embrace and learn from these elemental, natural realities.

---

[8] From the foreword to *The Metamorphosis, In the Penal Colony, and Other Stories by Franz Kafka* (1995).

Be true to your *felt* experience. Actually felt experience is that palpable coldness—preternatural, mysterious, and creepy—when our eight-year-old fingers touch the lips of the dead. Or feel the heaviness of death in the form of a coffined body, or the incongruous weightlessness of a dead body burned to a handful of ash. The cultural mind blunts and ducks the truth with euphemism; creaturely memory holds its truths in the palpable. In every life situation we can either write the equivalent of 'passed away' or we can invite our reader to feel the mysterious cold lips of death. The best memoir writers make us feel that coldness.[9]

Take advantage of your private writer's journal and first drafts. Here is how Patti Miller describes the nature and importance of private writing: 'There is a raw energy, a fierceness of experience, which can be lost when you focus entirely on the [more finished] word. Then you may need to write with your heart and with your gut, pegging the bloody mess out on the page without concern for appearance. Write wildly, fiercely, unrestrainedly, disturbingly, passionately. Write without respect, write inappropriately, scream if you want to. Write with only the fierce discipline of the desire for truth to guide you' (*Writing True Stories*). Letting go in journals and first drafts can reach truths you might otherwise not reach, or help unblock things you haven't been able to say but need to express.

Imagine what you want from another person's memoir. In particular, imagine reading the memoir of your grandfather or mother or father or sister or closest friend. Do you want to feel that they are working to be true to their actually felt experience—or merely writing to impress, to be 'interesting' and 'informative,' to make you feel good, to 'keep everyone happy,' or some combination of these? Don't we, as caring, curious readers, want to feel the memoirist's effort to be true to their actually felt experience—particularly on matters of significance in their life? Like that postnatal depression, or that feeling of lostness on retirement. Or what it was like to suddenly live in a 'adult' sexual body,

---

[9] Each culture and individual draws their own lines around the 'crude,' 'rude,' 'impolite,' 'risqué,' and 'embarrassing.' In modern Western culture, such lines still encircle sexuality, excreta, and death.

to be a 'teen,' to fall in love, to feel that a relationship was 'serious,' to come face-to-face with the death of a loved one. Or those times of existential inner questioning: *Am I happy? What does happiness, what could happiness mean? Why am I here? Have I lived as I should have?* Don't we as readers want the memoirist to let their actually lived life speak? Don't we want to experience something of their personally important life questions, surprises, quandaries, highs and lows, impulsiveness, doubts, longings, sadness, ragings, passions, and struggles? Don't we want memoirists being interestingly human, not busy shoring up their self-ideas? Don't we want memoirists who reassure us—hearten us? console us?—by writing about and learning from not only their goodness and achievements and what excites them, but their foibles, fears, regrets, and struggles? Write the memoir you want others who are important to you to leave behind, the one your curious, creaturely self recognizes is the real thing.

Trust your reader. Always write to a thoughtful, creaturely reader. Trust your reader's empathetic judgement. Good readers know about the difficulty of being true and will appreciate your own best efforts.

Be attentive to your tone. As the saying goes, 'It's not what he said, it's how he said it that matters.' If you write with bitterness, in an accusing tone, or as if everything is someone else's fault, you will lose the sympathies of your reader and the opportunity to make your truth more palatable. Be clear, direct, considered, and respectful, and your chances of being listened to will likely increase. If you are bitter or angry, get this out in your personal journal and first draft, then decide what to do next.

Qualify your certainties. Claiming the truth with unqualified certainty creates doubts and resistance. There's a saying from the Galicia region in Eastern Europe that goes something like this: When someone is honestly 55% right, that's very good and there's no use in wrangling. If someone is 60% right, then that's wonderful and great luck. But 75% right? Wise people say this is suspicious. And 100%? Whoever says he's 100% right is a fanatic, a thug, and the worst kind of rascal. Allow for contending versions of events, especially around interpersonal conflicts. Create room for readers to consider their own perspective—and to see your own as another perspective. Sometimes 'being true' needs to sound like this: *I'm not certain, but it went something like this.* Or: *My sister remembers this differently. Here's how I remember it.*

Being true to your experience is not about being 'nice' or 'liked.' Being true will sometimes make you seem unlikable or impolite or curmudgeonly. If life were about being liked, there'd be even more than the usual dissembling and confusion—and even more specious memoirs. Life and relationships are or can be rough. People disagree. We can do awful things. Natalie Goldberg: 'The things that make you a functional citizen in society—manners, discretion, cordiality—don't necessarily make you a good writer. Writing needs raw truth, wants your suffering and darkness on the table' (*Old Friend from Far Away*). *Truth* is more reliable—and in the end has a more constructive effect—than *nice*.[10]

Let go of the desire to impress—to sound in control or 'good' or smart. Don't perform. Patti Miller calls the desire to impress 'the greatest pollutant of the truth,' and for good reason.

Celebrate the positive. Distressing events can be preoccupying. Without avoiding them, remember to also tell stories of your experiences of achievement and fulfilment. Overcoming a fear of public speaking. Persevering to the bitter, exhausting end of that 10K race. Giving birth. Lovingly nurturing a child living with a cognitive or physical challenge. Helping to welcome a new neighbour from a 'different' culture when everyone else was suspicious. Standing up alone for your values. Remember to celebrate the truths of this courageous, caring you.

---

[10] In *Bird by Bird* Anne Lamott sometimes shifts the responsibility for angry reactions to truth-telling to those being written about: 'If people wanted you to write warmly about them, they should have behaved better.'

Towards an ethic of considering others

When our memoir writing refers to other people, as it so often does, how do we decide what to say and not say, how to say it, and address what we are not saying? Rules don't help here, not least because each situation is unique. What seems more useful is a kind of ethical framework within which to make considered choices, case by case. I invite you to build your own 'ethic of considering others' by using the following points[12]:

Check your motives. Why are you saying this? Because it is important, even critical to the personal expression of this particular experience? Because it may be personally healing? Because you need to 'look good'? Because this is a chance to 'get back' at your sister or father? On 'getting back,' it's worth recalling Annie Dillard's quip that '[w]riting is an art, not a martial art.'

Is it important? Is this truth critical to your life story—for example, a personal experience of abuse—or extraneous and unnecessary? Weigh its importance.

Who will you hurt—and how? Include yourself in this consideration. Are you ready to live with the emotional storms that might be set off in your family, among your friends, or within yourself?

Who will you help—and how? Again, include yourself in this consideration. Truth-telling can be liberating and healing. By saying what others dare not, your family members and friends might be helped by your courage to speak out.

Consider the unreliability of memory. Check your facts. Speak with others. Allow room for other possibilities.

---

[12] I have adapted some of the points in this and the next section from Patti Miller's excellent discussions of truth-telling in *Writing True Stories*.

Consider the privacy of others and yourself. Respect confidences told you by others. Reflect carefully on whether to reveal information based on events you have observed that may be embarrassing to those involved.

Opening a door you've never dared go through

Actually lived life is made up of 'light' and 'dark' times, times of pathless uncertainty, times of contentment and discontent, of elation and depression, of happiness and sadness, of fulfilment and want, of love and rage, of oneness with others (and life) and utter aloneness. It's easy enough to write about the 'positive,' the collectively familiar, and what culture conceives of as a 'regular' life. More difficult is to write about times of anguish, vulnerability, failure, disappointment, acts of folly, or 'falling apart'—those times in particular that can turn into what Anne Lamott calls our inner monsters that we hold in the locked rooms of our soul.

The 'monstrous' might have been monstrous in the original, or might have become so through its shuttered, shadowy hiddenness. Whatever the case, memoir writing is an opportunity to unlock the doors, to see what's actually in those closed rooms, to express the hitherto inexpressible, and thereby begin to diminish its power. Writing and story-sharing can also help us realize how similar many of our monsters are. As Anne Lamott writes in her demanding but helpfully blunt way, 'If there is one door in the castle you have been told not to go through, you must. Otherwise, you'll just be rearranging furniture in rooms you've already been in. Most human beings are dedicated to keeping that one door shut. But the writer's job is to see what's behind it, to see the bleak unspeakable stuff, and to turn the unspeakable into words—not just into any words but if we can, into rhythm and blues' (*Bird by Bird*).

But how to use writing to crack open that door you've never gone through? Here is what I suggest:

- Begin by acknowledging the difficulty of doing so—even, at first thought, the misery and possibly the futility of doing so.

- Remember that truth and the deep, live creaturely self are the best of friends. Truth wants expression on behalf of our creaturely self. It wants to be 'seen'—seen and heard and understood—for what it actually is.

- Take courage from what truth wants—from the wisdom of truth-seeking and truth-naming.[13]

- Take advantage of the safe, understanding, courage-giving space of your memoir writing group.

- Use the safety of your writer's journal.

- Remember those times when you really did pull yourself up from 'dark' places.

- Don't simply replay a painful moment from the past; critically *explore* it in the light of your current wisdom. Understand it anew.

- Trust the surprising power of your creaturely, reflective self to name what you feel and need to understand more fully. Listen to this self. What is it feeling? What is it saying?

- Talk truth out with a trusted friend who listens well and knows what questions to ask. 'Talking it out' through dialogue helps us find and voice the words leading to understanding.

- Explore distressing experiences in the entirely reasonable hope that writing out the distress—expressing and shaping it as personal story or essay—can lessen its grip and give you new reparative energy. Truth *does* want expression, for good reason.

---

[13] See Chapter 4 on courage.

Is there an angel in your life? If so, what are the stories shared by you and it? Angels, creatures of human need, come in many forms. Some become cultural types detached from their human origins, like the cherubic figure pictured on the left. By contrast, the *Poor Angel* (right), painted by Paul Klee, emerges directly from human experience. Klee painted many angels late in his life, around 1939. By then he had been conscripted in the First World War, experienced the violent deaths of friends, and lived through the grim interwar years. Klee's angels have names like Forgetful, Still Ugly, Incomplete, Weeping, Precocious, In Crisis, Petulant, and Hopeful. Each one feels like an expression of the grievous work of learning from and making accommodations with the world as it is—and, no less so, of Klee's determination to create breathing holes for creaturely hope, despite the world as it is. And you? What in your experience has given birth to your angels? And what do your angels express on your behalf? Photograph (left) courtesy Plato Terentev (pexels.com), photograph (right) from author's collection.

PART V

CHAPTER 22

THE MEMOIR WRITING WORKSHOP

The materials in this book emerged from my facilitation of a nine-month memoir writing workshop offered in various forms over several years. Most workshop participants have been retirees. We meet weekly for two hours during the first few months, then continue with this schedule or move to fortnightly sessions. Each workshop has a maximum of eight to ten participants. Face-to-face meetings, limited numbers, and weekly sessions help develop camaraderie, mutual trust, and self-confidence early in the workshop. Weekly meetings also introduce participants to a routine of regular writing. Workshop members are given weekly writing assignments of 500–800 words. They are given a topic from those listed in Chapter 5 or they can choose one based on their personal memoir project.

The importance of the writing workshop

Personal writing, including memoir writing, is a solitary and interior activity. The memoirist needs a place and time to be with their own memories and thoughts, to explore what is important in their life, and to develop a personal voice to express this importance. Yes we might discuss our writing with others. In the end, however, our words come from within ourselves on a journey we walk in single file. The memoir writing workshop is meant to be a reviving stopover—a place of supportive accompaniment—along this journey.

Each workshop is designed to bolster the memoir writer's curiosity, skills, and courage—and to sustain their commitment to writing their life stories. Workshop participants come together as writers and work as partners. We discuss our challenges and successes. We hear our own storytelling and essaying voice, and we feel its effect through the responses of others.

Personal writing includes times of doubt, drought, and dead ends. The workshop is a place to share these times and together find a way forward. Reading our personal work to others, and commenting on another's writing, cannot be done without feeling exposed, without moments of unease and clumsiness, without risk, and without courage. Anyone around the workshop table might stumble, anyone might feel self-doubt. This is why I call the workshops places of 'supportive accompaniment': we help each other get back on our feet and move ahead.

I sometimes imagine that we workshop participants are like Mnemosyne's (Memory's) literary midwives, helping each other give birth to our life stories. We stir up memories in one another. We encourage each other to explore our experiences anew, reflect on their meaning and meaningfulness, and find their most effective expression. We bolster the courage needed to express complex or difficult truths that need expressing. We care about one another's success. We cheer each other on.

Workshop goals

The writing workshop is a place of planned learning through participant readings, feedback, and guided discussions. We have three goals:

- Develop the skills and confidence to tell our life stories in ways that are true to our life experiences.

- Learn to use personal writing to explore our life experiences and enrich our self-understanding.

- Create a place of mutual interest, learning, and trust, and thereby offer each other the encouragement and courage to do our best possible writing.

The bargain

The workshop series is based on a bargain. Participants commit to write each week (or attend to their memoir writing in some form), actively participate in the workshop as regularly as possible, offer thoughtful feedback on the work of fellow writers, come prepared to discuss the learning materials, and be well on their way towards completing their memoir by the end of the workshop series. In turn, the workshop facilitator commits to coordinating the group's activities, preparing learning materials, and offering the best possible guidance, advice, and support to participants. Overall, we make decisions and work together as equals.

A typical workshop

Participants prepare tea and gather in a circle, usually around a table, to ensure that we can talk comfortably face-to-face. We begin with a roundtable 'check-in' and discussion of challenges, successes, and questions we have faced as writers during the week. After that the order of activities is fluid. Several participants read from their ongoing work. This is followed by feedback from the group. We also discuss the week's learning material and agree on the coming week's writing task. Each two-hour session includes a mid-workshop break.

Mutual support, confidentiality, and trust

Critical to the workshop's success is an environment based on mutual support and trust. Given this, workshop members discuss and agree to their own form of these three rules:

- I respect the validity of each person's experience. I do not question or judge in ways that might undermine any person's interpretation of their life.

- I respect the privacy of each person's stories and do not repeat them or related discussions outside the workshop unless given permission by an individual writer. What is said and heard in the workshop stays in the workshop.

- I focus my feedback and other comments on the writing and not on the writer or their life, and I do not offer personal advice on their life.

In the world of memoir writing, the lines between writer and person, and writing and one's life are naturally porous. Comments on 'skill' or 'style' can quickly scrape the exposed, creaturely self. Judgments on writing can easily feel like judgments on the writer's life. Mutual trust is essential. As trust develops between workshop participants, there comes to be a greater willingness to follow discussions into more challenging topics. What motivates such discussions, however, must always be the same thing that brings us together: to support each other as memoir writers.

Giving and receiving feedback

The purpose of feedback—giving it and listening to it—is to strengthen our writing and the self-understanding that feeds effective writing. Feedback discussions take place in a supportive, encouraging atmosphere. Each of us is invested in our own success and the success of our fellow writers.

Giving feedback as a listener

See the detailed feedback checklist at the end of this chapter.

- Begin by commenting on what you like or what you think works well.

- Ask about what you don't find clear or don't understand.

- Suggest what in your view might need further attention. Perhaps suggest changes you might make, or an alternative approach you might take.

- Above all, be respectful, be direct, and give the kind of feedback that you would find helpful as a writer.

Receiving feedback as a writer

- Listen. Listen. Listen.

- Resist explaining or justifying why you wrote something as you did.

- Ask clarifying questions.

- As needed, ask for advice or suggestions on alternative ways of expressing an element of your writing.

- Write with a thin skin but listen to feedback with a thick skin.

Listen, really listen to the writing

Focus feedback discussions on what was actually read: the subject matter and the writing. This point needs underlining because memoir writing discussions are a natural invitation to listeners to talk about their own associated memories and anecdotes. 'Feedback' on the writing can easily digress into anecdotes on who lived where, who knew whom, and who did what where. Discussions like these have their place. They stir our personal memories and build camaraderie in the group. But if we are only thinking about our own experience instead of really listening to or reflecting on the written experiences of others, we are not being as helpful as we need to be. Good feedback begins with active, attentive listening—then focusing your comments on what you have heard.

Feedback checklist

Feedback focuses on writing's experiential and expressive qualities, matters both of craft and of art. Not all the qualities listed here apply in equal measure to each story or personal essay. Adapt this list as needed. A number of terms ('aboutness', 'show' versus 'tell,' 'dramatic scenes') are discussed in more detail throughout this book.

- What specific elements and qualities really 'work' for me as I listen to this story or essay? What attracts my interest? What qualities do I find most appealing?

- Am I immediately engaged and kept engaged in the story or essay's unfolding world, situation, argument, drama?

- Setting and narrative thread. Do I know where I am: place, time, people, situation? Can I follow the story?

- Voice. Do I hear the writer's voice in the writing? Is the voice distinctly this writer's?

- Meaningfulness. Do I 'get' the importance of this story for the writer and their life?

- Does the writing convince me that the writer is authentically, self-reflectively exploring their experience, and working towards the truth of this experience?

- Focus. Does the writer keep everything (words, details, information, narrative thread) economically focused on the essential 'aboutness' of the story? Every word is needed, everything else is left out.

- Are the pacing and scale—amounts of attention to particular aspects—appropriate to the subject matter?

- Do certain qualities of the story or essay contribute to a lasting impression? How would I describe this impression?

- Am I moved to see things in a new way?

Does the writer make effective use of the following:

- 'Telling' and 'showing'?

- 'Dramatic scenes' and 'narrative bridges' and 'summaries'?

- Sentence structures and lengths to vary the writing's rhythms?

- Selected, evocative, telling 'realia': the concrete, sensory rendering of people, situations, objects, places?

- Spoken and inner voice, direct or paraphrased dialogue?

- Varied, even contradictory points of view and perspectives?

- Changing moods and tones?

- Moving between external events, people, and voices and inner reflection?

- Narrative, or how the material unfolds: begins, is arranged, recollected, developed, argued, ends?

- Humour?

- Figurative language?

SELECTED READINGS

On Writing Memoir Stories and Personal Essays

Included here are titles related to memoir writing that I have found especially helpful in writing this book.

Walter Benjamin, *The Storyteller Essays*.

Natalie Goldberg, *Old Friend from Far Away: The Practice of Writing Memoir*.

Vivian Gornick, *The Situation and the Story: The Art of Personal Narrative*.

Patricia Hampl, *I Could Tell You Stories: Sojourns in the Land of Memory*, especially the chapter 'Memory and Imagination.'

Mary Karr, *The Art of Memoir*.

Anne Lamott, *Bird by Bird: Some Instructions on Writing and Life*.

Phillip Lopate (ed.), *The Art of the Personal Essay: An Anthology from the Classical Era to the Present*. Excellent Introduction.

Phillip Lopate, *To Show and to Tell: The Craft of Literary Nonfiction*.

Jane Taylor McDonnell, *Living to Tell the Tale: A Guide to Writing Memoir*.

Patti Miller, *Writing True Stories*.

Tristine Rainer, *Your Life as Story.*

Marion Roach Smith, *The Memoir Project: A Thoroughly Non-Standardized Text for Writing and Life.*

William Zinsser, *Writing About Your Life: A Journey into the Past.*

William Zinsser (ed.), *Inventing the Truth: The Art and Craft of Memoir.*

Memoirs and other examples of personal writing

The number of memoirs and personal essays is not yet countless, although it is getting close. The titles included here are evidence of personal preferences, and the happenstance that shapes many reading lists.

Edward Abbey, *Desert Solitaire: A Season in the Wilderness.* Also: *Down the River* and *The Journey Home.*

Jordan Abel, *Nishga.*

T.W. Adorno, *Minima Moralia: Reflections from Damaged Life.*

Carmen Aguirre, *Something Fierce: Memoirs of a Revolutionary Daughter.*

Kamal Al-Solaylee, *Intolerable: A Memoir of Extremes.*

Maya Angelou, *I Know Why the Caged Bird Sings.*

James Baldwin, *Notes of a Native Son.*

Russell Baker, *Growing Up.*

Alison Bechdel, *Fun Home: A Family Tragicomic.* Also: *Are You My Mother?*

Walter Benjamin, *A Berlin Childhood Around 1900* and *One-Way Street.*

Eavan Boland, *Object Lessons: The Life of the Woman and the Poet in our Time.*

Dionne Brand, *A Map to the Door of No Return: Notes to Belonging.*

Hugh Brody, *The Other Side of Eden.* Also: *Maps and Dreams.*

Rebecca Busselle, *An Exposure of the Heart.*

Elias Canetti, *The Tongue Set Free* and *The Torch in My Ear.*

David Chariandy, *I've Been Meaning to Tell You.*

Wayson Choy, *Paper Shadows.*

Denise Chong, *The Concubine's Children.*

Frank Conroy, *Stop-Time: A Memoir.*

Jill Ker Conway, *The Road from Coorain.*

Harry Crews, *A Childhood: The Biography of a Place.*

Laura Cumming, *On Chapel Sands.*

Roald Dahl, *Boy: Tales of Childhood.*

Thomas DeBaggio, *Losing My Mind: An Intimate Look at Life with Alzheimer's.*

Robert Dessaix, *A Mother's Disgrace.*

Joan Didion, *The Year of Magical Thinking* and *Blue Nights.*

Annie Dillard, *An American Childhood.* Also: *Pilgrim at Tinker Creek* and *The Abundance: Narrative Essays Old and New.*

Annie Ernaux, *The Years.*

Loren Eiseley, *All the Strange Hours: The Excavation of a Life.*

Terese Marie Mailhot, *Heart Berries: A Memoir*.

Nadezhda Mandelstam, *Hope Against Hope: A Memoir*.

Sally Mann, *Hold Still: A Memoir with Photographs*.

Wendy Mitchell, *About Somebody I Used to Know*.

Michel de Montaigne, *The Complete Works*. Trans. Donald M. Frame.

Jan Morris, *Conundrum*.

Vladimir Nabokov, *Speak, Memory*.

Bill Neidjie, *Story About Feeling* and *Gagudju Man*.

Joyce Carol Oates, *A Widow's Story*.

Michael Ondaatje, *Running in the Family*.

Orhan Pamuk, *Istanbul: Memories and the City*.

Irina Ratushinskaya, *Grey is the Colour of Hope*.

W.G. Sebald, *The Rings of Saturn*. Also: *The Emergence of Memory: Conversations with W.G. Sebald*.

Raja Shehadeh, *Palestinian Walks: Forays into a Vanishing Landscape*.

Gary Shteyngart, *Little Failure*.

Andrew Solomon, *The Noonday Demon: An Atlas of Depression*.

Wole Soyinka, *Aké: The Years of Childhood*.

Gloria Steinem, 'Ruth's Song (Because She Could Not Sing It)' in Steinem, *Outrageous Acts and Everyday Rebellions*.

Cheryl Strayed, *Wild: From Lost to Found on the Pacific Crest Trail*.

Colin Thubron, *To a Mountain in Tibet*.

Leo Tolstoy, *Childhood, Boyhood, Youth*.

Eudora Welty, *One Writer's Beginnings*.

Edmund White, *My Lives*.

Helen Waldstein Wilkes, *Letters from the Lost: A Memoir of Discovery*.

Ian Williams, *Disorientation: Being Black in the World*.

Jeanette Winterson, *Why Be Happy When You Could Be Normal?*

Tim Winton, *Island Home: A Landscape Memoir*.

Christa Wolf, *Patterns of Childhood* (also translated as *A Model Childhood*, from the German title *Kindheitsmuster*).

Tobias Wolff, *This Boy's Life: A Memoir*.

Geoffrey Wolff, *A Day at the Beach* and *The Duke of Deception: Memories of My Father*.

Richard Wright, *Black Boy*.

Online Sources for Personal Writing

The online world is constantly changing. Here are several suggestions as of this printing.

Globe and Mail: First Person.

The New Yorker: Personal History.

The New York Times: Lives, Rites of Passage, and other personal writing columns. The *Times'* personal writing columns change their names and subject matter from time to time. Search their archives for examples from earlier columns.

The following websites feature examples and reviews of personal nonfiction writing, as well as discussions of memoir writing challenges and craft: *Brevity: A Journal of Concise Literary Nonfiction* (brevitymag.com), *Creative Nonfiction* (creativenonfiction.org), The Electric Typewriter (tetw.org), and the pages on memoir writing at *Literary Hub* (lithub.com/story-type/memoir).

CPSIA information can be obtained
at www.ICGtesting.com
Printed in the USA
BVHW071931191121
622014BV00002B/5